VOICES FROM
STALINGRAD

VOICES FROM
STALINGRAD

UNIQUE FIRST-HAND ACCOUNTS FROM WORLD WAR II'S CRUELLEST BATTLE

Jonathan Bastable

David and Charles

For my splendid family – Kim, Jacob and Eliza

A DAVID & CHARLES BOOK
Copyright © David & Charles Limited 2006, 2007

David & Charles is an F+W Publications Inc. company
4700 East Galbraith Road
Cincinnati, OH 45236

First published in the UK in 2007

Text copyright Jonathan Bastable 2006, 2007

A catalogue record for this book is available from the British Library.

ISBN-13: 978-0-7153-2176-8 hardback
ISBN-10: 0-7153-2176-5 hardback

ISBN-13: 978-0-7153-2725-8 paperback
ISBN-10: 0-7153-2725-9 paperback

Printed in and bound by Creative Print & Design Group,
Ebbw Vale, Wales, UK
for David & Charles
Brunel House, Newton Abbot, Devon

Commissioning Editor: Ruth Binney
Editor: Ame Verso
Project Editor: Christopher Summerville
Art Editor: Mike Moule
Designer: Sarah Clark
Production Controller: Kelly Smith

Original translations from Russian and German by the author, Robert Goldie and Alisa Jaffa.

Visit our website at www.davidandcharles.co.uk

David & Charles books are available from all good bookshops; alternatively you
can contact our Orderline on 0870 9908222 or write to us at FREEPOST EX2 110,
D&C Direct, Newton Abbot, TQ12 4ZZ (no stamp required UK only); US customers
call 800-289-0963 and Canadian customers call 800-840-5220.

CONTENTS

REMEMBERING STALINGRAD

Most visitors to Stalingrad – Volgograd as it is now – make the sad pilgrimage to Mamayev Kurgan. This tall hill, a Tatar burial mound, was the white-hot crucible of the battle. At the end of the war there was so much shrapnel embedded in the earth that no grass grew here, but today it is, as it was before the war, a quiet green park. It is also a war cemetery for thousands of Russian dead. A cavernous hall of remembrance has been carved out of the eastern face of the hillside. All must pass through it, filing past the eternal flame and the honour guard, on their way to view the astonishing object at the summit.

For on the crown of Mamayev Kurgan stands the colossal statue of a female figure. *Rodina-Mat'* – 'Motherland' – is the largest free-standing sculpture in the world. This furious giantess, 160ft (49m) tall, strains forward and holds aloft an avenging sword. She is an overpowering sight: it is as if the Statue of Liberty had leaped down from her pedestal and charged screaming into battle.

Some people find this kind of Communist monumentalism rather tasteless. But the towering Motherland figure certainly does what any work of art should: it tells a compelling and worthwhile story. It says that something of unbelievable enormity happened here, something as immense, unique and awesome as the statue itself.

But the statue does not tell the whole story. In its vastness it conveys little of the ordinary combatants' experience of Stalingrad (and says nothing about the German ordeal). Those stories are compelling and worthwhile too. And the aim of this book is to give an account of the epic of Stalingrad from the standpoint of those who were there: Germans and Russians, men and women, soldiers and citizens.

The war archives in Volgograd contain thousands of accounts written by Russian servicemen. Some are barely literate, and that is why they have never been published. Other accounts have gathered dust because the writers speak of incidents in a way that would have been considered un-Soviet by the regime at the time. In recent decades, a small proportion of this material has seen the light of day, but only in Russian and in tiny print-runs.

So Russian accounts are a rich resource. But German testimony is comparatively scarce, because barely one in a hundred of the German soldiers who fought at Stalingrad came through it. Consequently, many German eyewitness stories are not after-the-event reminiscences, but extracts from letters written to loved ones during the fighting. Sackloads of these intimate documents were captured by the Russians, and a few that reached their addressees later found their way into German archives. In this book, the names of certain letter writers have been obscured at the archives' request (hence, 'Hans S— wrote ...'), because the young soldiers often express Nazi views that they might have lived to regret, had they lived at all. And their objectionable opinions still have the power to distress or embarrass living relatives.

It is not just what they said; it's what they did. Some of the *Wehrmacht* soldiers whose voices are heard here surely committed appalling crimes in Russia. But as one reads anguished first-hand descriptions of the Germans' suffering at Stalingrad, there is little way of knowing who is receiving a dose of something like poetic justice, and who is a hapless pawn caught up in Hitler's megalomanic scheme. This is not just a Nazi conundrum: though right was ultimately on the side of the Russians, Red Army men too were implacably brutal – to the enemy and to each other, and subsequently to blameless German civilians.

As I gathered voices from Stalingrad, I was often confronted by this problem of pity. How far can one sympathize with an individual, not knowing what horrors he had seen or done, or might yet do? I decided that the answer was not to judge. And I choose to pity both the misguided henchman and the wretched victim, because in this most cruel encounter, they were all too often one and the same man.

Jonathan Bastable

1

FROM REDBEARD TO BLUE

The war between Nazi Germany and the Soviet Union was a clash of ideologies, a tussle between empires, and a continuation of the age-old struggle between the European West and the Asiatic East. It was also a collision of two psychopathic personalities. At the nub of the war on the eastern front was the rivalry between the criminally xenophobic person of Adolf Hitler and the morbidly paranoid figure of Joseph Stalin. The battle between them took on a grandiose and fearsome life of its own at Stalingrad in 1942. It became a monster that consumed as many as two million men.

Years before he came to power, Hitler had made plans for a crusade against the barbaric Bolshevik east. It is all set out in his early autobiography *Mein Kampf* ('My Struggle'). Hitler wrote the book in 1924, while serving a prison sentence for attempting a coup in Bavaria. It consisted of a queasy mix of anti-Jewish and anti-Communist rants, self-pitying or self-aggrandizing reminiscences, and dull lectures on German politics. It was an indigestible recipe for a book, and even Hitler's closest friends and allies admitted in private that they had not been able to finish it.

But for all its ghastliness as a piece of writing, *Mein Kampf* does express the fullness of its author's philosophy. And with a true politician's instinct, Hitler reduces his theories to a series of easy slogans. Among the catchwords is *Volk*, which means 'the people' but contains the quasi-mystical notion that the Germanic peoples represent the peak of humanity's cultural evolution, and so have a special destiny to rule over lesser nations. Then there is *Lebensraum* – 'living space' – the idea that there was not room enough in Germany for the energetic Germans, that the nation needed to expand. A third slogan is *Drang nach Osten* – roughly 'the urge to the east' – which is the proposition that the natural annexe of Greater Germany lies in the fertile farmland of Poland and the Western Ukraine. Add to all this such martial contentions as 'the German people owes its existence solely to its determination to fight,' and you have a programme for robbing the Slavic peoples of their ancestral territory. Once Hitler was at the helm, war with Russia was always going to happen.

Hitler was happier performing to an audience than writing books (even *Mein Kampf* was dictated to his doggish underling, Rudolf Hess), and in his speeches he occasionally came out with an arresting turn of phrase. In 1936, for example, while addressing a gathering of the Nazi party faithful in Munich, he made this strangely intimate remark:

> **I follow the path that Providence has ordained with the assurance of a sleepwalker.**

That single sentence says a great deal about the man. The path of fate is laid out in advance – so whatever Hitler does on that path is by definition right, and the idea that he might make mistakes becomes a logical impossibility. Meanwhile, the sleeping Hitler sees only his dream, which is both his inspiration and his own creation. There is no question that he is responsible for what he does in his dreaming state, or that those actions might be morally wrong. However nightmarish the sleepwalker's vision, he has a perfect right to live it out.

THE TWO DICTATORS

Hitler was democratically elected Chancellor of Germany on 30 January 1933. At that time, Joseph Stalin had been master of the Kremlin for some years. It has been pointed out that there are some striking parallels between the lives of Hitler and Stalin. Both had experience of war in their youth – Hitler was a lowly infantryman on the Western Front in World War I; Stalin was a commander in the Russian Civil War. Both men served time in prison for their revolutionary activities in the countries that they came to lead.

Intriguingly, both were from national minorities. Hitler was an Austrian, not a German; Stalin came from the Caucasian province of Georgia, and Georgian was his native language (he spoke Russian with a marked foreign accent all his life).

Once they came to power, both men were tyrants – and both used their great personal power to boost the standing of their respective nations. Stalin, for his part, inaugurated the rapid industrialization of the Soviet Union by means of 'five-year plans', and in so doing made the USSR into a modern superpower. In February 1931 he said:

> Those that lag behind are beaten. We do not want to
> be beaten. Old Russia was ceaselessly beaten for her
> backwardness. She was beaten by the Mongol khans, she was
> beaten by Swedish feudal lords, she was beaten by Polish-
> Lithuanian *Pans*, she was beaten by Anglo-French capitalists,
> she was beaten by Japanese barons, she was beaten by all for
> her backwardness. We are fifty or a hundred years behind the
> advanced countries. We must make good this lag in ten
> years. Either we do it or they will crush us.

Stalin was right to link the necessity for modernization to the threat of war, to all the wars that Russia had fought and lost. And his guess that he had a decade to catch up was spot on, as the German invasion was to come ten years and four months after he spoke those words. By then, Stalin had succeeded in dragging the new Soviet state into the 20th century. The first five-year plans effectively put the country's economy on a war footing, though the war was yet to come. Factory cities were built in the ore-rich regions, and these new cities were populated by enthusiastic young migrants. Entire new industries were planted and took root in Siberia. Medieval farming methods were abolished – the tractor drove out the horse-drawn plough – and agriculture was brought under state control. A modern army and air force were created.

But these changes came at immense cost. When the mass of Russian peasants were herded into large state-run collective farms, they lost their livestock and their right to sell privately. The better-off peasants resisted the process fiercely, and so felt the full force of the Socialist state's determination to industrialize. Millions of these 'kulaks' were liquidated; a famine was engineered in the western Ukraine to break the resistance of the Ukraine people to Soviet rule and to collectivization.

The educated classes – the intelligentsia – were also seen by the new regime as a brake on the process of modernization, as reluctant bystanders to the historic triumph of the working classes. In the Great Terror of the 1930s they were arrested in their hundreds of thousands. The process became a kind of mass psychosis, in which Stalin's own suspicious and vengeful personality was magnified and let loose on the populace. 'Enemies of the people' were deemed to be at work in every factory and office. People denounced their neighbours, and the arrestees, under torture, denounced anyone they could think of, thereby providing a fresh crop of enemies for the secret police – the NKVD – to gather in. Victims of this process were shot or else shipped to the gulag, where they worked as slave labourers on immense industrial projects such as the building of the White Sea Canal.

Disastrously for the conduct of the war that was yet to come, there was a mighty purge of the armed forces in 1937 and 1938. Officers were arrested and eliminated in their thousands. Almost half of the entire officer corps was shot or deported to the camps. Among the victims were many of the highest-ranking soldiers: 60 out of 85 corps commanders, 110 out of 195 divisional commanders, 220 out of 406 brigade commanders. No foreign enemy could have caused such attrition: Stalin had decapitated his own army on the eve of war.

Soon after the purges, a system of 'dual command' was introduced in the Red Army: every officer, from the highest general to the lowliest lieutenant, was to be shadowed by a 'commissar', a politically minded officer who would act as the ideological conscience of the commander. Commissars were first used in the Russian Civil War, when many officers in the Red Army were former Tsarist soldiers – good at their jobs, but not necessarily committed to the Bolshevik cause. The need for political overseers had died away in the 1920s, once the state ideology permeated through the officer corps. So the reintroduction of the commissar system now was a measure of the distrust Stalin felt for his own armed forces.

Hitler's revival of Germany meanwhile was, one might almost say, spiritual in character. He aimed to change the German people's idea of itself, and – to the immense detriment of Germany and the peoples of Europe – he succeeded brilliantly. Many Germans of Hitler's generation were bitter about their country's defeat in the Great War. They saw the peace terms imposed by the Western Allies at Versailles as a stain on their national honour. Hitler's impassioned rhetoric seemed to acknowledge those old hurts, but he also had a practical remedy to hand. As soon as Hitler took power, he got down to rebuilding Germany's armed forces, the *Wehrmacht*. Rearmament was in direct contravention of the Versailles treaty, but Allied governments turned a blind eye, not wanting to provoke the irascible new leader of Germany. This allowed Hitler to increase the number of men under arms from barely 100,000 to almost four million between 1932 and 1939. At the same time he, like Stalin, devoted resources to the construction of a powerful air force and large numbers of tanks.

There was one man who quickly realized that it was not just the number but also the nature of Hitler's new soldiers that gave cause for alarm. As early as 1934 Winston Churchill said: 'Germany is now equipping itself with the technical apparatus of modern war, and at the same time is instilling into the hearts of its youths and manhood the most extreme patriotic, nationalist and militarist conceptions.' Not just a new generation of footsoldiers, then, but fanatical Nazi stormtroopers – eager for glory and conquest. Churchill's insight was shrewd, but at this time he was out of government and out of favour. Hardly anyone heeded his warning.

THE ROAD TO WAR
Hitler tested his strength, and his future enemies' will to resist him, in an incremental series of aggressive foreign-policy adventures. First, he withdrew Germany from the League of Nations and refused to continue paying reparations to the victors of the Great War. In 1935

he wrested the coal-rich Saarland from French control; in 1936 he sent troops into the demilitarized zone west of the Rhine, bringing his army up to the Dutch and Belgian borders. In March 1938 he annexed Austria to Germany. Hitler claimed he was merely bringing ethnic Germans back under the protection of the Reich, and that he was doing so at those peoples' own request. The same argument justified the takeover of the Sudetenland, German-speaking borderlands of Czechoslovakia, in September 1938.

This gradual expansion was achieved more or less peacefully, with the acquiescence of the Western powers. After the Sudetenland, Hitler declared that he had no more territorial claims in Europe, and many people across Europe breathed a sigh of relief. The British prime minister, Neville Chamberlain, went to Munich and extracted a promise from the Führer that his appetite was sated, and got him to put his signature to it. Chamberlain came back triumphant from Germany, and waved that flimsy paper above his head. 'It's peace in our time,' he announced.

But time was running out. Hitler thought nothing of breaking the undertaking he had signed with Chamberlain, and in 1939 he began to put pressure on Poland to allow a corridor across its territory to the German-speaking city of Danzig on the Baltic coast, and to the little enclave of East Prussia beyond it. The Poles refused to cede any territory to Germany, and so Hitler threatened to take a chunk of Poland by force.

But first he had some business to conclude with Stalin, who for years had been railing against Hitler's land-greed and the Western powers' cowardly policy of appeasement. Hitler needed to reassure Stalin that his drive to the east represented no threat to the Soviet Union. The two leaders did not meet in person, but their respective foreign ministers, Joachim Ribbentrop for Germany and Vyacheslav Molotov for Russia, negotiated a non-aggression treaty that was signed in August 1939. This was a stunning event: 'The sinister news broke upon the world like an explosion,' wrote Churchill. In the House of Commons Chamberlain said with almost comical understatement that: 'I do not attempt to conceal from the House that the announcement came to the government as a surprise, and a surprise of a very unpleasant character.'

But the most outrageous and sinister part of the treaty remained secret. Hitler and Stalin had agreed to share out the lands that lay between their two empires. When Hitler invaded Poland from the west, Stalin was to take possession of the eastern half of the country. Stalin would also be free to occupy the three free Baltic states – Latvia, Lithuania and Estonia – and in the south he would grab the Romanian-speaking province of Bessarabia (soon to be renamed Moldavia). This cynical division of the spoils made war in Europe not only inevitable, but also imminent.

A week after the pact was sealed, German troops marched into Poland. This provoked Britain, which had no means of helping the Poles, into making an impotent declaration of war. Stalin waited a couple of weeks until the Germans had completed their blitzkrieg campaign, then sent his troops across the western border of the USSR. Within a few days Russian and German troops faced each other along a new frontier running north to south across what had been Polish territory. Poland itself had effectively ceased to exist.

Stalin could now relax. It seemed that the war would play itself out in Western Europe. In 1940 he watched from the Kremlin as Hitler unleashed his shiny new war machine on Denmark, the Netherlands, Belgium and France. He observed from a distance the air battle over Britain and the subsequent bombing of British cities. True enough, Stalin took some military precautions in 1941, as reports came in that Germany was planning to break the non-aggression treaty, and he was alarmed and angered by an obvious build-up of German forces on his western borders. But like Chamberlain and other leaders in the 1930s, Stalin did not want to rile Hitler, especially now that the Wehrmacht had been tempered in battle and had all the resources of Europe behind it.

In the middle of June 1941 Stalin received a frantic message from his most reliable foreign spy, saying that the Germans were definitely going to invade in one week's time. It was a golden piece of intelligence – but Stalin refused to believe it.

BARBAROSSA – 'REDBEARD'

The German attack on Russia was launched before dawn on the morning of 22 June 1941. It was the largest invasion in the history of warfare. Some four million men smashed through the Soviet defences at three points along the lengthy Russian border. Army Group North struck across the Baltic states towards Leningrad; Army Group Centre headed due east from Warsaw towards Minsk, Smolensk and, beyond them, Moscow; Army Group South, backed up by Hungarian and Romanian forces, punched its way into the Ukraine. This vast onslaught was code-named 'Barbarossa' – Redbeard – in honour of Frederick I, the great German king who led the Third Crusade against Saladin in 1189. For Hitler, this was a no less glorious and sanctified undertaking. He was going to rid the world of the heresy of Bolshevism.

Stalin, for his part, was shocked to the core by the treacherous attack. He seems to have had some kind of breakdown, for he disappeared into his apartment and did not emerge for days. In effect, he deserted his post as commander-in-chief. To the dismay and bewilderment of the Soviet people, it was foreign minister Molotov who made the radio announcement on the first day of the invasion, informing them that the country was at war. But within the fortnight Stalin somehow pulled himself together, and emerged from his dark hidey-hole. On 3 July he addressed his people in a radio broadcast. Erskine Caldwell, an American living in Moscow, was up early to hear the speech. This is what he wrote in his diary:

At 6.30 am practically every person in the city was within
earshot of a radio, either home set or street loudspeaker.
Red Square and the surrounding plazas, usually partially
deserted at that hour, were filled with crowds. When Stalin's
speech began, his words resounded from all directions,
indicating that amplifiers were carrying the message to
every nook and cranny of the city. This was Stalin's first
speech to the people through a microphone since 1938. His
intervening ones had been delivered either to government
gatherings or for recording machines.

Stalin's guttural Georgian consonants would have grated on Russian ears had he not been so feared and revered. His tone was flat and his delivery was halting, but his first words were emotional, replete with the paternal condescension of the tsars of old: 'Comrades, citizens, brothers and sisters, fighting men of our army and navy. I am speaking to you, my friends ...' He began with a great lie. He said that 'the enemy's finest divisions had already been smashed and met their doom on the field of battle', adding the contradictory admission that 'the enemy continues to push forward'. Then he summed up the Germans' war aims as he saw them, or as he wanted his simple people to understand them:

> The enemy is cruel and implacable. He is out to seize our lands watered by the sweat of our brow, to seize our grain and oil, secured by the labour of our hands. He is out to restore the rule of the landlords, to restore tsarism, to Germanize our people, to turn them into the slaves of German princes and barons.

All this was true, given a little poetic licence. But everything Stalin had said up to this point was a preamble for his call to arms, his summons to destroy the enemy or, failing that, to destroy everything in his path, to 'scorch the earth' of Russia and make life hell for the invader.

> In case of a forced retreat, all rolling stock must be evacuated, the enemy must not be left a single engine, a single railway car, a single pound of grain or gallon of fuel. The collective farmers must drive all their cattle and turn over their grain to the safe keeping of the authorities for transport to the rear. All valuable property, including metals, grain and fuel, that cannot be withdrawn, must be destroyed without fail.
> In areas occupied by the enemy, guerrilla units, mounted and on foot, must be formed. Sabotage groups must be organized to combat the enemy, to foment guerrilla warfare

everywhere, to blow up bridges and roads, to damage
telephone and telegraph lines, to set fire to forests, stores
and transport. In occupied regions conditions must be
made unbearable for the enemy and his accomplices. They
must be hounded and annihilated at every step, and all their
measures frustrated.

Caldwell, listening on the street in Moscow, was impressed both by
Stalin's words and by the instant reaction to them.

As an observer, I had the feeling that this announcement
immediately brought about the beginning of a new era in
Soviet life. The people have heard for the first time since the
war began a fighting speech by their leader. As a Russian
said to me, you may be sure that from this moment a
grapple to the death has begun. From what I have seen
during the day in the hotels and on the streets, I would not
be surprised if the entire population of Moscow suddenly
besieged the military offices for permission to move *en masse*
to the front. A Russian girl told me today, and it is typical of
sidewalk conversation, that the winning of this war was now
the sole objective of her life. If there is any such thing as so-
called total war, this is to be it. The battle of the Russian
Steppes will make all previous conflicts seem like rehearsals.

Without doubt, Stalin's dry rhetoric, along with the very fact of the
invasion, had raised the Russian people to heights of righteous fury.
The universal popular conviction that this was a sacred war helped the
Soviet government's efforts throughout the long years of conflict that
were to come. This patriotic outrage was an intangible factor, but in
the end perhaps the decisive one in their eventual victory.

But for now, the Germans were entirely in the ascendant. Harald
Henry, a 20-year-old infantryman, crossed into Russian territory on
25 June, in the second wave of the invasion. He was taken aback by the
havoc that his comrades had already wrought.

The sight of the line of retreat of their army, wrecked by our tanks and our stukas, is truly awful and shocking. Huge craters left by the stuka bombs all along the edges of the road that had blown even the largest and heaviest of their tanks up in the air and swivelled them round. Their army was taken by surprise, and was finished off by our tanks. And now we've been marching for 25 kilometres past images of terrible destruction. About 200 smashed-up, burnt-out tanks turned upside down, guns, lorries, field kitchens, motor-cycles, anti-tank guns, a sea of weapons, helmets, items of equipment of all kinds, pianos and radios, filming vehicles, medical equipment, boxes of munitions and books, grenades, blankets, coats, knapsacks. In among them, corpses already turning black.

Worst of all are the horses, torn to pieces, bloated, their intestines hanging out, their bloody muzzles torn away, gruesomely halfway between slaughtered and rotting, giving off a stench of putrefaction that hangs numbingly over our columns. The worst was a pig that was gnawing away with such relish at one of these dead horses that it made me think I might like a taste of horsemeat too.

Henry could not have imagined that a time would come when German soldiers would be glad of a piece of rotting horsemeat. In these first, hot weeks of the war in the east, everything seemed to be going better than any *Landser* – German trooper – could have hoped. Their problems were the problems of success: the advance was so swift that the infantry was almost constantly exhausted. They could not go forwards as fast as the Russians were retreating. The day after Stalin's speech, Henry was well on his way to the city of Mogilev, but suffering from the intense summer heat.

Endless hours of marching ahead, 25 or 30 kilometres past shattered and burnt-out tanks, vehicle after vehicle, passing the skeletons of shot-up and totally scorched villages.

The walls that remain rise up black and ghostly, with a few bright orange lilies still flowering in a small garden – quite eerie. The strange smell everywhere, a mixture of fire, sweat and horse corpses that will probably remain with me forever as part of this campaign. The dust shrouds us all. The body is wet all over, wide rivers run down one's face – not just sweat, but sometimes tears as well, tears of helpless rage, despair and pain, squeezed out of us by the unremitting strain. No one can tell me that a non-infantryman can have the remotest idea of what we are going through here. Imagine the very worst extreme exhaustion that you've ever experienced, the burning pain of open, inflamed foot wounds and that's the condition I was in – not by the end, but at the beginning of a 45-kilometre march.

Others found the going easier, and were exhilarated by the fast pace with its promise of an early victory. Bernhard Ritter, in Army Group South, even found time to get interested in the strange land he had come to conquer.

On the move, 30th July 1941. It's now nearly six weeks that we've been marching and fighting here in Russia, and yet it seems like hardly three to me. That's probably due to the pace at which we're racing forward. We're now a good bit further east of the Dnieper and will probably soon be catching up with the panzers, so that they can then move further ahead. There just don't seem to be any days off, although our people are in sore need of them after the strenuous fighting that is now behind us at last. But this vast area can probably only be defeated by extreme effort.

Judging by my map, we seem to be leaving the impoverished White Russia behind and advancing into a somewhat better country, the villages are larger and situated closer together. The farmers make a reasonable impression. It is gratifying at last to see people that appear to have enough to eat after the pitiful wretches, to see people that are *pleasant* to look at.

19th August 1941, early. We're on the march again. This unending eastern land is so vast, it's quite impossible to try to gauge its extent. As one wave follows another at the beach, here it is always the same following on from the same. It's still not possible for us to grasp it, the only thing is to rejoice at details, a clump of flowers in an abandoned garden, a meadow, trees. Here the featureless spaces flow endlessly as far as the horizon.

German flyboys had it easier still. The unblooded Soviet Air Force was no match for the battle-hardened Luftwaffe. More than 2,000 Russian planes were destroyed in the air or on the ground in the first week of the invasion. Russian fighter pilots were so naive in their battle tactics that the German field marshal Albert Kesselring was moved to call the war in the air 'pure infanticide'. German bomber pilots such as Hans August Vowinckel went about their work unopposed. Eight days into the campaign he was bombing the ancient city of Smolensk, well over halfway between the start line and the goal of Moscow.

Smolensk is burning – it's been a spectacular sight all night long! After a two and a half hour flight we didn't need to search for our target, as gigantic fires lit up the night from afar as we approached. The colossal searching arms of the searchlights and the bright streaks of the anti-aircraft guns met high above the town – and we had to get through them in order to add our bit to the annihilation.

We flew in a wide arc over this fire dome. Then we set a course right into the centre of it. Inside the plane it was as light as day. The flames below drew one's gaze with magnetic force, as if they wanted to pull men and machines into them. But the engines kept up an even drone, and the plane continued on an even path. The light of the searchlights entered the plane, without stopping it; the flak

fire exploded without hitting us. Our bombs fell and
punched out new fires in the town.

But the battle for Smolensk, 250 miles (400km) west of Moscow, was
a kind of turning point. When the German ground troops reached the
city in July, they encountered strong resistance for almost the first
time. Here, where 121 years before the troops of Napoleon's *Grande
Armée* had paused on their way to Moscow, the Russians found the
strength to land the kind of blow that would at least slow the Germans
down. 'At the front events are not developing at all as they had been
planned,' noted Franz Halder, Chief of the General Staff and one of
Hitler's key advisers. Optimistic forecasts that Barbarossa would be
over in a month – or two at most – were forgotten or hastily revised.

Nevertheless, Moscow was still in danger. A strong thrust by Army
Group Centre could certainly have taken the city in August, and this
would have paralysed the entire Russian war effort. The war in the east
could still have been won during the summer, as had always been
Hitler's aim. But at this critical moment, Hitler made one of the
characteristically rash interventions that so infuriated his commanders.
He stripped Army Group Centre of its tanks, sending half north to
assist the attack on Leningrad and the other half south to bolster the
Ukrainian campaign. The battle-weary German infantry would now
have to march on Moscow without the support of armour.

As summer gave way to autumn, German soldiers in the field
began to worry that they might be following too closely in Napoleon's
footsteps. They had no greatcoats or warm kit, and were keen to finish
with Barbarossa before the long chill nights came. Unfortunately for
them, the snows and bitter winds arrived unusually early in 1941. By
mid-October Harald Henry, the soldier who had complained so
bitterly about marching in the heat, was in the open land before
Moscow, suffering from the even more painful ravages of cold.

From a quarter to six until two in the morning, with only a
short pause, we were out in a blizzard. It penetrated our
coats, our clothing gradually got soaked through, freezing

stiff against our bodies. We were feeling unbelievably ill in the stomach and bowel. The cold soon exceeded all bounds. Lice! Frost gripped my pus-infected fingers.

We advanced into the forests, up to our knees in snow that filled our boots. My gloves were so wet I couldn't bear them any longer. I wrapped a towel round my ravaged hands. It was enough to make you want to bawl. My face was contorted with tears, and I was already in a kind of a trance. I trudged on, my eyes shut, babbling meaningless words, and thinking all this was just happening in a dream. There was shooting, you fell into the snow, staggered on, turned in a circle, stood, waiting for orders. Torment without end.

Now it was nearly dark, we'd got through the forest. Then came the order: everyone to move on forward again. By now it was five o'clock. In the following nine hours we marched about 15 kilometres, the rest of the time we stood. Stood, wet and frozen, hands wrapped, in the open hour after hour. Boots froze solidly to the ground, we were wet through to the skin and stood, stood, stood, waited, marched on a bit, then stood again. I'm shattered in every fibre of my being, but will probably have to carry on when the onward march starts again tomorrow morning.

Lieutenant Willi Thomas was a 27-year-old infantry lieutenant. He too had remained happy and confident while the good weather lasted, but now his mood began to dip with the falling temperature. On 16 October 1941, he wrote a letter home to his girlfriend, Ingrid, and one can sense his soldierly optimism draining away almost sentence by sentence. His first taste of cold and hunger, and his alarm at the prospect of being surrounded, are a tiny presentiment of the horrors that his comrades would endure at Stalingrad the following year.

How can I begin to tell you, there is nothing I can say, began Thomas. My heart is still so full of the cruelty and difficulty of the last days and hours that I need to be holding your

hand, so as to free myself of it all in the telling. But I know
that just writing it to you will give me peace and strength ...

We broke through a line of steel and concrete bunkers
and there we tasted war in all its rigour and pitilessness.
Besides much else, that day took a particularly dear
comrade of mine. His laugh and his peculiarly rough
handshake will remain with me.

Though we were hoping for a little rest after this battle,
the forward march went on without a break. A thick blanket
of snow had fallen; it was almost as if heaven wanted to
cover all trace of the blood and death that were there to be
seen on that battlefield. The snow no longer melts, and the
frost is growing harder all the time. This is the beginning of
the Russian winter. After a good strong march we dug in at
last – in one of the few villages that is not burning. But
nothing came of the longed-for rest. At two o'clock in the
night we received the order to push on eastward.

In the vast open spaces of Russia, neither side knew when or where
they might encounter an enemy force. The skirmishing was sometimes
more like a naval battle than an infantry advance. The Germans
might spot a Russian grouping in the distance and engage it.
Or, like a submerging submarine, a Russian column might melt into
the landscape before battle could be joined. On this occasion both
sides were surprised to find themselves suddenly in the fray:

Before it had even got light, in thick icy fog, we ploughed
into the enemy, wrote Thomas. There ensued a battle
which was tougher and more brutal than anything I had
experienced until now. The acting commander, who was
standing in for Oberleutnant B., was not on the spot –
so I was leading the battalion almost single-handed.

We were attacking through a dense thicket. We were
making good progress until suddenly we were being shot at
from three sides, and were in danger of being boxed in by

the Russians, which is the last thing you want. The battle raged backwards and forwards until midday, when the main danger seemed to be over. Until nightfall we lay on the ground – the enemy fifty metres away opposite us – and even then we had a lot to deal with. More and more comrades fell both to the left and the right of me, and I often felt that I was practically alone in the field.

At one point a shot glanced off my helmet, knocking me to one side. I heard corporal Klein, who was lying next to me, shout out: 'Now our lieutenant is dead too.' But it wasn't that bad. A metal sliver had just ripped the skin by my left eye.

We were all wet through from rolling around in the snow. There was of course no chance of getting anything to eat. And so the night came – the worst night I have ever spent. It is impossible to describe how frozen cold we were. Once we had seen to our dead and wounded we huddled together in our foxholes and tried to warm up. Around dawn more snow fell, and the frost eased up a little.

Fortunately our wretched situation now came to an end, because the enemy had withdrawn – as they often do when they have received a bloody nose.

Hitler was hoping to deliver more than just a bloody nose. The decisive battle for Moscow, Operation Typhoon, had begun at the start of October. Almost two million German troops were ranged on a 500-mile (800km) front that formed a wide arc around the city. Stalin appointed the 45-year-old Georgy Zhukov to organize the defence of the capital. General Zhukov accomplished the task with panache and efficiency, establishing himself as Stalin's most useful and gifted commander. Nevertheless, by the end of October the Germans were close enough to the city to see its golden domes, and its nervous population could hear the sounds of battle coming from the west.

In an act of defiance, Stalin staged the traditional military parade through Red Square on Revolution Day, 7 November. The tanks and men that passed by Lenin's mausoleum, under the Kremlin wall, proceeded straight from the square to the battlefront. The Germans, meanwhile, were planning a decisive offensive, one last attempt to take the city before the year was out. That attack came on 15 November. It rocked the Russian defences, but petered out within a fortnight without penetrating the city. By now the temperature had fallen to 35 degrees below zero: the winter was not just early, it was one of the coldest in memory.

Zhukov's bold temperament was not content with merely fighting the enemy to a standstill. On 5 December, he launched a counter attack using fresh troops from Siberia. These men, who knew all about coping with cold, struck back hard at the shivering, demoralized Germans, who were stunned to find themselves on the sharp end of a Soviet offensive and could not hold their front line. Half a million German soldiers were killed in this one battle, and within ten days the Wehrmacht had been pushed back more than 100 miles (160km). It was now clear that the threat to Moscow had been removed until spring at least. Operation Barbarossa, the plan to defeat the USSR in a summer, had ended in failure. The war would resume come warmer weather. And the year 1942, the 'hinge of fate' as Churchill later called it, would see a different kind of struggle.

THE CHANGING SHAPE OF BLUE

Springtime in Russia is not a pleasant season. A damp and clammy cold replaces the crisp, dry frost of winter. The deep, crusty carpet of old snow melts, new snows fall, and together they turn the bleak countryside into a vast ocean of mire. The heavy topsoil remains saturated for weeks. It stinks of stagnation and sticks like glue. At the high tide of this swampy period, a man can sink into the ground up to his thighs, and the ground will suck the boots off his feet when he is pulled out. Even horses cannot wade through it, and travelling by wheeled vehicles becomes impossible. Russians call this annual flood of mud the *rasputitsa* – 'the time of no roads'.

Hitler's campaign of 1942 could not begin until the rasputitsa had run its course, since the Wehrmacht supply lines depended heavily on columns of trucks. The Germans also made extensive use of 'panje wagons', horse-drawn carts of almost medieval appearance that – unlike lorries and half-tracks – rarely broke down on the rutted dirt tracks that passed for roads in Russia.

But much planning was done in Berlin before the next round of the eastern war began. Despite the setbacks of winter, Germany was in a commanding position. The Wehrmacht had occupied a vast swathe of Soviet territory. Belorussia and the Ukraine – with all their industrial and agricultural resources – were in German hands. Kiev and Kharkov, the USSR's third and fourth largest cities, were deep inside enemy territory. The three Baltic states, granted to Stalin under the worthless non-aggression pact, were now in Hitler's domain. Leningrad – the second city of Russia – had spent its first winter under siege. And the front ran for more than 1,000 miles (1,600km) in a wavy line from Lake Ladoga in the north to the Sea of Azov in the south.

There was not strength enough in the Wehrmacht to wage war along this extended front. German strategists all agreed that a single *Schwerpunkt* – point of maximum attack – must be selected for the campaign. Hitler's generals, looking at the situation map, felt strongly that the best course of action was to strike a second blow at Moscow with Army Group Centre, the strongest prong of the German trident. Hitler disagreed. His plan was to use Army Group South to drive south-east from the Ukraine towards the oilfields of Maikop on the Black Sea and Grozny in the Caucasus. If he could do this, he would starve the Russians of fuel for their war effort, and so force them into submission. At the same time he could use the oil himself to continue the war in the west. So winning on this front would *ipso facto* provide the means of winning on the other. This was the kind of bold all-encompassing stroke that Hitler loved. He knew it was a gamble, but inspired rolls of the dice were his forte, the practical proof of his special genius. It was with relish rather than trepidation that he told his officers: 'Either I get the oil of Maikop and Grozny, or I must put an end to this war.'

The plan to seize Russia's oil was given the codename *Fall Blau* – 'Case Blue'. General Ewald von Kleist was the commander of the First Panzer Army, one of the units that was to spearhead the attack.

The capture of Stalingrad was subsidiary to the main aim, said Kleist after the war. It was only of importance as a convenient place, in the bottleneck between the Don and the Volga, where we could block an attack on our flank by Russian forces coming from the east. At the start, Stalingrad was no more than a name on the map to us.

Hitler said that we must capture the oilfields by the autumn, because Germany could not continue the war without them. When I pointed out the risks of leaving such a long flank exposed he said he was going to draw on Romania, Hungary and Italy for troops to cover it. I warned him, and so did others, that it was rash to rely on such troops, but he would not listen. He told me that these troops would only be used to hold the flank along the Don from Voronezh to its southerly bend, and beyond Stalingrad to the Caspian, which, he said, were the easiest sectors to hold.

No one could persuade Hitler that these foreign troops, far from home and lacking a commitment to the grand Nazi design, could turn out to be the Achilles' heel of the Wehrmacht. The Sleepwalker was too wrapped up in his dreams of conquest to hear other voices.

Case Blue was due to begin on 22 June, a year to the day after Barbarossa. But on the 19th a strange incident caused an unexpected delay, and nearly scuppered the entire operation. On that day a staff officer named Major Joachim Reichel took a flight along the front line to check the disposition of the opposing armies. He had foolishly taken with him a briefcase containing the plans for Blau in his sector of the front. But he flew too near to the Russian line and was shot down in no-man's-land. A German search party was sent out to find the wreckage. They located it without encountering the Russians, but they had been beaten to the finish line: the pilot's body was there; Reichel and his briefcase were gone. The foolhardy Major Reichel was in fact dead and buried. He had survived the crash, but was killed by the Russians who found him when he refused to surrender. His briefcase with its precious plans was already on its way to Stalin.

The Germans were plunged into a frenzied debate by Reichel's fatal blunder: should Blau be cancelled now that the Russians had the plans? Could the plan be adapted to take account of this security breach? They need not have worried. As Stalin pored over Reichel's maps in the Kremlin, his chary mind could not believe that the plane wreck and its booty were anything other than a deliberate deception. Perversely, seeing the evidence of the German intention to strike for oil in the south confirmed his belief that the Germans' real goal for 1942 was the centre, Moscow. He refused to shore up the line in the south by moving forces away from the capital. That, surely, was what the Germans wanted him to do.

So with Stalin's unwitting help, Operation Blue got off to a cracking start. On 28 June, the German Second Army and the Fourth Panzer Army poured into the gap between the parallel courses of the rivers Donets and Don. This strike force was supported by the Sixth Army under General Friedrich Paulus, which set out from the more southerly starting point of Kharkov. At first everything seemed to be going according to plan. 'The Russian is finished,' said Hitler to General Halder in July, and the normally cautious Halder could not disagree: 'It certainly looks like it,' he said.

But precisely because things were going so well, Hitler started meddling with the plan. He decided that the unexpectedly good progress meant that his armies were too generously deployed: if he split them up, he could achieve all the objectives of Blau and more. So Army Group South was divided in two. Group A was to rush to the Caucasus and seize the oilfields of Maikop, then perhaps head on to the jackpot prize of Baku on the Caspian coast, which produced four-fifths of Soviet oil. Army Group B was to destroy the Russian armies west of the Don. These tasks were now to take place simultaneously rather than one after the other. This meant that two Army Groups would function independently rather than support each other: their aggregate fighting strength would consequently be halved.

Moreover, Paulus's Sixth Army, the largest formation in Group B, was stripped of the support of Fourth Panzer – a move very reminiscent of the denuding of Army Group Centre at Moscow the previous summer. The tanks were sent south to join Army Group A. But late in July Hitler reversed that decision and sent the tanks back to the north, because something on the operational charts had caught his eye. Stalingrad, the city that bore the name of his wily adversary, was beginning to look like a personal affront. It was a nasty blot on the map. With a stroke of the pen Hitler decreed that the city would not just be neutralized: it must be occupied, conquered. This now became the primary task of the Sixth Army, which was presently battling its way down to the great south-westerly bend in the River Don.

NOT ONE STEP BACK

Stalin was alive to the threat facing his city even before it began to worm its way into Hitler's greedy consciousness. Martial law was declared in Stalingrad in the middle of July: from that time the city was under its jurisdiction, and the civilian population was put to work digging trenches and building tank traps on the western approaches to the city.

On 28 July, the Soviet high command, the *Stavka*, issued Order No. 227, the directive known as 'Not One Step Back', which was distributed to every unit in the Russian armed forces and solemnly read out loud to the troops. It reads like a sermon, and its question-and-answer format is the stylistic hallmark of the former seminarian Stalin. His personal signature invested the order with almost scriptural authority. The lesson begins with a reproach from on high.

> The people of our country, for all the love and respect that they have for the Red Army, are beginning to feel disappointment in it; they are losing faith in it, and many curse the Red Army for giving our people over to the yoke of the German oppressors while the Army runs away to the east.
>
> Some foolish people at the front comfort themselves by saying that we can always retreat further east, since we have much territory, much land and manpower, and that we will always have more than enough grain. They say this to

excuse their shameful conduct at the front. But such talk is lies and falsehood, and only helps our enemies.

After the loss of the Ukraine, Belorussia, the Baltic lands, the Donbass and other regions, we have much less territory, far fewer people, much less grain and metal, fewer factories and industrial plants. To retreat any further would be to ruin ourselves and our Motherland. Every little scrap of land that we give up strengthens our enemy and weakens our defence, our Motherland.

And so the time for retreating is over. Not one step back! – that must now be our watchword.

Can we take the blows of the enemy and push them back to the west? Yes we can, because the factories in the rear are doing excellent work and the front is receiving ever more aircraft, tanks, artillery and mortars.

Is there something we lack? We lack order and discipline. This is our main shortcoming. We must establish the strictest order and iron discipline in our army if we want to rescue the situation and defend the Motherland. Panickers and cowards will be eliminated on the spot. Commanders of companies, battalions, regiments and divisions, along with their commissars and political workers, will be considered traitors to the Motherland if they retreat without orders from above.

The document went on to spell out some practical measures. Any officer or soldier guilty of a disciplinary offence would be sent to a *shtrafbat*, a penal battalion. These units were used for suicidal tasks such as attacking across minefields. The only way out of such a unit was to be wounded, that is 'to atone with blood for crimes against the Motherland'. The shtrafbat was, in other words, nearly always a death sentence. Another new kind of unit was instituted by Order No. 227 – the 'blocking battalion' or *zagradbat*. The job of these formations was to linger at the back in any attack, and shoot any soldier who looked as if he was retreating or not advancing fast enough. In the course of the upcoming battle for Stalingrad, thousands of Russian soldiers were summarily executed or shot on the battlefield by other Russians, the unforgiving disciplinarians of the zagradbats.

Stalin's order certainly put the fear of God into the Red Army and perhaps added some steel to the Russian defence. 'If this order had been issued at the beginning of June,' said one Soviet infantryman, 'then our division would have fought harder in the Ukraine and may not have ended up in the Stalingrad region.' But Stalin's cajoling of his army could not stop the enemy advance down the Donets corridor. The Germans had caught the Russians in the crook of the Don and were chewing them up relentlessly. Hans S— was a corporal in the 546th Regiment, 389th Infantry Division. His unit was making headway but he was finding the going tough, as his letters home show.

> August 7th. For the last two days we've been positioned
> here, first we were supposed to attack, then that was called
> off, and at about 8 o'clock another regiment at the ready
> behind us attacked. Just a word about where we are.
> Two days ago we reached this immense plain. Not a village,
> not a bush, not a tree anywhere, and the worst thing, no
> water. On the other hand, not a cloud in the sky, and the
> hot rays of the sun are beating down mercilessly on our
> foxholes. As a result of our rapid advance and the thinly
> populated area (we're in the Don bend) rations are very
> limited. We Landsers ended up getting half a slice of bread
> a day. The last two days we haven't had any at all, just three-
> quarters of a billycan of soup from the kitchen once a day.
> But worst of all is coping with thirst in the August heat. We
> watch for the field kitchen a hundred times a day and wait
> from hour to hour to see whether there's any coffee coming
> to wet our tongues. The tarpaulin does provide some shade,
> but all the same it's terribly hot under it, as it has to be
> pitched so low to prevent the enemy seeing it.

The paucity of Russian villages was a real problem. Marauding the local population was the Sixth Army's main means of feeding itself.

This is why the corporal was complaining to his wife about having to go hungry.

August 8th, Saturday. I'm going to carry on with yesterday's letter now. We were pulled back three kilometres and got our water bottles filled. There we heard that the previous night the Russians forced their way into the village behind us and went wild. But they were pinned down and were finished off to the last man. These bastards – a whole unit of them – happened to find a position where the Landsers on guard duty had fallen asleep.

We stayed lying in a small hollow till twelve o'clock and then followed the unit that had been attacked earlier. Unbearable heat, and by six o'clock we'd reached our destination. Now we're positioned in an abandoned field of oats that would probably take a hundred days to harvest. We immediately came under heavy fire. Everyone's so thirsty, we can hardly get our holes dug. But it's got to be done, even though the ground is rock hard from the unending heat ... We are tense, waiting to find out if they're advancing in our direction. From what we've been told by deserters, the Russians have very good forces and have no intention of letting themselves be beaten.

August 13th. We took part in two attacks on the great Don bend. For once our unit was in reserve, which was very lucky for us, as there were many deaths. So we have a unit in our regiment which is left with 28 riflemen. As we passed by the graves in the battle area, we had to thank God that things went as they did for us, even though all leave is cancelled. For the past few days we've been getting plenty to eat again. What's more, the post arrived.

The intensity of the fighting was beginning to give Hans intimations of mortality. That, and the sweet melancholy of a letter from home, put him in a maudlin frame of mind.

Now, my dear wife, there's something I must tell you, in case it should come about and it is the will of divine Providence that I shouldn't return home, you have done everything for me that you could. I don't want this sentence to upset you or make you cry, my dear wife, when one is stuck here in the thick of things, as our regiment is, you have to reckon with everything, even though we and you don't want it to happen.

With his next letter, Hans sent some of the propaganda leaflets that the Russians were producing to try to demoralize the Germans. At this stage, before the Russians had taken many prisoners who were willing to help them with the text, the quality of the German in the leaflets was often poor. This naturally amused the Germans and made them think their enemy was inferior and stupid – the very opposite of the intended effect. In any case it was the Germans who were taking all the prisoners at this stage, and a pretty sorry lot they were in the eyes of their captors.

20th August, Thursday. I'm sending you a few leaflets along with this letter to show you what these bastards are up to – they must be really desperate. They seem to think that we Landsers should give ourselves up and change sides. We would rather not have to catch so many of them: all they do is grumble about Stalin. Yesterday one of these Russkies had the cheek to ask me for cigarettes. You should have seen the look on his face when I reached for my pistol. The nerve of these fellows is really too much at times, so that one of them occasionally gets a kick up the arse ...

Don't show these leaflets to anyone!

22nd August. Yesterday our unit was badly hit. Two comrades from my group were killed in action, and my good friend Zap was shot in the lung. You've no idea how we all feel, especially as the unit is about to go on the attack again early this morning. We're very tense. The Russians defend themselves fiercely. Now there's talk of our being pulled out, and that this was the regiment's last attack. I only hope so, since we're war-weary. Now let's see how things carry on and hope for the best ...

We've just learned that our commander also got severely wounded. Such a smart, able officer, what a shame. Our sarge, who's always been so courageous, is very depressed. Now here's our commander wounded, it's just beyond description. He's saying that if the unit does attack there won't be many men left.

Though Hans S——'s regiment had been badly mauled, the Sixth Army as a whole was rampant. They were battling two Russian armies: the 64th and the 62nd. Both were in full flight. The 64th Army had withdrawn across the river late in July and blown up the bridge behind them. Alexander Utvenko, a Ukrainian colonel with the 33rd Guards Division, had taken part in that battling retreat across terrain as dry as desert, and he had struggled to manage it in good order. Progress was impeded by the many natural ravines, deep cracks in the baked crust of the steppe, called *balkas* in the local Russian dialect.

When I took command of the division, it was already on the defensive, said Utvenko. On the 23rd of July the Germans had launched a massive attack with several divisions across a 22-kilometre stretch of our front. On our right flank, their tanks had broken through, and the division on our left flank had fallen back. I bent the flanks to form a circular defence. I deployed the mobile reserve in the defence: 17 tanks with machinegunners. On the 24th of July communications with the army were lost. They were restored on the 27th of July, only to be severed for good on the 6th of August.

The divisions to the right and left of us had moved out across the Don. I stood my ground, both because I had been ordered to, and because I saw my division as a strong point that our troops could make use of to take the offensive. I

had one German division completely pinned down, and
another two partially. We would soon have been overrun if
we hadn't dug in below head height. We were running out
of munitions and provisions. The wounded were sent to the
rear by night, on carts and camels. Right from the outset, we
were short of food. We started boiling and eating wheat.
By the 9th there was nothing left to eat at all.

That evening Utvenko received an order over the radio to cross the
Don rather than be annihilated where he stood. He now commanded
3,000 or so stragglers from the battles in the Donets corridor. Only
about one in 20 of them were to survive the retreat to Stalingrad.

The Germans sustained heavy losses, too. In just one sector,
we threw 513 German corpses into a balka. We had counter-
attacked and held our ground, leaving a lot of dead
Germans deep in our defence, and you couldn't breathe
for the stench of them.

We moved across the balkas in two columns. We broke
through on a narrow front, losing around 300 men. During
the night and morning, the Germans deployed an infantry
regiment to the east, closing the ring around us once again.
On the 11th, at four o'clock in the morning, the battle
resumed. We were bombed, and attacked by tanks.

The battle went on until midday. I myself reloaded my
Mauser five times. Some commanders blew their own brains
out. We lost maybe a thousand men. But one soldier took a
leaflet out of his pocket and started walking towards the
Germans. Galya, our interpreter at division headquarters,
shouted 'Look, that rat's surrendering!' And she shot him
with her Mauser.

Tanks were shooting at us point-blank. I was firing from
the last gun. The gun ran out of shells, six gun crews were
knocked out. The Germans ran up to the gun, and I jumped
from the precipice to a marsh about nine metres below.

A shell hit me in the legs, completely covering me with mud. The Germans were sitting up on the precipice, and I could hear them talking as I drifted in and out of consciousness. When it was dark, I and two other soldiers crawled out up to the next precipice, where we found another four men, and then more, until there were twenty of us. We sat out the day in a field of sunflowers.

Hidden among the flowers, Utvenko recalled another tight spot he had been in during the previous year's fighting. The memory of it made him believe that he could get out of this predicament too.

We had broken out of encirclement in 1941, too. That autumn, I swam across the river Ugra, breaking the crust of ice as I swam. The shards of ice were as sharp as needles, but I had to make it, I had to make it ... and I made it! But that was a picnic compared to the encirclement of this summer, when every drop of water had to be fought for. We were throwing grenades just to capture the German soldiers' water bottles.

I never took off my soldier's tunic. I escaped from the encirclement still wearing my insignia. If you're going to die, you should die in your uniform. To have a colonel's uniform but die in civvies would be miserable, shameful! If it weren't for Soviet power, I'd be nothing but a farm-labourer.

So we ended up with 120 armed men. We swam across the Don. Eight men drowned. By night, we mustered. I had a temperature of nearly 104. My new aide-de-camp, Vasya Khudobkin, was an obstetrician by training: he should have been caring for women, but he ended up treating men. But he killed more Germans than he cured our lads. He swam over the Don with his machinegun. After we crossed the Don, I assembled 600 armed men, and from the 16th to the 25th of August we held the line near Alexeyevka. At the end of it all, there were 160 men left in my division.

I haven't yet lived for myself, everything has been for the cause. Until the war, I didn't know what kind of a man I was. But now all I have left is to fight. No one will ever write to me 'Look after yourself!' All I can think about is that I want to die in Kiev.

The Russian 62nd and 64th Armies crowded into the isthmus between the Don and the Volga. Individual units and single soldiers drifted towards Stalingrad as the Germans massed on the far bank of the Don behind them. Alexander Fatyushenkov was one of the soldiers who had been chased across the river.

The heights on the right bank of the Don commanded a view of the entire region, and artillery and mortar batteries poured a sea of fire down onto our regiments, which were out in the open. The fascists were completely hidden in the woodland along the bank of the Don. The river was close by, but to quench our thirst we had to drink out of a bog. This bog was filled, everywhere you looked, with dead bodies of soldiers. It was hard to clear them away, because there were minefields all around too.

The Russians hit back with a new weapon, which the soldiers had christened *katyusha* – 'little Kate'. This was a battery of rockets that were fired simultaneously from a metal rack mounted on the back of a truck. On launch they flew into the air with a terrifying whooshing noise and a sheet of flame. A loaded rack vaguely resembled the pipes of a church organ – hence the German nickname for these weapons: *Stalinorgeln* – 'Stalin's organs'. Mikhail Alexeyev, a Russian infantryman with the 29th Rifle Division near Abganerovo, remembers his first encounter with their awesome music, before dawn on 20 August.

I had heard about the katyushas, but never seen them in action. And so when I heard that hideous screech and hiss coming from somewhere behind me I couldn't help

hunching down into my shoulders. I guessed what the noise
meant, so I looked round and saw a majestic and awe-
inspiring spectacle. It was as if some kind of steppeland
whales had come swimming out of the dark, lined up in
a row, and then let loose fountains of fire all at the same
time. Then we saw something no less terrifying ahead of us:
a line of flaming tornadoes, a good half a kilometre wide.
It seemed that the village of Abganerovo itself was hopping
around in some kind of mad, demented dance. That was the
rockets exploding.

By this time the Germans had already crossed the Don down to the
south-west, beyond the great left-hand bend. The Fourth Panzer Army
was wheeling round near Kotelnikovo to attack Stalingrad from
below. Russian units in the Kalmuck steppe south of the city were
doing their best to block the Germans' progress. Among them was the
10th NKVD Division, the police garrison of Stalingrad. Their normal
duties in the totalitarian state were to maintain order among the
civilian population.

Alexandra Batova was a nurse attached to these troops. She already
had experience of battle, as she had been a student in Minsk the
previous June. While she was sitting in a lecture hall, taking her final
medical exam, the bombs started to fall on the city around her. Now
she was in the small town of Aksai, 50 miles (80km) south of
Stalingrad, with a team of female nurses. And the German bombers
were above her once again.

Medical staff – surgeons, dressers and orderlies – worked
side by side with military personnel. When the bombing
abated towards evening they would go to the aid of
wounded civilians. I remember the enemy's terrible
bombardment of the villages of Aksai and Abganerovo.
The enemy bombed and strafed with such ferocity that
it was difficult to lift your head. Nevertheless Raisa
Shestakova (the youngest member of the battalion at

the time), Klava Shipovalova and Sasha Zhidok fearlessly bandaged the wounded where they lay on the battlefield, even when shrapnel was flying like hail.

I remember an occasion when I was told there were wounded civilians inside the school in Aksai. Raisa Shestakova and I went out to help. Watching Raisa bandage the injured women and children, it was obvious that her attentions were giving them new hope. Raisa and I worked through the night. Every last wounded civilian was given the help they needed. The following morning, our battalion had to fall back temporarily towards Abganerovo. When we returned to Aksai the next day, we were greeted by a terrible sight: the Germans had taken savage reprisals against the wounded civilians whom Raisa and I had tended during the night. They had all been shot – except for the Komsomol and Party members, who had been hung from trees in front of the school. That is a sight I will never forget.

So the stage was set for the battle of Stalingrad. To the south, the Panzers were poised to pierce the underbelly of the city like a lance. In the west, the Germans were in full possession of the sharp Don bend, where it points like an arrow towards Stalingrad.

It so happens that this right-angle turn in the flow of the Don is mirrored by a similar dogleg in the flow of the Volga, so on a map the separate courses of the two rivers form an hourglass shape. Here, and only here, the Don and the Volga are a mere 40 miles (65km) apart. On 22 August, when the vanguard of the 16th Panzer Division crossed the slow-flowing Don at Kalach, the tankmen knew that they were just one hard day's drive away from the goal.

2
ENEMY AT THE GATES

Tsaritsyn, the city later renamed Stalingrad, was one of a chain of fortified settlements founded on the banks of the Volga by Ivan the Terrible. He was the first Russian prince to use the title 'tsar', and to a Russian eye the name of the city seems to commemorate that fact: Tsaritsyn suggests 'tsar's town'. But in actuality, the fortified town he planted here in 1555 takes its name from the word *tsaritsa*, which is a corrupted form of the Tatar *sari su* – 'yellow river'. This is what the Mongol rulers of southern Russia called the tributary that flows into the Volga from the west at this point.

The Volga is more than a mile wide at its confluence with the little Tsaritsa. This is far too great a distance to bridge, so the town grew up on only one side of the great river. It spread thinly along the high west bank of the Volga (the right bank as you head downstream). As a consequence, Tsaritsyn was always a peculiar long and thin shape: on a map, the town alongside the broad river looks like a fat caterpillar on a tree trunk.

Throughout the 17th and 18th centuries, Tsaritsyn lived by the trade that flowed up the Volga from the south. Merchants came from Bukhara in Central Asia, and from India and Persia. Their ships docked here, and the town became a hub of the transport and postal network for Russia's southern provinces. Tsaritsyn prospered, but it was occasionally shaken by the paroxysms of civil strife that came on Russia like a recurrent fever. In 1606, Cossack supporters of the pretender known as 'the false Dmitry' gathered here with the intention of marching on Moscow. Fifty years later, the town garrison declared for the peasant revolt led by Stenka Razin: this uprising was more a year-long riot of destruction than a popular revolution, and it ended with Razin's public execution on Red Square in Moscow. When, a century later, a very similar rebellion occurred under the leadership of Emelyan Pugachev, Tsaritsyn was twice besieged by Cossack armies.

In the 19th century, a different kind of revolution came to the city: modern industry transformed the face of Tsaritsyn. Brick-making factories, breweries and a river port were built. In 1867, railway tracks were laid to Moscow, and Tsaritsyn acquired a fine neoclassical terminus in the heart of the so-called 'business district'. A refinery was built, and the largest fuel containers in Russia were constructed on the riverbank to hold the crude oil that was ferried here from Baku. Shipbuilders' yards, fisheries, sawmills and warehouses jostled for space on the riverbank.

Foreign investors began to take an interest in Tsaritsyn at the end of the century. In 1898, a French joint stock company built a metallurgical plant to the north of the established city. In 1914, on the eve of war, the Anglo-Belgian Vickers company put up the money for a machine-tool factory, which was built right next to the smoking chimneys of the French concern. These turned out to be poor investments: when the Russian Revolution came three years later, the new Bolshevik government promptly nationalized all foreign-owned companies. The French metallurgical factory was given the resonant name *Krasny Oktyabr* – Red October – and the Vickers factory was rechristened *Barrikady* – Barricades – a word ringing with romance for Communist revolutionaries.

In the wake of the Revolution, the old fever of insurgency racked Tsaritsyn once more. It was the focus of fierce fighting in the Civil War of 1918–20. While it was under siege by anti-Bolshevik forces in 1918, one of the Red commanders organizing the defence of the city was the man Lenin called his 'marvellous Georgian' – Joseph Stalin.

In 1925, as Stalin was installing himself as Lenin's successor, Tsaritsyn was renamed Stalingrad in his honour. This was ostensibly in recognition of the part that Stalin had played in Tsaritsyn's fate during the Civil War. But intentionally or not, there is a subliminal message in the circumstance that the 'city of the tsar' became the 'city of Stalin'. It is at least an appropriate coincidence, because to the Russian people the name seemed to say: I, Stalin, am your tsar now.

At any rate, once it bore the name of the leader of the world proletariat, the city had to shine. As the population of Stalingrad reached the half-million mark, the architecture of the city centre was renewed. Fusty old churches and monasteries were torn down, and gleaming white apartment blocks built in their place. The Victorian hotels and municipal buildings of the city centre were joined by the quasi-classical mansion blocks decorated with the stolid balconies, concrete urns and hammer-and-sickle mouldings that were much favoured by the best Moscow architects at the time. There were also some almost Modernist school buildings and hospitals: clean, boxy white façades with large plate-glass windows.

The men and women who laboured in the factories were provided with all the prerequisites of a workers' paradise: west of the Red October and Barricades plants were extensive 'garden cities' of workers' cottages. Outside the factory gates was a new circus, and the city also boasted a zoo. In the town centre and in the residential districts to the south there were sports stadiums, cinemas and 'palaces of culture' containing theatres and lecture halls. There were large open spaces, chief among which was the ancient Tatar burial mound of Mamayev Kurgan, which sat like a big green dome between the old town and the factory district. The kurgan was planted with fruit trees and dotted with cafés. On summer evenings lovers would climb the 100 metres (330ft) to the summit and listen to the military bands or watch the lazy boats on the river a mile away to the east, beyond which stretched the hazy steppe, flat and featureless like a dry ocean bed.

Turning a little to the left, they would see that the process of industrialization in Stalingrad had continued apace under the Soviet regime. A tractor factory – the *Stalingradsky Traktorny Zavod* or STZ – had been constructed north of the huge Red October and Barricades complexes. (The 'factory district' now stretched for 5 miles (8km) from the kurgan to the village of Rynok, and was a kind of town in its own right.) The machines produced by the STZ were the workhorses of the new Socialist agriculture. They won prizes at industrial exhibitions around the world, and to the mass of pro-Soviet Russians were the very symbol of the transformation of their country from a feudal society into a modern agro-industrial giant.

When war broke out, the STZ switched to production of the equally iconic T-34 tank – a case of beating ploughshares into swords. The factory had been sending tanks to the front for a year. Now, in August 1942, the front had come to the factory.

BLACK SUNDAY

Stalingrad was destroyed in a day. On Sunday 23 August, the Luftwaffe carried out a merciless and devastating raid. Nikolai Razuvayev was one of the few soldiers stationed in the city. Most were fighting the Germans out on the steppe.

The twenty-third of August 1942 is a day I will never forget, said Razuvayev. The unit I was serving in was deployed in Stalingrad, in the market district beyond the river Tsaritsa. It was around three or four in the afternoon, and I remember that the market was still buzzing with people, and children were bustling around the Prizyv cinema, waiting for the performance to start. All of a sudden, a voice boomed out of a loud-speaker: 'Attention, citizens – air-raid warning!'

The people thronging the market and walking along the streets looked up anxiously, but didn't particularly hurry to get to the shelters, as they were already used to such alarms. Two or three minutes later, anti-aircraft guns opened up, and five minutes after that thousands of bombs started dropping on the city. After ten minutes the sun was blocked out; everything was covered in smoke and dust. The ground beneath my feet was shaking. There was a continuous roaring on all sides, and fragments of bombs and broken stone were falling from the sky. It went on like this until darkness fell. The voice from the loud-speaker was still saying: 'Citizens, the air-raid warning is still in effect!'

The bombing was indiscriminate. All parts of the town were targeted, and no attempt was made to avoid residential districts. The workers' settlements with their little wooden cottages went up in smoke in the first hours. All that was left was a forest of blackened brick-built chimney-breasts.

Sowing terror among the civilian population was a large part of the Germans' intention. As many as 40,000 civilians were killed in two days. The death toll was perhaps greater because up to this point Stalin had forbidden large-scale evacuation. He had said that the retreating army would fight harder for a 'living town'. So on that sunny afternoon, most people were on the street or at home with their families. Larisa Ladnaya was a teenager living with her mother and a younger brother and sister in the south of the city. The raid changed her family forever.

My mother went into labour when the bombs started falling. A new baby brother was born. We all went to shelter in a railway tunnel. There must have been about thirty people in there. But they started to bomb the railway line, and shrapnel flew into the tunnel. Many people were killed in that tunnel in the first days. My mother was wounded in the chest while she was feeding the baby. My mother was bleeding and the baby was crying. Still, we spent that night there, and in the morning we buried the dead. Soon there was another raid. My three-year-old brother was wounded by a piece of shrapnel which went right through his shoulder. Two weeks later he died in my arms.

There was nothing to eat. We would run to the burning grain elevator and get some scorched wheat. Shells were bursting all around, but we had to try and get something to feed the wounded and the little children, who were crying and asking for food. Since I was older, they all turned to me for help. We could only prepare food and bring water at night. It was impossible to leave the hiding-place in daylight. A friend of mine was killed with her entire family

when her apartment block took a direct hit. Many of the
girls in my class were killed too.

The city had many wooden buildings which burned easily.
The oil tanks made a terrifying fire. Everything was bathed
in the glow of fires. The whole city was covered in smoke
and ash. Wooden houses burned, factories burned, the
jetties burned. The cannery in Yelshanka burned. We ran
there and tried to bring back some tins of food, but they
had all exploded in the heat. We came back with very little.

My mother would burst into tears whenever she looked at
us. A thick strand of my younger sister's hair turned grey.

On the 25th, an emergency one-page edition of *Stalingradskaya Pravda*
warned that looters would be shot on sight. Larisa, out on the hunt
for food, was as much at risk of being killed by her own side as by the
Germans. The same day's news-sheet published 'Resolution 404a' of
the City Defence Committee. This was the decision of the city
authorities to allow the evacuation of women and children. It was like
locking the stable door after the stable had been razed to the ground,
but it was the right move all the same. Until this point, leaving the
city, or even considering going over to the left bank of the river, had
been considered a criminal act of defeatism.

The newspaper, which was the official mouthpiece of the
Communist party, tried to make sure that its own resolution did not
look like desertion: 'We will destroy the enemy at the gates of
Stalingrad,' it declared. But the enemy had already kicked down the
gates, and was busy demolishing the walls. In the choking smoke and
impassable rubble that used to be a busy city, the paper's words
sounded like a very empty boast.

Survivors of the bombing now made their way by whatever means
to the river. Elizaveta Krekhova was alone in the city with her toddler
son. Her husband, an engineer at the STZ tractor factory, had gone off
to the front as a civilian volunteer. She had no idea if he was alive or
dead. So Elizaveta decided to do what was best for her child, and
embarked on a hazardous journey to the river station.

I dressed my son up warmly. He had only just learned to walk. I packed five kilos of wheat, and also my mincer, so that I would be able to make food along the way. That is all I took with me. I had only my own back and my own hands to rely on.

I saw a tractor with a trailer coming towards us. I ran out into the road, and lifted up my baby to the tractor driver, trying to explain with gestures that we needed to get to the Volga. He understood, stopped the tractor, and helped me to get into the trailer with the baby. There was another woman with a baby sitting in the cabin of the tractor. As I clambered up into the trailer I saw that it was full of artillery shells. I sat down on the neat rows of shells, and on we went. But to my horror, we got caught up in a bombing raid. The tractor stopped, and we all hid in a nearby ditch. I lay on top of my child. I was so scared: all it would have taken was for one bomb fragment to hit the trailer and we would all have been blown sky high. We couldn't crawl any further away from the tractor at that moment. And when we eventually crawled out we could not believe that the storm had passed over us for now at least. I climbed back into the trailer on the tractor, and we carried on.

Breathtaking, terrifying scenes greeted the people who made it to the Volga. The oil tanks embedded in the high right bank of the river had burst open. Broad streams of burning fuel flowed down into the water, so that the very river seemed to be afire. So the first survivors found themselves staring at the unnatural sight of flames leaping out of the waves, and of boats lighting up like matches and sinking before they could come to the rescue of the crowds at the river's edge.

The whole bank was full of children, said KS Bogdanova. There were very many children. People were trying to dig holes with spades or with their bare hands – to give themselves some protection from the bullets and shrapnel. As soon as it was light, German planes appeared over the

Volga. Flying low they swooped down on the river station, dropping bombs and shooting with their machineguns. The pilots must have been able to see that all the people on the riverbank were civilians. But they were acting like professional assassins. They opened fire on defenceless women and children, and chose their targets so as to kill the maximum number of people. They dropped their bombs on the crowds just as the people were beginning to get on the ferries, they strafed the decks, they bombed the islands where there were hundreds of wounded. People tried to make the crossing not only on ferries and barges. They went on overloaded rowing boats, even on logs and barrels or planks lashed together with wire. And the Nazis opened fire from the air on everything that floated. It was like a hunt.

The people were so tightly packed on the embankment that, as they jostled forward, those nearest the edge toppled into the water. Some drowned, others were crushed by boats at the jetty. People would take desperate leaps to a boat's deck as soon as any vessel came close enough. The boats did not moor, but lingered alongside the quay until they were packed to the gunnels, then simply moved away so that no more people could risk the jump. OK Selyankin was a senior lieutenant on a river trawler that was part of the rescue effort. He lost his ship, and had a close brush with death in this Russian Dunkirk.

All the usual naval concepts such as safety margins, stability on the water, and maximum capacity were thrown to the wind. All the ships had so many people on board that their portholes were beneath the water line. As we made our way to the left bank we tried to avoid making sharp turns of the wheel. And if we could, we avoided the waves made by exploding bombs and by passing cutters – they could easily have capsized us. But there was no way we could have taken on any fewer people, not when we saw the expressions of hope on their faces as we came in to dock.

We made four trips successfully, but during the fifth crossing an enemy bomb turned us upside-down. The explosion blew me into the water, and when I came up to the surface our trawler had already gone down. Only eight people were left bobbing about, trying to find something to grab onto. I undressed in the water, and put my komsomol card and my identification papers under my hat. Then we helped each other to swim to the left bank, which was about 400 metres away. The Nazi planes had run out of ammunition, and that was what saved us.

It goes without saying that there was no time to sit and recover from the ordeal. There was work to be done for anyone who was alive and unharmed. Some clothes were found for me and I was assigned to a little boat. I worked it for the rest of the day, and returned to base in the small hours of that night.

From the relative safety of the left bank, civilians and soldiers watched the long immolation of the city. The fires burned over a frontage of 8 miles (13km), and did not abate through 24 and 25 August.

On the third day, wrote the war reporter Konstantin Simonov, when the fires started to die down, you began to smell in Stalingrad that special heavy odour of ashes which from then on never left the city through all the months of siege. The smells of hot iron, charcoal and burned brick mixed themselves into a single, heavy, caustic stench. Cinders and ash settled quickly on the ground, but as soon as even the lightest breeze came off the Volga this black dust began to roll in puffs along the burned-out streets, and then it seemed that the town was smoking again.

But work went on despite the destruction. The tractor plant continued to churn out tanks, which went straight from the factory floor and into battle – unpainted, and driven by the men who had just bolted and welded them together. The distinction between a worker and a soldier all but disappeared. Fyodor Yerofeyev started the week as an employee of the factory, and ended it in the ranks of the Red Army.

I was working in assembly shop No. 2 as a controller.
My brother worked in the plant's steel-shaping shop.
The fascists had broken through to the Volga and were attacking from the north. They had taken the village of Orlovka, and had occupied the heights above the village of Spartanovka, where I lived at the time at 28 Tersk Street. Despite this, I went off to work.

It was eight in the evening when I began my shift. A gearbox was being finished off, and the fitter Anatoly Devyatov was adjusting clutches. It was then that the Germans swooped down. The bombs hit the pattern shop, killing many workers. After a deafening explosion, the blast wave ripped out all the frames in our shop, which was only ten metres from the pattern shop. They made several more attempts to drop bombs, but were driven away from the plant by our anti-aircraft guns.

We spent an agonizing night taking cover in the shop's oil tanks, in total darkness. When dawn came, the barrage of our anti-aircraft artillery subsided, and by morning we were able to leave the plant. The Germans were firing on the workers from the hill above Spartanovka. Me and my senior foreman, Pyotr Smolkov, got out through the garden. Once outside, I heard people saying that the Germans had already taken Spartanovka. My heart stopped, as that was where my house was, and my family too – not to mention all my documents: my military card, my passport, and my card exempting me from military service. But I still decided to find out what had happened in person, since it was only two kilometres to the village.

I got to the lower end of the village, and turned onto the concrete bridge where our militia were manning an observation post. They told me that I could go across, so I sprinted across the cement bridge and went to my house, where I found my 89-year-old grandmother and her daughter-in-law. I dug a slit trench to hide from the bombing, grabbed my documents, and went straight to the regional military commissariat. I presented my documents and asked to be enlisted in an active army unit so I could defend my plant, which had nurtured me ever since I was a pupil at the works school.

They assigned me to a 120-millimetre mortar battery that was part of the 149th rifle brigade commanded by Brigade Commander Bolvinov. The brigade commissar was a Georgian, I don't remember his surname. He later died by the circus outside the tractor plant. I was given a uniform and ordered to take my civvies home. I grabbed a carbine, and set off home with one of my comrades.

On the way there we caught up with my brother, who was walking home from the plant. He and I decided that I'd ask my commander to enlist him in my unit, and he joined our battery. After three days of relentless bombing – our baptism of fire – we took the oath. A crew of three pairs of brothers was formed to man our mortar: the Sibiryak brothers, the Banchekovs, and we two Yerofeyevs, Dmitry and Fyodor. I was appointed the commander of the unit.

No drill, no training. Fyodor Yerofeyev and his band of brothers were now in the war for the duration.

IN THE SKIES OVER STALINGRAD

The planes that rained terror and destruction on Stalingrad all belonged to the Fourth Air Fleet, the air arm of Paulus's attack force. The commanding officer of the Fourth Air Fleet was Colonel-General Baron Wolfram von Richthofen. He was a cousin of the 'Red Baron' of World War I, and had flown in his famous relative's squadron. His illustrious name and distinguished record had taken him to the top of the Luftwaffe, but he had nothing but contempt for the new Nazi élite. Like many aristocrats in the Wehrmacht, he took the view that Hitler was an over-promoted corporal, Göring a preening buffoon, and Goebbels a poisonous little toad. Richthofen seems to have had a fairly low opinion of Paulus too, whom he regarded as a rather timid, middle-class bureaucrat. In his waspish diary he constantly railed at the army's reluctance to seize the moment. This lack of fighting spirit, he felt, was largely down to Paulus's cautious personality.

Richthofen was equally contemptuous of the Russians. On the eve of the bombardment he dismissed both his own side and the defenders of Stalingrad in one sentence. 'Enemy much weaker than I expected,' he wrote in his diary on 21 August. 'Army always seems to have far too high an opinion of the enemy.' Richthofen had fought in Spain during the Civil War, where he led the notorious bombardment of Guernica in 1937. He was so inured to aerial bombing that the inferno at Stalingrad barely merited notice: 'Put the whole of Air Fleet Four in the air, with the result that we simply paralysed the Russians and helped Wietersheim's Panzer corps to advance 60 kilometres almost without firing a shot. At 1600 hours they reached the Volga.'

The Russian Air Force, it was true, was struggling to make any headway against the Luftwaffe. German fighter pilots were finding it almost too easy. Heinrich von Einsiedel was a Messerschmitt pilot and, like his commanding officer, a high-born German nobleman. He was a descendant of Otto Bismarck, the 'Iron Chancellor' who had made Germany a world power in the 19th century. (This family connection amazed the Russians when he was later captured: 'You are Bismarck's son?' they kept asking him.) Alone in his aeroplane, Einsiedel positively enjoyed the first days of the attack on Stalingrad.

> The waters of the Don and Volga reflected the sky of a scorching day. A light haze lay over the steppes as I circled high over them in my Messerschmitt 109. My eyes scanned the horizon which faded into formless mists. For a few seconds I gave myself completely to the joy of flying, that proud intoxication which is complete liberation from

earthly ties. But this was no time for dreaming. For the expanse beneath me was the town of Stalingrad and it was the 24th August, 1942, the day on which the battle for the town, the climax of the summer offensive, was launched.

Far beneath me, like so many columns of busy ants, I recognized battalions, regiments, divisions, vehicles, tanks: the German troops advancing on the Volga and Russian tanks counter-attacking on both flanks. A sudden call in my headphone brought me back to reality: 'Einsiedel! Over Pitomnik!' The Russians were behind the Stukas. Like meteors two Messerschmitts fell from the sky and crashed to the ground. The expanse between heaven and earth, which a few minutes ago had seemed infinite, suddenly became small. Our aeroplanes plunged into the few square miles of condensed space where Russians and Germans were locked in battle.

The day before, when the German combat squadron began its first daylight mass-attack on Stalingrad, not a single Russian plane had appeared. The city had remained undefended, open to destruction. But now the Russian command had seen what was happening. The Soviets put all their available planes into battle and an air-battle developed on a scale so far only seen in the West over the Channel. Every German Stuka, every combat aeroplane, was surrounded by clusters of Russian fighters which swarmed behind their own *stormoviks* in close formation.

We threw ourselves into the tumult at random. A two-star Rata crossed my track. The Russian saw me, went into a nose dive and tried to get away by flying low. Fear seemed to have crippled him. He raced ten feet above ground on a straight course and did not defend himself. My machine vibrated with the recoil of its guns. A streak of flame short from the petrol tank of the Russian plane. It exploded and rolled over on the ground. A broad, long strip of scorched steppe-land was all that it left behind.

Einsiedel was slightly wounded in the leg later the same day, but for him this was barely more than a sporting injury – something to tell his friends and team-mates about back at base.

> The pilots gathered at the squadron command post and reviewed the engagement. Thirty pilots, their sunburnt faces tense and full of expectation, their hair blowing in the wind, were standing before their commander, 'the Prince' as we called him. His head had something of the expression of those medieval statues to be seen in the great cathedrals of Western Europe. This group presented a colourful picture in the red glow of the evening sun. One was dressed like a trapper, in leather from head to foot, another in fur boots and shorts, a third with a coloured scarf and embroidered Ukrainian cap. One might have thought they looked a little played out, if one had not seen the passion and excitement of the battle on their radiant faces and if one had not known what this little group had only just achieved.
>
> Forty enemy planes were down for certain, and not one of the Il-2s had reached its base. I tried to imagine the same discussion among the Russians. How often it must have happened to them that a whole squadron did not return to base, and yet they seemed to become more and more numerous, and to fly better from week to week. How they managed this in view of such losses was a mystery to me, and even a greater mystery when one saw the captured Soviet pilots who, as a rule, had such dull and primitive faces. 'The Russians are simply too stupid to run away,' Goebbels had written in *Das Reich*. We had taken this as an insult to the front. But whence that country derived its strength, which seemed to increase with each day of the war, I did not know. It was like the fairy tale of the great undefeated giant who draws his unconquerable strength from the mother earth.

Einsiedel was justified in feeling insulted. The Russian pilots were not stupid (or dull or primitive); they were utterly determined – but they were outclassed. The attitude of AP Chubarov, flying in the same skies as Einsiedel, was typical: try to get at least one German before they kill you. He piloted an Ilyushin-2, a low-flying fighter-bomber designed to attack ground targets. The Russians called them 'aerial tanks'.

On August 18th we were given orders to bomb the Don crossings, said Chubarov. We set off in three groups, each of which consisted of six aircraft. This was my fifth or sixth combat mission. I confidently held my position in the wing, never taking my eyes off the lead plane. Our six Ilyushins soon encountered heavy German flak, and there were enemy fighters all over the sky. But all six of us made it through to the target just south of Kalach, and successfully attacked the bridge. I can't say that my bombs hit the bridge, but I am sure I hit a concentration of enemy forces. I saw that with my own eyes, so I am sure that the attack was effective.

As I came out of the dive I felt something strike my Il-2. The plane shuddered, a smell of burning filled the cockpit along with the sharp stench of an exploded shell. At first I thought I had been hit by flak from the ground, but then I saw that two 'Messers' were attacking me. My plane was out of control, and I began to go into a downward spin. I had reached an altitude of about 700 metres on the way out of the dive, and I was fairly sure that I was over our territory. I knew there was no way I could land the burning plane, that I would burn with it, so clearly I had to jump. With some difficulty I got out of the cabin, leaped into the air and pulled the ripcord. The parachute opened fine, and a kind of silence descended on me. Once I had taken a moment to calm down, I looked up and saw that holes had appeared in the parachute. The Messerschmitts were coming round to attack me again. I felt something hit my leg, and then there was a searing pain. But I managed to land near one of our own anti-aircraft guns. The ack-ack men gave me some first aid: a bullet had passed diagonally through my left leg and nicked the shinbone. It was not enough to put me out of action.

That night I left the anti-aircraft battery and hitched a lift on the road. That's how I got back to the airfield at Gumrak.

So a plane was lost, and the pilot was lucky to escape with his life. But with Russian pilots going down like swatted flies, it is hardly surprising the Luftwaffe felt it was on the high road to victory.

GERMANY ON THE VOLGA

The greatest German success of those August days was not their easy dominance of the air or even the pulverization of the city. The arrival of Panzers on the Volga at Rynok, mentioned in passing by Richthofen in his diary entry for the 23rd, was the really momentous event. That morning, as the Fourth Air Fleet was revving its engines ready to fly in and flatten the city, elements of General Wietersheim's 14th Panzer Corps set off on a dash from the Don to the Volga. In the forefront was General Hans Hube's 16th Panzer Division. Hube was a good choice for this piece of bravado. He was a grizzled veteran of the Great War, in which he had lost his left arm. The black prosthetic hand he wore lent a sinister air to his already imposing appearance. Hitler held him in high esteem because he was a commander who could get results. His troops loved and respected him and called him (not to his face) Papa Hube or, more reverently, *der Mensch* – 'The Man'.

The forward lunge by General Hube's 16th Panzer Division reached the Volga late in the afternoon of the 23rd. To the right of them was the flaming metropolis of Stalingrad. News that the Volga had been reached quickly spread back along the German line, and heartened the advancing troops. 'We'll soon be singing "A soldier stands on the banks of the Volga" for real,' wrote Berthold G——, quoting the song by Franz Léhar. This was on the 24th, while the air attack was still going on. The sights Berthold was seeing for himself, as he waited on the steppe for the land-borne assault against the city, were equally encouraging.

There's only one more range of hills, occupied and fiercely defended by the Russians, between us and the Volga. It's only 45 kilometres to Stalingrad. For the past two days our division's been very thinly spread out in a hilly area, as the artillery and the air force has to clear the way beforehand to some extent. And they're setting about it in a thoroughly German fashion. Yesterday we watched through binoculars as the Russians were retreating with their artillery. It'll be another few days yet before the attack on Stalingrad actually begins. The infantry divisions aren't as far ahead as we are, and it seems we have to stay here and wait for them. The Russians have wagered everything on Stalingrad. It's vital for the outcome of the Russian campaign. Stalin has apparently taken over the defence of the city in person. But even that won't change the fate of the city.

Berthold G— continued his letter home a few days later. Nothing had happened to dent his optimism.

28th August, Friday. The entire Russian front to the Urals and the Caucasus and as far as Stalingrad is being penetrated from the south by our Panzer and mechanized troops. You simply can't imagine the speed of our wonderful motorized comrades. Plus the assaults on the defending Russians by our aircraft. What a secure feeling when our pilots are in the air, as there are no Russian planes to be seen then. I want to send you a small glimmer of hope – first, as soon as Stalingrad has fallen, our division will have completed its mission. Apart from that, we won't be setting up winter quarters in Russia, as we haven't been supplied with winter clothing. So, God willing, you, our loved ones, will be seeing us again this year. Once Stalingrad has fallen, the Russian army in the south is finished.

The rumour about Stalin being in the city was wishful nonsense, as was the idea that the Germans were at the Ural mountains. But

Berthold G——'s assessment was sober enough: Stalingrad certainly looked close to collapse. The German presence at Rynok meant that the Russian 62nd Army, as it retreated into the city, was cut off from Russian forces north of the corridor. For the Germans, this opened up the possibility that they might strike south through the city along the riverbank, choking off the supply line that was already half strangled by the air attacks on river traffic. It would then be a relatively simple task to finish off the Russians in the ruins of the city.

But the motorized force at Rynok had not yet dug in. The Russians had to try to prise the Germans' grip away from the river before it was too late. Captain G. Pravilenko was part of a counter-attacking force, hastily put together from elements of the Volga military flotilla.

Under cover of darkness the naval cutters ferried our battalion of sailors to the Spartanovka area. Here they took up position on the right flank, next to a unit made up of Stalingrad workers. By morning the naval infantry had dug themselves foxholes on the edge of a deep balka. On the far side of the balka was the village of Rynok, where the Germans were running riot. We could hear shots coming from there, and we could even hear some heart-rending screams. German trucks were heading west out of the village. The trucks were filled with stolen booty.

Our task was to push the Germans back, to get them as far as possible away from the Tractor Factory. The sailors were all keen to get down to the job. All the more so as they had seen the fascists shoot up the steamer *I.V. Stalin* as it headed upriver with evacuees. The Germans had brought a cannon up to the corner of the Latoshinsky garden, and for the fun of it had blasted away at the steamer. The crippled ship had floated back down stream, burning. The Germans had not stopped shooting at it until it disappeared round the curve in the river. Lots of women and children died on that ship. All night we could hear the terrible cries of people struggling to stay afloat in the water, slowly losing hope.

They were calling for help, but many drowned. 'Is the attack starting soon, sir,' one sailor asked me. 'I can't stand this.'

The order to attack came at dawn. A company under the command of Engineer-Captain Grigory Rechkin, attacking along the riverbank, was first to reach Rynok and to engage the Germans on its eastern edge. The fascists were knocked back on their heels, and the German line of defence buckled. When our third company struck at the western end of the village, the enemy began to fall back, fighting fiercely as he went.

A searing battle blew up in the Latoshinsky garden, between Rynok and the hamlet of Latoshinka itself. The company in which I served as commissar was pinned down by enemy fire, and there was a danger that the whole attack would lose its momentum. But once again the tanks came to our rescue. One of the tanks rushed forward, smashed into the German line and trampled a machinegun nest under its caterpillar tracks. But a few minutes later we again came under fire from the side, which cut us off from our tanks. But the tanks came up again and led the advance. They pushed through the German defence. The soldiers rode into Latoshinka on the shoulders of the tanks.

Grigory Rechkin, who was the first man into Rynok and who was loved by all the men, died in the attack. Sergeant Avdeyev was fatally wounded by a shell blast. It took off both his legs. Even after he was wounded he found the strength to throw one last grenade at the Germans, and to shout a word of encouragement to his men ...

We captured much enemy equipment, including guns. In many of the enemy positions we found uniforms – they had retreated in their underwear. At the corner of the Latoshinsky garden we found a staff car, and inside it there was a briefcase containing documents. Here too was a table laid with food and wine, and near that the cannon that had shot at the steamer *I.V. Stalin.*

This Russian attack was the first of many that took place over the coming days. But in the event, none of them was entirely successful: it proved impossible to dislodge the Germans from the high ground around Rynok. The Germans in the advance guard were reeling under the Russians' constant blows, however. At one point things looked so bad that General Hube considered disobeying a direct order from Hitler to hold the bridgehead, and was about to withdraw his men. Reinforcements arrived just in time to make him change his mind.

By the end of August the Germans had fortified their corridor to the Volga. No Russian reinforcements could now flow into the city from the north. On 3 September the Germans linked up south of the city too. The tattered, battered men of the 62nd Army were surrounded, tied up tight inside the city like cats in a sack. And Hitler had every intention of tossing them into the river.

THE SIEGE BEGINS

Once the Russians were locked in, German propaganda units got to work churning out leaflets calling on them to surrender. These fliers depicted a solid ring of tanks around a sketch of the city. They also functioned as a *laissez-passer*: an accompanying text, in Russian and German, said that the bearer was to be allowed to pass through the German lines and must be treated as a POW according to the rules of war. Many demoralized Russians were persuaded to risk it. Berthold G——, still stationed some way outside the city, saw the defeated enemy coming in.

> September 2nd, Wednesday. The summer's nearly over and
> then it'll be back to winter again. Nothing much has
> changed here. We're still advancing towards Stalingrad.
>   The day before yesterday there was a massive assault.
> First stukas and all kinds of bombers, laying their eggs non-
> stop. Then they dropped leaflets urging surrender, with
> fairly good results. The Russian comrades held out for a
> short while, and then they threw in the towel. Long columns
> of prisoners in their thousands came wandering back.

Lads of 16 or 17, and 60-year-old men. There are also some
women among them, but those were all nurses. Nothing
will be done to them. On the contrary, they'll be useful for
taking care of the prisoners. There are dreadful scenes to be
witnessed in this parade of horror. It's beyond description.

It was clear to Berthold G—— that Russian resistance had stiffened as
the 62nd Army fell back towards the city, so at the beginning of
September he was less hopeful of catching Stalin in his own nest.
But otherwise he was happy regarding the progress of the campaign.

We're supposed to be pulled out of here, and placed elsewhere
for another action. After all, we're mechanized troops, and they
get bounced from one sector to another. We just drive along
one behind the other, and then by night when it comes to
announcing our position, we're told 'Another major enemy
troop has been encircled.' That's all we're ever told. We very
seldom know what is actually going on.

In any case, today we're 25 kilometres outside Stalingrad, and
at night we see the Russians fiddling about with umpteen
searchlights, but they mostly light up their own aircraft, which
usually go into action at night. In the day they come flying
surprisingly low from time to time, and then they're greeted
with showers of flak, and all hell is let loose. But our light
infantry is always at the ready too, and only this morning they
brought two Russians down very neatly.

3rd September, Thursday. I couldn't write any more yesterday
as the attack on Stalingrad is continuing. We're now only 15
kilometres away at most. You can now see the radio towers and
one huge water tower. Up at the front line I imagine they are
going at it hammer and tongs. All the same, Stalingrad will fall
in the next few days. We should be able to catch Comrade
Stalin then – who has taken over personal command of the
defence of Stalingrad, according to what we've heard. But the
old dog is bound to clear off in good time.

Stalin was far away in Moscow. But he had plenty of eyes and ears in the city and he did not like what they were telling him. On 3 September he dashed off a threatening and panicky telegram to Zhukov, whom he had sent down on 28 August to supervise the defence of the city:

> The situation at Stalingrad has deteriorated further. The enemy stands three versts from the city. Stalingrad may fall today or tomorrow if the northern group of forces does not give immediate assistance. See to it that the commanders north and north-west of Stalingrad strike the enemy at once and come to the aid of the Stalingraders. No delay can be tolerated. To delay now is tantamount to a crime. Throw all your air power to the aid of Stalingrad. The city has few planes left.

Stalin was demanding that the Russian forces north of the Rynok corridor break through and relieve the ten-day-old siege of the city. Zhukov thought it was crazy to try to do this right away. He was one of the few men – perhaps the only man – who could stand up to Stalin and contradict his judgment. He telephoned Stalin and told him that it would be pointless to start the battle without first taking the time to coordinate the actions of the air force and the artillery. As for the infantry, that had not yet even received supplies of ammunition for their rifles. 'Do you think the enemy is going to wait while you get yourself organized?' Stalin shouted down the phone. 'Yeremenko says the enemy is going to take the city at the first attempt unless you strike from the north.'

Zhukov calmly disagreed with the assessment of the commander of the Stalingrad Front, who was in any case his subordinate. He insisted that the attack wait for two more days. It was launched on 5 September and lasted for 72 hours – but barely made a dent in the German line. It did, however, force the Germans to transfer some forces from their continuing drive into the city, and so slowed up their relentless advance a little.

It was a small gain won at great cost, and it was not enough to help the Stalingraders. Natalya Tikhonova was a medical student who lived on the western edge of the city. When the bombing began on 23 August she was at home celebrating her birthday with her parents and sister. She had failed to get across the Volga, so she returned to the ruins of her home, where she had a strange meeting with the enemy.

> We were living in the cellars of wrecked buildings.
> There were five of us, two children and three adults, and
> we were sitting there and keeping silent. Then we heard
> Germans talking, lots of voices. Suddenly a German officer
> came in and said to us in broken Russian: 'Stay quiet, go
> nowhere, the SS are coming,' – and then he went away.
> He left us alone and said loudly: 'There's no one here.'
> I understood that much German.

She was unbelievably lucky. It was a rare German officer who would show mercy to a Russian – Tikhonova's guardian angel was certainly risking his life by doing so. But she could not stay in the cellar for ever, and when she emerged she found herself in Nazi-occupied territory.

> A few days after the bombing we left the cellar to look for
> water and something to eat. We had to eat anything that
> was half-way edible. Once we found a dead horse, and that
> for us was a real feast. Some of the cellars were flooded.
> We boiled the floodwater and drank it.
>   At the end of August it became easier to move freely in the
> city. The city was terrible to behold: everything was in ruins,
> blackened, and everywhere there lay dead bodies of civilians
> and soldiers, of Germans and Russians. At the beginning of
> September the Germans announced over loudspeakers that
> all able-bodied people were to go and register at the German
> *Kommandantur,* and that anyone who failed to do so would
> be shot. By that time we were already like robots, and we
> made sure that we did all that we were told. In any case, we
> could not bear to sit in the cellar any longer. Everybody who
> went to be registered was sent to a collection point guarded

by German soldiers. It was impossible to get away from
there – and those who tried it were shot. There were very
many of us there, and they informed us that we were to be
sent to Germany and put to work. We hardly cared. We were
all befuddled, like in a dream.

KILL AND ENJOY IT

The foot soldiers of the Wehrmacht brought terror to Stalingrad, just
as the Luftwaffe had before them. The bombardment and the SS-
orchestrated deportations were only part of it. There were reprisals
against civilians who were suspected of helping their own armed
forces; there were random acts of callousness or downright sadism.
And there was the fact that German troops were under orders from
Paulus to live off the land. This meant that stealing the food and (later
on) the warm clothing of the civilian population was an everyday
necessity for the men of the Sixth Army. If the Russians starved or
froze to death as a result, then so what?

But the cruel actions of the Germans at Stalingrad were not merely
an outworking of the vagaries of war. They were part of an intentional
Nazi policy to subjugate the Soviet people as a whole. The 'extreme
conceptions' that Winston Churchill had remarked upon before the
war – an utter lack of compassion towards non-combatants, and
complete contempt for the normal rules of engagement – were now
part of the military philosophy of the German armed forces. Hitler
had spelled this out explicitly. In March 1941, when plans for
Barbarossa were far advanced, he had warned his field commanders
that this conflict was to be something of an entirely different nature
from previous campaigns.

> The war against Russia cannot be fought in knightly
> fashion. The struggle is one of ideologies and racial
> differences and will have to be waged with unprecedented,
> unmerciful, and unrelenting harshness. All officers will
> have to get rid of any old-fashioned ideas they may have.
> I realize that the necessity for conducting such warfare is

beyond the comprehension of you generals, but I must
insist that my orders be followed without complaint.
The commissars hold views directly opposite to those
of National Socialism. Hence these commissars must be
eliminated. Any German soldier who breaks international
law will be pardoned. Russia did not take part in the Hague
Convention and, therefore, has no rights under it.

In other words, brutality was to be a difficult but necessary part of the
German soldier's task in Russia.

The speech in which Hitler made these remarks became known as
'the commissar order'. Communist party members, civilian or military,
were to be eliminated wherever they were encountered, because (in
Hitler's febrile mind) Bolsheviks were nearly all Jews, and all Jews were
by nature Bolsheviks. This vicious philosophy was spelled out explicitly
to the mass of ordinary German soldiers in a publication called
Mitteilungen für die Truppe, 'Information for the Troops'.

Anyone who has ever looked at the face of a red commissar
knows what the Bolsheviks are like. Here there is no need
for theoretical expressions. We would be insulting the
animals if we were to describe these men, who are mostly
Jewish, as beasts. They are the embodiment of a satanic and
insane hatred for the whole of noble humanity. The shape
of these commissars reveals to us the rebellion of the
Untermenschen against noble blood. The masses, whom they
have sent to their deaths by making use of all means at their
disposal such as cold terror and insane incitement, would
have brought an end to all meaningful life, had this
eruption not been dammed at the last moment.

Here was a formula for mass murder, and its results were noted in the
first year of the war. In Moscow in 1941, a young British foreign
reporter named Christine Haldane bumped into the Jewish Soviet
writer and journalist Ilya Ehrenburg. He was using his extensive

contacts in the army and the government to document Nazi atrocities in occupied regions of the USSR.

Ehrenburg, wrote Haldane, was deeply interested in the strange mentality of the younger Nazis and SS men, ruling-class Germans. To them, according to the conversations he had had with them, and the documents he had studied, war, this horrible, ghastly slaughter they have instigated, was merely a sport; the most exciting in the world. One diary was a day-to-day record of shootings, lootings, and drunken orgies in France, Poland, and Russia. Its author, a German lieutenant, wound up the description of one such happy day's activities as follows: 'Had a hell of a lot to drink, and got very tight. We then went to the cemetery and dug up the skull of an old Jew, with which we had a game of football in the moonlight. Grand fun.'

The Russians, who had studied many of these Nazis in the prisoners-of-war camps, were frankly at their wits' ends to understand their mentality. They were also appalled at the problem of what to do, when we shall have won the war, with such a nation, in which the minds of nine-tenths of the younger men and lads have been corrupted and polluted by this poisonous Nazi doctrine, which violates the elementary decencies of life. The ten commandments no longer have any validity in Germany. 'Thou shalt not kill' has been replaced by 'Kill, and enjoy it', when it comes to Poles, Czechs, or Russians. Harmless civilians, old men and women, young girls, little children, are natural prey to these Huns with guns. The Poles and Czechs in Moscow amply confirmed the facts told by Ehrenburg and the other Russian war correspondents. People in Britain – even though we have been at war with Germany now for more than two years – and still more in America, simply do not realize the orgy of sadism that Hitler has let loose in Europe.

I happened to remember, when I heard those horrible stories, that the German language contains a word for which I know no equivalent in any other – the word *Lustmord* or to translate it as nearly as possible, murder for pleasure; the adjective *lustig* means gay. Short of postulating some strange and unknown mental disease as having attacked the majority of the German nation, it is difficult to find a rational explanation for the conduct of this incomprehensible people, in thrall to Schickelgruber, the Viennese house-painter, who has made himself their devilish master. This problem of Germany's moral degeneracy was much discussed in Moscow; not only by politicians and writers but also by the scientists ... Thousands of Russians were firmly convinced that the German troops were always drunk and even systematically doped by their commanders before being sent into battle.

Most of the stories were all too true, and by the summer of 1942, Ehrenburg's intellectual curiosity had been replaced by a raw, undiluted hatred for Germans. In July, as the battle for Stalingrad was getting under way, he published an article in *Pravda* which recounted some of the dreadful tales of slaughter and cruelty that he had investigated. He ended his piece with the thought that the time had come to fight fire with fire, that a little native Russian *Lustmord* was required. In this, the concluding passage of Ehrenburg's article, the chillingly repetitive exhortation to kill falls as starkly as a drumbeat at an execution:

If a day goes by when you have not killed a German, then that is a wasted day. If you imagine that your neighbour is going to kill a German on your behalf, then you have not appreciated the threat. If you don't kill a German, then a German will kill you. He'll take your loved ones and will torment them in his accursed Germany. If you can't kill a German with a bullet, kill him with a bayonet. If things are quiet where you are, if you are waiting for the battle to come to you, then kill a German before the battle. If you allow a German to live, that German will hang a Russian man and rape a Russian woman. If you already have killed a German, kill another one – for us there is nothing jollier than German corpses.

Don't count the days passed or the miles travelled. Just count the Germans you have killed. Kill a German – that is what your old mother asks of you. Kill a German – that is what your child begs from you. Kill a German – the earth that bore you is crying out for you to do it. Don't miss. Don't hesitate. Kill.

The bloodthirstiness of the prose is shocking. But it is somehow more astonishing to find almost exactly the same sentiments expressed in verse. Konstantin Simonov, one of *Red Star*'s special correspondents in Stalingrad, published a poem entitled 'Kill Him' in the same week as Ehrenburg's icy diatribe. (This apparent coincidence, and the similarity in tone to Ehrenburg's piece, suggests hate literature was a deliberate new strand in Soviet propaganda.) Simonov's poetry reads like a kind of blood-soaked version of Kipling's 'If'. It is a coldly unforgiving crescendo of hatred. Here it is in a prose translation:

If your home is precious to you,
The place where you grew up a Russian;
If you love the log ceiling under which
You once were rocked to sleep;
And if you hold its walls and corners dear,
And remember its warm stove,
And the floors that have been worn smooth
By the feet of your father and grandfather;
And if you are fond of the poor little garden
With its spring flowers and buzzing bees;
And if you like the ancient table
Which your grandfather planted beneath the tree;
And if you do not want some German
To stamp his feet on your old floor,

To sit at your grandfather's table,
Or to fell the trees in your garden;

And if you love the mother who fed you at her breast;
A breast that is long since dry, but which you still embrace;
And if you cannot bear the thought
That a German stands before her now,
Grabbing her plaited hair and slapping her wrinkled face;
That the hands which bore you to your cradle
Should wash that viper's clothes and make his bed;

If you have not forgotten the father
Who held you in his arms,
Who was a good soldier in his time,
Who fell in the Carpathian snows,
Who died for the Volga and the Don,
For the sake of your homeland;
If you don't want him to turn in his grave,
If you don't want a fascist soldier
To grab his portrait and throw it to the ground,
To put a heel in your father's face
Before the very eyes of your mother;

If you do not want to give away
The one you walked with hand in hand,
The one you dared not kiss
Because you loved her too much;
If you do not want the fascists to have her,
To push her into a corner,
To crucify her three at a time, naked on the floor;
That those three dogs should take,
In pain and hate and blood,
The very thing you held so sacred
With all the strength of your love;
If you do not want some Nazi to take from you forever

The house where you lived,
The home of your wife and mother,
And all you call your motherland –
Then know this: no one will save them if you do not save them.
Know this: no one will kill him if you do not kill him.
If you do not kill him – until you have killed him –
Do not presume to speak of your love.
Do not call the place you grew up,
The house where you lived, your home.
If your brother has killed a fascist,
If your neighbour has killed a fascist,
Then that is their revenge, not yours,
And it does not pay your dues.
You cannot hide behind another man's back,
Or avenge through another man's gun.
If your brother kills a fascist,
Then he is the soldier – not you.

So kill a German. Let him, not you,
Be the one who is rotting in the ground.
Let the wails of mourning sound
In his house, not in yours.
Let his home burn, and let his wife be the widow.
Let his mother be the mother who weeps,
Not yours, and not your children.
Let his family be the family that waits in vain.
Kill a German, one at least,
Kill him as fast as you can.
As often as you see a German,
That is how often you must kill him.

Here on the Volga, Ehrenburg and Simonov were preaching to the converted. From now until the battle's end, killing was to be the city's only industry. Stalingrad was about to become a vast slaughterhouse, a rolling production line of death.

3
WAR OF THE RATS

On 12 September Hitler ordered General Paulus to fly to a council of war at his *Werewolf* command centre in Vinnitsa. This complex of log cabins in the Ukrainian forest, Hitler's forward headquarters, was a full 700 miles (1,100km) behind the front line at Stalingrad, but being here made him feel close to the action.

The Führer was upbeat, almost hopping with anticipation. He had just had a reshuffle of his top commanders, in which he had weeded out the defeatists and weaklings as he saw them. Among those to go was Franz Halder, who was the closest thing to a voice of reason in Hitler's immediate entourage. Other victims were Field Marshal Sigmund List, whose progress in conquering the Caucasus was deemed too slow. Two of the Panzer corps commanders at Stalingrad were also sacked for dawdling. Now, with right-thinking Nazis in all the key posts, and with his Sixth Army poised for a massive assault, Hitler was certain that Stalingrad would soon cease to be a problem. He had made plans for after the battle: the entire male population of this 'shrine of communism' was to be shot. As for the women and children, Hitler gave no specific orders. Presumably they were to be deported to the west as slave labour, like other unfortunate civilians captured in the earlier phase of Operation Blue.

Paulus, before his arrival at the Vinnitsa conference, had assured his master in a memo that the subjugation of the city should not take more than ten days at most once the offensive began. He had 170,000 men on the start line, ready and waiting to punch their way through the city to the Volga landing stages. The massive infantry force was supported by 500 tanks and 3,000 big guns and mortars. Behind this mailed fist was an equal number of reserves. Moreover, German air superiority was overwhelming: von Richthofen's planes ruled the polluted skies over the city. The Russians, on the other hand, had only 54,000 trained soldiers inside Stalingrad. They possessed barely 100 tanks, and most of their artillery was on the far side of the Volga. And many of the people manning the outer defences were women and factory workers who barely knew how to use a gun.

If, on the eve of battle, Paulus had any personal doubts about his ten-day timetable, he kept them to himself. The odds seemed stacked in his favour, and in any case he had half an eye on the promotion he was hoping to receive once the Stalingrad campaign was over: he had heard rumours that he was in line for the post of Chief of the German Armed Forces High Command. So all in all, firm-jawed optimism was the order of the day at Werewolf HQ.

By coincidence, on that same day – 12 September – Stalin summoned General Zhukov to a crisis meeting at the Kremlin in Moscow. The previous week, Zhukov had failed to slice through the German corridor north of Stalingrad. Three Russian armies – the First Guards, the 21st and the 66th – had been held off by a very professional German defence. This meant the enemy now had a strong grip on the Volga and could impede the supply line from the far bank: a choking hand at the throat of the city. The 62nd Army inside Stalingrad was completely cut off, and weakening by the hour. Stalin wanted to know what Zhukov planned to do about it.

The session was held late in the evening – Stalin's favourite time for holding court and for desk work. The Red Army's General Chief of Staff, Alexander Vasilievsky, was also there. Like Halder for Hitler, he was wont to express the sensible military view of matters when political considerations were too much to the fore; unlike Halder, he was on his way up rather than on the way out. Vasilievsky was a natural ally for Zhukov, who recalled the meeting in his post-war memoirs.

Vasilievsky reported on the movement of new German forces toward Stalingrad from the direction of Kotelnikovo, on fighting near Novorossisk, and on the German drive

THE GERMAN ADVANCE

BESIEGING THE RUSSIANS

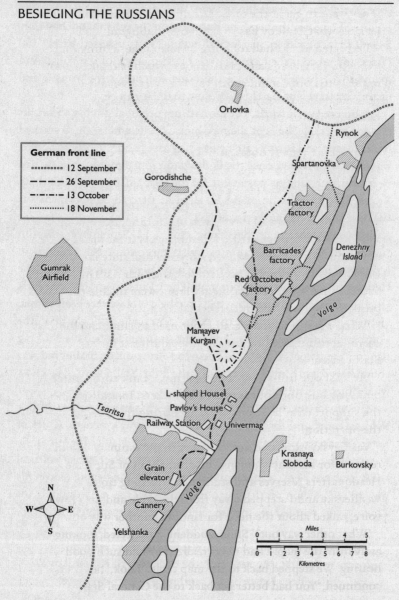

Orlovka

Rynok

Spartanovka

German front line
- 12 September
- 26 September
- 13 October
- 18 November

Gorodishche

Tractor factory

Denezhny Island

Gumrak Airfield

Barricades factory

Red October factory

Volga

Mamayev Kurgan

L-shaped House

Pavlov's House

Tsaritsa

Railway Station

Univermag

Krasnaya Sloboda

Burkovsky

Grain elevator

Volga

N
W E
S

Cannery

Miles
0 1 2 3 4 5

Yelshanka

0 1 2 3 4 5 6 7 8
Kilometres

toward Grozny. Stalin listened closely and then summed up: 'They want to get at the oil of Grozny at any price. Well, now let's see what Zhukov has to say about Stalingrad.'

I repeated what I had told him by telephone, adding that the 24th, 1st Guards and 66th armies, which had taken part in the battle of September 5th to 11th, were basically good fighting units. Their main weakness was the absence of reinforcements and the shortage of howitzers and tanks needed for infantry support. The terrain on the Stalingrad Front was extremely unfavourable to us – it was open terrain dissected by deep gullies that provided excellent cover for the enemy. Having occupied a number of commanding heights, the Germans could now manoeuvre their artillery fire in all directions. In addition, they could also direct long-range artillery at our forces from the area of Kuzmichi, Akatovka and the experimental state farm. Under those conditions, I concluded, the 24th, 1st Guards and 66th armies of the Stalingrad Front were unable to break through the enemy defences.

'What would the Stalingrad Front need to eliminate the enemy corridor and link up with the Southeast Front?' Stalin asked.

'At least one full-strength field army, a tank corps, three tank brigades and four hundred howitzers. In addition, the support of at least one air army during the time of the operation.'

Vasilievsky expressed agreement with my estimate. Stalin reached for his map showing the disposition of Supreme Headquarters reserves and studied it for a long time. Vasilievsky and I stepped away from the table and, in a low voice, talked about the need for finding another way out.

'What other way out?' Stalin suddenly interjected, looking away from the map. I had never realized he had such good hearing. We stepped back to the map table. 'Look,' he continued, 'You had better get back to the General Staff and give some thought to what can be done at Stalingrad and how many reserves, and from where, we will need to reinforce the Stalingrad group. And don't forget about the Caucasus Front. We will meet again tomorrow evening at nine.'

Zhukov and Vasilievsky spent all the next day sketching out a plan that was far grander and more ambitious than merely breaking through to Stalingrad from the north. In the course of that single day they came up with the blueprint for a massive counter-offensive, a giant encirclement deep in the rear of the German Sixth Army. They envisaged a pincer movement that would swallow the Germans whole, like the jaws of a python stretching around a big fat rat. Once the Germans were held tight, Zhukov would lay siege to the besiegers of Stalingrad and destroy them.

But this plan, dizzying in its scope, depended entirely on one highly suspect assumption: that the Germans would not be able to take Stalingrad while it was being prepared. Zhukov and Vasilievsky calculated that it would take six weeks to amass the vast numbers of men and tanks required – and yet there was every chance that Stalingrad would fall in the next 48 hours. But Zhukov thought it could be done, and was sure that this one big blow was a better idea than frittering away army after army on a series of small-scale operations. All the same, there was no way of knowing if Stalin would agree. Zhukov recorded that:

In the evening of September 13th, Vasilievsky called Stalin and said we were ready to report. Stalin said he would be busy until ten o'clock and that we should come at that time. We were in his office at the appointed hour.

He greeted us by shaking hands (which he seldom did) and said with an air of annoyance: 'Tens and hundreds of thousands of Soviet people are giving their lives in the fight against fascism, and Churchill is haggling over twenty Hurricanes. And those Hurricanes aren't even that good. Our pilots don't like them.' Then, in a quiet tone without any transition, he continued: 'Well, what did you come up with? Who's making the report?'

'Either of us,' Vasilievsky said. 'We are of the same opinion.'

Stalin stepped up to the our map. 'What have you got here?' he asked.

'These are our preliminary notes for a counteroffensive at Stalingrad,' Vasilievsky replied.

'What are the troops at Serafimovich?'

'That would be a new front. We will have to set it up to launch a powerful thrust into the rear of the German forces at Stalingrad.'

'We don't have the forces now for such a big operation.'

I said that according to our calculations we would have the necessary forces and could thoroughly prepare the operation in forty-five days.

'Wouldn't it be better to limit ourselves to a thrust from north to south and from south to north along the Don?' Stalin said.

I explained that the Germans would then be able to shift their armoured forces from Stalingrad and parry our thrusts. An attack west of Don, on the other hand, would prevent the enemy from quickly manoeuvring his forces and bringing up the reserves – because of the river obstacle.

'Aren't you out too far with your striking forces?' Stalin said.

Vasilievsky and I explained that the operation would proceed in two stages: after a breakthrough of the German defences, the enemy's forces at Stalingrad would be surrounded and a strong outer front would be created, isolating his forces from the outside; then we would proceed to destroy the trapped Germans and stop any attempts to come to their aid.

'We will have to think about this some more and see what our resources are,' Stalin said. 'Our main task now is to hold Stalingrad and to keep the enemy from advancing toward Kamyshin.'

At that point Poskrebyshev walked in and said Yeremenko was on the phone.

After his talk with Yeremenko, Stalin said, ' Yeremenko says the enemy is bringing up tank forces near the city. He expects an attack tomorrow.'

Turning to Vasilievsky Stalin added 'Issue orders immediately to have Rodimtsev's 13th Guards Division cross the Volga, and see what else you can send across the river tomorrow.'

So on that September night, when the full might of the Sixth Army was about to be unleashed on Stalingrad, the foundation stone of the eventual Russian triumph was laid. To adopt the plan for a counter-attack in November was an enormous act of faith on the part of Stalin and his generals. It was a seed of victory sown in secret.

But another event occurred on that day of meetings, one that went unremarked at the Kremlin but was almost as significant for the outcome of the battle as Zhukov's grand design. On 12 September, Vasily Chuikov formally took command of the 62nd Army inside Stalingrad, and so became Paulus's chief adversary.

The two opposing generals could hardly have been more different. Paulus was aloof, fastidious, always immaculately turned out. He was a gifted administrator rather than a front-line commander, and sometimes seemed to find the passion and squalor of war somewhat distasteful. Chuikov, on the other hand, was a son of the peasantry. In uniform he was irredeemably scruffy – something his contemporaries always joked about. He was naturally pugnacious and had the broad nose and beetle brow of a boxer or a street fighter (his father was locally famous as a wrestler). As a commander, Chuikov was ruthless and unforgiving towards subordinates who failed him. At the same time, he was congenitally incapable of despair. Most of all, he had the special gift, granted to some war leaders, of being able to imbue his army with his personality, to make it an extension of his own stern will. Almost from the moment Chuikov appeared in their midst, the men of the battered 62nd became as unshakeable and indomitable as Chuikov himself. And they needed to be, because on the morning of 13 September the Germans smashed into their lines like a giant steam hammer crashing into a brick wall.

ANNA, A PRISONER OF WAR

On 12 September 1942, the German front line at Stalingrad was 30 miles (48km) long. In the north it formed a wide loop around the factory district, taking in the village of Orlovka. But a little further to the south the Germans were ranged closer to the city. Their forward positions formed an undulating line that ran more or less parallel to the Volga at a distance of about 5 miles (8km). South of the Tsaritsa they were nearer still – about 2 miles (3.2km) from the river – and they had contact with the Volga beyond the southern reaches of the town. So on the eve of battle the Germans were still some way outside the city limits. But that was about to change.

The two-pronged German attack began on the 13th, and was directed mainly at the southern half of the city. First came a day-long artillery bombardment that created a dirty pink fog of smoke and brick dust over the city. Then, while the German 295th Infantry Division raced for the hilltop of Mamayev Kurgan, the 71st and 76th Divisions struck out diagonally from Gumrak towards the central landing stage. Meanwhile, the 94th Infantry Division and the 24th Panzer Division drove like a steel nail through the southern suburbs of the city, heading north-east towards the same finish point on the riverside.

Anna Andreyevskaya was a nurse attached to a Russian unit south-west of the city. When the Germans reached her on the first morning of the attack, she was plunged into an ordeal that she survived only by bringing her own courage and quick-wittedness to bear.

> We had nothing to respond to the Germans' fire with – only the commanders had machineguns, said Andreyevskaya. All our signallers had been killed. So when at nine o'clock in

the morning the Germans went through us with their infantry and tanks, it was all over. We were taken prisoner.

I had crawled into the observation post to bandage the wounds of the deputy company commander. He died in my arms. I stayed in the observation post. It would have been madness to leave it, since the Germans were outside, only 20 metres away.

Merzlov, the regiment's senior political officer, jumped into the observation post along with four signallers. In addition to myself, there were another three signallers in the observation post, two of them wounded in the legs. The senior political officer said that he would admit anyone who so wished into the Communist Youth League, but it turned out that we were all already members. 'If I die, consider me a Party member,' I said to Merzlov. 'Very well, from this moment on you are a member of the Communist Party,' he replied. We shook hands.

The political officer was in the process of telling us where to direct our fire when I heard a terrifying noise, like a loud crack. When I lifted my head, the dugout was full of suffocating smoke and dust. And at the entrance where Merzlov and the four signallers had been standing there was now a gruesome pile of lumps of flesh, bones, clothes and smashed rifles.

By some miracle, I was still alive, though I had a pain in my side from being hit by something. I sat down on a shelf that had been made in the dugout wall, and when the Germans started throwing grenades into the dugout's passage I instinctively bent my head down onto the chest of the dead deputy company commander. I remained sitting in this position, as if frozen. I could hear German voices around the dugout. I was afraid the Germans would rape me.

I pulled out my revolver and put the muzzle to my temple. I could already feel the touch of the steel when I realized that it was preposterous for a strong, healthy person to end her own life. Captivity would be terrible, but perhaps I could be of some use to the Motherland even in captivity? Perhaps I would be able to escape. Perhaps the regiment would send reinforcements and save us. If I were already dead, it would all be in vain. No then. What will be will be. I put my revolver back in its holster.

Then a German officer jumped into the dugout. He started picking up map-cases, weapons and compasses. When he spotted me, his eyes widened. '*Weib? Weib?* Woman?' he said, and made a grab at my chest. I pushed his hands away. 'Weib,' I said, and told him to stop touching me. I took off my map-case and handed over my revolver. He was especially pleased with the map-case. He shook everything inside it straight onto the bloody pile, taking only my diary. '*Das ist Dokument,*' he said.

Anna was kept under guard for some time in the dugout where her comrades had been killed. Around midday she was joined by some other prisoners-of-war, men from her own unit.

A German radio operator had set up his equipment in the dugout's passage (I could hear its cheeping sound), and he was sitting on a shovel that he had rammed into a slope in the dugout's walls. Then three soldiers from my company jumped into the dugout. 'Anna, you're alive!' they shouted in utter amazement. 'The Germans have taken two of our battalions prisoner ...' Until that moment, I had been sitting there completely motionless, frozen to the spot. To block out what was happening to me and what might lie in store for me, I instinctively distracted myself from all terrifying thoughts. I started thinking about the words I would use 'later on' to describe what was happening to me. I have always considered myself a writer. But on hearing my comrades' words I took heart: 'Well there's something to live for, there's a purpose!'

Towards evening, the Germans settled down to eat their dinner. They were talking quietly. Several men peeped into my bunker, one at a time, and looked at me as if I were some kind of exotic wonder. I started to be gripped with fear: would I still be here when night came? Finally, I made up my mind.

I stood up, went out of the dugout and addressed one of the soldiers in German: 'I wish to speak to your officer.' He listened to me attentively and immediately fetched an officer. I saluted him and said: 'I wish to see your most senior commander. Take me to him.' And this officer took me to the very dugout in which I had lived before the Germans came. Only now it was different: they had already replaced some of the furniture. There were many officers in this dugout, all of them handsome and cultured-looking. I couldn't help noticing this.

The officer offered me a chair and asked me to wait. Finally, someone came up to me who I assume was their most senior commander, as everyone else there leapt to their feet and stood to attention. He sat down at a table and said to me, *'Was wollen Sie?* What do you want?'

I replied, in German, that I wanted him to send me to the wounded Russian prisoners. The German officer listened to me approvingly and then switched to Russian. He said that he had lived in Russia for a while, and ordered some officer to drive me to the Russian prisoners. I thanked him, saluted, and headed for the exit. 'Perhaps there's something else you want?' I heard this same officer say (I never did make out his rank). I turned around: 'Nothing! Thank you.'

Half an hour later, I was with my fellow Russians! They greeted me as if I was one of the family. I immediately did the rounds of everyone there. There were many wounded. They had had nothing to eat or drink since the morning, and it was a hot day. The following day, the Germans lined us up into a column. They had gathered all their wounded from the battlefield and they forced us Russians to carry them, on either our capes or our overcoats. We spent the night in Novoalexeyevka, on an empty patch of land surrounded by barbed wire, and in the morning we were driven to a camp for Soviet POWs, in Kalach.

THE GRAIN ELEVATOR

By now the offensive had moved up the edge of the city. On the second day of the onslaught, the men of the 94th Infantry and the 24th Panzer could see the huge bulk of Stalingrad's grain elevator, looking like a beached aircraft carrier on the near horizon. Willi Hoffman was with the 267th Regiment of the 94th Infantry Division as it marched into the city. 'We can see the Volga,' he wrote in his diary. 'But everywhere you look there is fire and flames. Russian cannon and guns shoot from within the burning city. They are fatalists, fanatics.' This note of grudging admiration for the enemy is a niggling presence in his diary entries over the next few days.

13th September. A bad date, our battalion was very unlucky. The katyushas inflicted heavy losses this morning: 27 killed and 50 wounded. The Russians fight with the desperation of wild beasts; they won't allow themselves be taken prisoner, but instead let you come up close and then they throw grenades. Lieutenant Kraus was killed yesterday, so now we have no company commander.

16th September. Our battalion is attacking the grain elevator with tanks. Smoke is pouring out of it. The grain is burning and it seems that the Russians inside set fire to it themselves. It's barbaric. The battalion is taking heavy losses. Those are not people in the elevator, they are devils and neither fire nor bullets can touch them.

The grain elevator was an unappealing piece of industrial architecture, about the size of a Norman castle, and just as impregnable. The concrete silos – about eight storeys high – stood side by side forming a solid, windowless mass. A kind of tower containing a staircase abutted one end of the concrete massif and led to a long flat storey atop the silos. This had a row of windows like the portholes on a ship – each one now bristling with guns. Inside the elevator was a small band of Red Army men – the apparently indestructible devils who so exasperated Hoffman. But they were a dwindling band: they could not hold out alone, so a section of the 92nd Independent Rifle Brigade, naval infantrymen of the Far Eastern Fleet, was on its way to reinforce them. When Stalin had told Vasilievsky to 'see what else you can come up with', these Siberian sailors were what he pulled out of the bag.

The 92nd Brigade arrived on the right bank of the Volga in their sailors' uniforms during the small hours of 16 September, when the German offensive was well under way. The sailors fought until nightfall. After this baptism of fire, one unit under the command of Andrei Khozyainov was given the elevator mission.

> On the night of the 17th, after a fierce battle, I was called
> to the battalion command post and given the order: take a
> platoon of machinegunners to the grain elevator and,
> together with men already there, hold it at all costs.
> That same night we arrived at the place we were told to go
> and report to the garrison commander. At that time, the
> elevator was being held by a battalion of not more than
> thirty to thirty-five guardsmen. There were also the
> wounded, some slightly, some seriously, who they had
> not yet been able to send back to the rear.

On the night that Khozyainov arrived in the elevator with his men, this building became the white-hot focus of the battle for Stalingrad. Forty-odd souls were holding out inside the elevator against the combined weight of three divisions. Khozyainov's arrival increased the tired defenders' fighting strength by a mere 18 men.

> The guardsmen were very pleased to see us, and immediately
> began cracking army jokes and making funny remarks. We

had two Maxim guns, one light machinegun, two anti-tank rifles, three tommyguns and a radio set.

At dawn on the 18th a German tank carrying a white flag approached from the south. 'What's going on?' we thought. Two men showed themselves from inside the tank, a Nazi officer and an interpreter. Through the interpreter the officer tried to persuade us to surrender to the 'glorious' German army, as defence was useless and there was no point in our sitting it out any longer. 'Get out of the elevator now,' insisted the German officer. 'If not we will show you no mercy. In one hour's time we will bomb you all flat.'

'What a cheek,' we thought, and gave the Nazi lieutenant a curt reply: Tell all your fascists they can go to hell in an open boat! You two 'voices of the people' can go back to your lines, but only on foot. The German tank tried to back away, but a volley from our two anti-tank rifles stopped it.

Soon after that enemy tanks and infantry about ten times our strength attacked from south and west. After the first attack was beaten back a second began, then a third, and all the while a reconnaissance plane circled over us. It corrected the fire and reported our position. Ten attacks were beaten off just on September 18th.

We were very careful with our ammunition, as it was a long way to bring up more, and a difficult trip. In the elevator the grain was on fire, and the water in the machineguns evaporated. The wounded kept asking for something to drink, but there was no water nearby. This was how we defended our position, day and night. Heat, thirst, smoke – everybody's lips were cracked.

During the day many of us climbed up to the high points in the elevator and from there fired on the Germans, especially at their snipers. At night we came down and made a defensive ring. Our radio set had been put out of action on the first day of the battle, so we had no contact with our units.

The Russians held out in their makeshift citadel in this way for a further three days and nights, until they were weak with hunger and half crazed with thirst. To keep their water-cooled machineguns from seizing up, they had to urinate into the casing. On 20 September the Germans launched their most determined and ferocious attack yet.

Around noon, twelve enemy tanks came up from the south and west, continued Khozyainov. To our dismay, we had already run out of ammunition for our anti-tank rifles, and we also had no grenades left. The tanks approached the elevator from two sides and began to fire at our garrison almost at point-blank range. We continued to fire our machineguns and tommyguns at the enemy's infantry, to stop them from entering the elevator. Then a Maxim was blown up by a shell together with its gunner, and in another part of the elevator the casing of the second Maxim was hit by a piece of shrapnel, bending the barrel. All we had left was one light machinegun. Concrete was raining down on us after each explosion, and the grain was in flames. Even at a metre's distance, we could not see one another for dust and smoke. We shouted to each other – 'Hurrah!' and 'All hands on deck' – to keep our spirits up.

Soon German tommygunners appeared from behind the tanks. There were about two hundred of them. They went into the attack very cautiously, throwing grenades ahead of themselves. We were able to catch some of the grenades and throw them straight back. Every time the Germans got close to the walls of the elevator we would shout out again: 'Hurrah!' 'Onward!' 'For the motherland!' 'For Stalin!'

On the west side of the elevator the Germans managed in spite of us to enter the building, but we immediately covered the areas they had occupied with gunfire. Fighting raged inside the building. We were so close to the enemy that we could feel and hear their breath, their every movement, but we could not see them. We fired at noises.

That evening, during a short lull, we counted our ammunition. It turned out there was not much left: one and a half drums for the machinegun, twenty to twenty-five rounds for each tommygun, and eight to ten rounds for each rifle. It was impossible to defend ourselves with that amount of ammunition. We were surrounded by tanks and infantry, no more than 60 metres away. We decided to break out to the south, towards Beketovka, as enemy tanks were cruising back and forth to the north and east of the elevator. We set off during the night of the 20th. To begin with all went well; the Germans were not expecting us here. We passed through the gully and crossed the railway line, then happened on an enemy mortar unit which was just taking up position in the darkness.

We overturned the three mortars and a wagon-load of bombs. The Germans scattered, leaving behind seven dead. They not only abandoned their weapons, but left behind bread and water too. And we were faint with thirst. 'Something to drink! Something to drink!' was all we could think. We drank our fill in the darkness.

And so the elevator was lost – but the defenders had done enough to hold the Germans up, to keep them from gaining a stronger foothold on the banks of the Volga. At the time, the Germans failed to see that this was a pyrrhic victory, won at far too high a cost. But the appalled Willi Hoffman almost admitted as much to his diary:

22 September. We have broken the resistance of the Russians in the elevator building. We have reached the Volga. We found about forty corpses in the elevator. About half of them are sailors – sea devils, they are. We took one prisoner. He is badly wounded and can't speak, or pretends he can't. Our battalion is now reduced to less than the ordinary complement of a company. None of our old soldiers can remember fighting as barbarous as this.

26th September. Our regiment is still engaged in
constant heavy fighting. The Russians continue to resist
just as stubbornly now that we have taken the elevator.
You can't see them: they hide in the buildings and
basements and strike at us from all sides – even from the
rear. Such barbarians, to use gangster tactics against us.
Russian soldiers have suddenly reappeared in a sector which
we occupied two days ago, and the battle has begun all over
again. Our people are getting killed not just in the front
line, but in rear sectors that we already have.

It was perhaps unreasonable of the Germans to expect the Russians to
fight in a civilized manner. But the 94th Infantry Division did not
care. They were just pleased to have cracked the hardest nut in this
part of town. General Paulus felt the same. He saw the capture of the
grain elevator as a symbolic victory for his men. So confident was
Paulus that he now found time to design a campaign badge for his
army. It took the form of a shield depicting the grain elevator as seen
from the west, the Germans' main direction of attack, and it had the
word 'Stalingrad' in bold Gothic script beneath it. Paulus gave his
sketch to a regimental artist to work up, but that was as far as it went.
The Sixth Army's victory badge remained on the drawing board. It was
never to be anything more than a general's doodle.

CITY ON THE BRINK
And yet three days into the attack, things were looking very good for
the Germans. The Luftwaffe continued to enjoy the easy pickings.
'The last few days have been pretty hectic, three to four assaults a day,'
wrote Manfred S——, a fighter pilot.

I've notched up two Russians that I brought down, and
others that don't count as I didn't have a witness, and I
couldn't keep my eyes on them as they crashed. We moved
our base forward a bit yesterday, to be closer at hand.
That means being constantly at the ready of course, and

here the nights are considerably noisier. It's quite amazing
how quickly we've settled into a new place. Up to now the
weather has been fantastic. It hasn't been decided yet
whether we'll be spending the winter here.

The protective wing of the Luftwaffe was much appreciated by the
ground troops as they advanced. One soldier wrote home: 'Yesterday
morning, after hard defensive battles north of Stalingrad, we went
back on the offensive towards the heavily defended city. The battle is
still very much under way, and the city is entirely obscured by clouds
of smoke. Above us, our Luftwaffe is working tirelessly, and fierce
dogfights can be seen all the time. We hope this bulwark of Bolshevism
will be in our hands very soon.' Even behind the front line there was
much evidence of destruction to cheer the heart of a German Landser
– even if now the prospect of a speedy return home was fading.

I had the opportunity to drive across the area where one
of the greatest Panzer battles over the last days took place,
wrote Corporal Otto K—— in a letter home. A vast, steppe-like,
slightly hilly terrain, and across it as far as the eye can see
shot-up and burnt-out tanks – and Russian ones at that.
There are hardly any German ones among them, I only saw a
single one, proof of the excellence of the German weapons.
    The general feeling is that the troops will be staying here
over the winter, so for the immediate future we don't expect
there to be much going on, so you needn't worry about me.
There are many German aircraft about, only the occasional
Russian one, so by and large the Russian Air Force doesn't
seem to be such a threat, at least not on this part of the
front. For days at a time the Russian brothers keep
themselves out of sight – Göring's boys are seeing to that.

The corporal will surely have come to rue his casual attitude to the
Russian winter: it was probably the death of him if he survived long
enough to see it. But for now it was the Russians who had reason to

be worried. Late in the evening of 16 September, an NKVD officer named Selivanovsky filed a secret report to Lavrenty Beria, Stalin's deeply sinister chief of police. Selivanovsky's job was to spy on his own side, and his report is first and foremost a summary of the state of morale inside the city and the army: are there traitors, wreckers or cowards? Is anyone voicing criticism of the country's leaders? Selivanovsky's notes are written in the dry, lugubrious tone adopted by policemen everywhere when they put pen to paper; and he is overly pessimistic about the loss at the grain elevator, which was very much still in the fight at this time. But despite these inaccuracies, the police report provides a vivid snapshot of the situation in Stalingrad at that precarious moment. It is a picture of a city on the very brink of defeat. Here is Selivanovsky's memorandum:

> As of 24.00 on the 15th of September, the enemy in Stalingrad has occupied the grain elevator, which has been penetrated by up to 40 enemy tanks and groups of enemy motorized infantry. The enemy also has the House of Specialists, situated right next to the Volga, 150–180 metres from the crossing. The enemy has moved more than 20 tanks, and groups of sub-machinegunners and mortar men up to this location.
>
> The railway depot, the former building of the State Bank and a number of other buildings have been occupied by enemy sub-machinegunners, who have turned them into strong points. The enemy has captured Mamayev Kurgan (which dominates all Stalingrad and the left bank of the Volga) thereby taking control of all the crossings and roads leading to Krasnaya Sloboda.
>
> Stalingrad was completely unprepared for its defence. No fortifications had been erected on the streets, and no underground depots of munitions, medical supplies and provisions had been dug. After only one day of street battles, the units completely ran out of munitions. Ammunition and provisions are now having to be

brought across the Volga, by the only crossing still in
operation, and only at night.

For several days now, the enemy has been shelling the
Volga crossings and raking them with sub-machinegun
fire, and three of the four working ferryboats are currently
disabled. Enemy aircraft are still subjecting our units and
the city of Stalingrad to continuous bombardment.

There are still instances of disorganization and
carelessness. On the night of the September 15th, I
personally went out into Stalingrad and established that the
command post of the 13th Guards' Infantry Division and
the communications post of the commander of the 62nd
Army, both located on the bank of the Volga by the NKVD
building, were completely undefended from the Volga side,
even though the enemy was only 100–150 metres away. I
pointed this out to the commander of the 13th Guards'
Division, comrade Rodimtsev, and steps have been taken
to strengthen the command post's defences.

Selivanovsky's report ends with accounts of a few mundane incidents
from the life of a Soviet secret policeman in wartime: it was a harsh
and cheerless round of arrests, interrogations, investigations and
summary executions.

At around 10pm on September 14th, a group of enemy sub-
machinegunners, having broken through to the area of
Medveditskaya Street, captured the command post of the
8th Independent Company of the city's Commandant
Directorate, which was located in a tunnel. Around eighty
men were taken prisoner when this command post was
captured, and they are now being used in small groups to
take ammunition to the German sub-machinegunners.
One such group was recaptured by NKVD operatives in the
area of the command post of the 13th Guards' Infantry
Division, and four of the six men in the group were shot

in front of the ranks as traitors to the Motherland. An investigation is under way.

On September 15th, a woman who spoke German was taken prisoner in the engagement outside the NKVD building. She said her name was Volodina, and she had actively participated in the engagement as a sub-machinegunner for the Germans. Since she was wounded she could not be interrogated, so Volodina was shot by our operatives.

The 62nd Army's Special NKVD Section, responsible for patrolling the city, has set up task forces of men from the regular army to detain those acting suspiciously. At 11pm on September 15th, one of these task forces was fired on from a building in the area of the city market. A search of the building found five soldiers dressed in Red Army uniforms. All five were arrested, and an investigation is under way.

Between September 13th and 15th, the Defence Detachment of the 62nd Army's Special Section detained 1218 soldiers, of whom 21 have been shot, 10 arrested, and the remainder sent back to their units.

Major Zhukov, commander of the signals regiment of the 399th Infantry Division, and Senior Political Officer Raspopov have been shot for cowardice: they had deserted the battlefield and abandoned their units.

It must surely have seemed to Selivanovsky that the fall of the city was inevitable, but he knew better than to say so. Others were foolish enough to voice such opinions out loud. One junior commissar wrote in a letter home that 'Hitler will take Moscow this year and take it easily. Stalingrad will clearly belong to the Germans in a couple of days' time.' (That gloomy but realistic prognosis will certainly have cost the commissar his life, as his letter was intercepted by one of Selivanovsky's watchful colleagues.)

The Germans, on the other hand, were in triumphant mood. Their vanguard was in the centre of the city and had advanced as far as the railway station, which they occupied. The loss of the rail terminus was a disaster for the Russians. 'The station was an advantageous spot from a tactical point of view,' said one Red Army man who fought there. 'It gave cover over the whole of the town centre, and for the Germans was the quickest way to occupy the centre and push on through to the river crossing. That's why they put so much effort into capturing it.' What is more, from the station the thick blue stripe of the Volga was plainly visible though the gaps between the buildings. Once they saw the river, the Germans sensed the battle was as good as over. German trucks came screeching to a halt in the city, soldiers piled out and began dancing drunkenly in the streets.

They were often in full view of Russians, who were too astonished by the sight of their opponents' celebrations to shoot them. One German, although he was a little way behind the front line, got wind of the jubilation of his fellow soldiers and began to nurse hopes for the future.

The Reich flag has been flying over the centre since yesterday. The centre and the area round the railway station are in German hands. You cannot imagine how we felt about the news as we lay in the earth holes wrapped in our blankets. The cold north-east wind came whistling through the canvas strips of the tent. It was pouring with rain. By way of celebration we cobbled together a mixture of flour, water and some grease (intended for lubricating guns) and fried up some pancakes. We rounded off this delicious meal with tea and the last cigarettes. We could give a housewife a tip or two.

Just as we finished – I was on night duty – the Russians attacked and tried to cut off the approach road into town. The firing didn't stop till early morning. Today it's a stormy, cold autumn day, and we're freezing even with our coats on, and are dreaming ahead of well-built winter quarters tucked into the earth, glowing little Hindenburg stoves, and a lot of letters from our beloved homeland.

THE 13TH GUARDS CROSS OVER

For the Russians, the capture of Mamayev Kurgan, 3 miles (4.8km) north of the city centre, was an even more catastrophic development than the loss of the railway station. This hill stood 335ft (102m) above the level of the river. From its rounded peak the Germans were able to survey the whole city and their artillery could rain fire on any boats that attempted to cross the river. They could not be allowed to hold the hill.

The only hope for stabilizing the front line inside the city rested with the reinforcements, who were coming across the river at a trickle during the night. The slow transfusion of new blood was just barely sufficient to keep the 62nd Army alive as a fighting force. The paucity of the reinforcements was due in part to the difficulties of crossing the river when it was under constant fire, and was partly a deliberate matter of policy. All available resources were now to be garnered for Zhukov's great counter-attack. General Chuikov's job (though Zhukov did not tell him so) was to keep the Germans busy until that time. He and his army were the bait in the big trap.

But the newcomers who came across the river from the east were often ill-prepared and under-equipped. The Soviet writer Viktor Nekrasov, who lived and fought through the hard September days, saw many of the green troops come over to the city from the left bank. It was a glorious and a tragic spectacle.

> There were times when these reinforcements were really pathetic. They'd bring across the river – with great difficulty – say, twenty new soldiers: either old chaps of fifty or fifty-five, or youngsters of eighteen or nineteen. They would stand there on the shore, shivering with cold and fear. They'd be given warm clothing and then taken to the front line. By the time these newcomers reached this line, five or ten out of twenty had already been killed by German shells – for with those German flares over the Volga and our front lines, there was never complete darkness. But the peculiar thing about these chaps is that those among them who

reached the front line very quickly became wonderfully
hardened soldiers. Real *frontoviks*.

Fortunately for the Russians, they still had one trump card to play.
The ace in their pack was the 13th Guards Division. This was the unit
that Stalin had personally ordered into the attack on the evening of
13 September, and whose inadequately defended command post was
noted by the beady-eyed Selivanovsky on the 15th. They entered the
fray at the moment when the survival of the 62nd Army was balanced
on a bayonet's edge.

The little iliad of the 13th Guards began with a waterborne assault
under heavy fire. Ten thousand men were crossing the river – a kind of
D-Day in miniature – after a forced march through the Kalmuck
steppe. One in ten of the guardsmen had no rifles, and those who were
armed had little ammunition. But there was no question of waiting
until they were properly kitted out. Every passing hour was an
opportunity for the Germans. So the 13th Guards embarked straight
away, their eyes and their boots still clogged with the dust of the
Central Asian desert. Vasily Grossman, a special correspondent with
the army's *Red Star* newspaper, described the entry of the Guards into
the city in an article published a few weeks after the event.

> The men climbed aboard the barges, ferryboats and motor
> launches. 'All set?' 'Full speed ahead,' called the captains of
> the launches, and the grey, rippling band of water between
> the boats and the bank began to grow, to widen. A little
> wave lapped the prow of the boats. The barges bounced
> on the waves, and the men of the landbound rifle division
> began to worry that the enemy was everywhere – in the sky
> and on the far bank – and that they were going into the
> encounter without the reassuring solidity of the earth
> beneath their feet.
>
> All heads turned in alarm, looking up at the sky. 'He's
> diving, the bastard,' someone shouted. About fifty metres
> from the barge a tall, thin, blue-white column, all flaky at

the top, suddenly rose up out of the water. The column collapsed, raining fat splashes on the men and washing over the deck. Then another column shot up rather closer, then a third. At the same time, the German mortars opened rapid fire on the division as it made its crossing. The mortars exploded on the surface of the water, and the Volga was covered with jagged, foaming wounds. Lumps of shrapnel thumped into the sides of the boats and the wounded cried out quietly – as if trying to hide the fact that they were wounded from their friends, from their enemies, from their own selves. And now rifle bullets were whistling across the water.

There was a terrible moment when a heavy mine struck the side of a small ferry. There was a flash of flame, and thick smoke covered the boat. You heard the sound of the explosion followed by another drawn-out noise that seemed to grow out of the booming sound of the first: it was the sound of men screaming. Thousands of men could see the heavy green steel helmets of other men trying to swim in the water amid the shards of wood. Twenty of the forty had died on the ferry, and it was a truly fearful moment when the guards division, strong as a Russian Hercules, knew that it could not help the remaining twenty wounded who were now slipping beneath the water.

The crossing continued through the night, and there has probably never been a time, while light and darkness have existed, that men have been so glad of the September gloom.

The motorized armada carrying the 13th Guards reached the far shore. The men clambered out of their boats and rushed straight into action, shooting as they clambered up the bank and into the dark maw of the city. Their commander, Alexander Rodimtsev, reported directly to Chuikov. Rodimtsev was tall and slim with grey hair sticking up like a bottle-brush on his narrow head. He looked like an intellectual, but he was a seasoned fighter, having experienced urban warfare as an 'adviser' to the anti-Franco forces in the Spanish Civil War. He was adored by his men, and held in high esteem by superior commanders. But now Chuikov gave him orders that were on the verge of the impossible. He and his men were to take back both the summit of Mamayev Kurgan and the railway station, and they were to do it right away.

The task of taking back the station was delegated to Lieutenant Anton Dragan, commander of the 1st Battalion of the 42nd Regiment in Rodimtsev's division. On the evening of 15 September he received his orders. The station was so close that Dragan and his men were there within a few minutes, and Chuikov knew by the sound of gunfire that his orders were being carried out.

> I had led my company to the railway station and began exchanging fire with the Germans, then battalion commander Chervyakov caught up with me, said Dragan. He came up close, and as he wiped his glasses he said to me: 'You have got to cut them off, those fascists, and hold them back. Hang on as long as you can. Get some grenades in.'
> I rounded up the company, and in the darkness we began to move round to the back of the station. It was night-time now, and there were noises of battle all around. Small groups of our forces dug themselves in inside half-ruined buildings.
> I could tell that the main station building was in enemy hands. We cut across the railway track to the left-hand side. At the crossing stood a damaged tank, one of ours, along with about ten tankmen. We gathered near the station building and then went in expecting hand-to-hand combat.
> It was a shock attack: grenade first, then a soldier right behind. The Germans made a run for it, shooting wildly in the dark. In the time it took for the Germans to realize that we were only one company we had set up strong defensive positions. And though they attacked from three sides several times in the course of the night, they did not manage to take back the station.

As dawn broke German dive-bombers began pouring hundreds of bombs on the station. And after the bombing came the artillery shells. The station building was in flames, walls were blown apart, iron buckled, but our people carried on fighting. By evening the Germans had still not managed to take the building. They finally realized that a frontal attack would get them nowhere, and so moved to surround us. Then we moved the fight to the square outside the station. There was a fierce fight around the fountain and along the railway track.

I remember one moment when the Germans had got behind us. They had gathered in a corner building on the square. We called this building the 'nail factory', because our reconnaissance people had said there was a large stock of nails there. The enemy was planning to attack at our back, but we guessed what they had in mind and launched a counter-attack. We were aided by a mortar company, which had arrived at the station by this time. We didn't manage to take the nail factory in its entirety, but we drove them out of one of the workshops. They were still in the workshop next door.

Now the fighting continued inside the building. Our company strength was almost used up. But it was not just our company: the whole battalion was now in an extremely difficult position. The Germans were pushing us back from three sides. We were running low on ammunition, and there was no question of eating or sleeping. But worst of all was the thirst. To get water, in the first instance for the machine guns, we fired at drainpipes to see if any water came out.

This battle had now entered its third day, but showed no sign of ending. Inside the nail factory, exhausted soldiers from the two armies tiptoed round each other, probing for some tiny tactical advantage, any fleeting opportunity to kill.

Plate 1. *The cult of Stalin reached new peaks in the course of the war. He was routinely described in the press as 'the genius organizer of our victories' and 'the great captain of the Soviet people'. He became a genuinely popular leader, the very embodiment of the Russian war effort.*

Plate 2. *Georgy Zhukov, Stalin's best general, was as ruthless as he was gifted. 'If we come to a minefield, our infantry attacks exactly as if it were not there,' he said. 'The losses we consider equal to those we would have had from guns if the Germans had chosen to defend the area.'*

Plate 3. *Hitler with his generals on the eve of Operation Blue. Friedrich Paulus, the recently appointed chief of the Sixth Army, is second from the right. Paulus was a gifted staff officer, but he had never commanded an army in the field. He did, however, have total belief in Hitler's genius.*

Plate 4. *German tanks made rapid progress in the summer of 1942, but it was not a comfortable ride for the tankmen. 'There is a fierce wind blowing that makes us all look like dusty millers on the sandy, unmade roads,' wrote one driver, 'And nothing but steppeland on every side.'*

Plate 5. *This playful sculpture stood outside Stalingrad's railway station, which can be seen burning in the background. In the month after the initial bombing of the city desperate hand-to-hand fighting took place here, under the eyes of the dancing children and the snapping crocodile.*

Plate 6. *In May 1942, German gunners accidentally fired on Wolfram von Richthofen's plane. He later sent a note to their commander: 'While it is a delight to see the fighting spirit of the German troops against aircraft, may I ask that they direct their fighting spirit against the Red Air Force?'*

Plate 7. *Many Germans thought the coming battle would be easy. 'We've crossed the Don and are now positioned a short distance from Stalingrad,' wrote one soldier. 'It has been hot, but at night it gets a little colder each day. But soon we will be standing on the banks of the Volga.'*

Plate 8. *This picture of the grain elevator was probably taken at the end of September, after it had at last fallen to the Germans. Massive damage had been inflicted on the corner at the south-west, which was the German direction of attack. The Volga is no more than a mile away.*

Plate 9. *In the days after the air raid on Stalingrad, thick plumes of poisonous smoke rose from burning oil tanks and blocked out the sun. The fires could be seen from 40 miles (65km) away. But the smoke was a blessing: it hid troop movements within the city from German eyes.*

Plate 10. *A German soldier sits in a cosy foxhole on high ground north of Stalingrad. His gun is trained on the Volga. The fact that the enemy occupied the riverbank at this point caused the Russians endless problems. It was almost nigh impossible to bring over reinforcements in daylight hours.*

Plate 11. *A band of Germans, adrift in the factory district, nervously scan the sky as a plane flies overhead. In the early days the Luftwaffe had control of the air, but by the end of October any passing plane was as likely to be a Russian fighter-bomber as a friendly Junkers.*

Plate 12. *General Vasily Chuikov (second from the left) holds a meeting in his cramped bunker. His HQ was at times within three hundred yards of the German front line. The grey-haired man on the right is Alexander Rodimtsev, commander of the celebrated 13th Guards Division.*

Plate 13. *Heavily armed Russian infantrymen share a loaf in some ruins. The man on guard has a Degtyarev machinegun – recognizable by its flat, frying-pan magazine. The two men on the left carry the ubiquitous and deadly Schpagin tommygun, while the man on the right has a long anti-tank rifle.*

Plate 14. *Russian artillery takes up position inside a factory workshop. 'The furnaces were a good place to take cover,' said one Russian soldier. 'Get inside there and the shrapnel can't touch you. And you're safe even if the bombs bring the walls and ceilings down on top of you.'*

Plate 15. 'Stalingrad is no longer a city,' wrote one German. 'By day it is a cloud of burning, blinding smoke. When night arrives, the dogs plunge into the Volga and swim desperately to the other bank. Animals flee this hell; the hardest stones cannot bear it for long; only men endure.'

The fighting in the nail factory would go quiet for a time then break out again even more fiercely, continued Dragan. In short skirmishes knives, spades and rifle-butts came in handy. Around daybreak, the Germans began to bring up reserves and company and they moved against us. It became difficult to hold them off. They were on three sides of us. I sent an urgent report on the situation to Senior Lieutenant Fedoseyev. The third rifle company, commanded by Junior Lieutenant Koleganov, was sent to help us out. On its way to us the company came under a storm of fire, it was attacked several times. But the tall, wiry figure of Koleganov got through with his company. His army greatcoat was covered in brickdust when he said laconically: 'Twenty men reporting.' In his report back to battalion headquarters this officer wrote: 'Arrived at nail factory. Situation difficult, but while I am alive no bastard will get through'.

Fierce fighting went on deep into the night. Small groups of German machinegunners and snipers began to get round behind us. They hid in attics, in ruins and in sewer pipes and hunted us from there.

Now began an odd game of leapfrog: Dragan was ordered to assemble a group of machinegunners who would try to get behind the Germans – who had already got behind the Russians – inside the nail factory. Dragan gathered a team of volunteers, but did not go with them on the mission. But perhaps he envied the men he sent out, because they at least got something to eat:

Each man received a five-day supply of food and ammunition, along with detailed instructions on what to do. Soon the German defence was in a state of alarm. It seemed they could not understand who had just blown up the lorry which had just brought them ammunition, or who had put their machinegun crew and their artillery auxiliaries out of action.

From morning till midday clouds of enemy planes hung over the city. Some of them would break away from the group and dive, then strafe the streets and the ruins with a hail of bullets. On the night of the 18th the Nazis blew up the wall separating our room from the rest of the nail factory, and started lobbing grenades through. Our guardsmen tried to throw the grenades back through the windows.

Dragan's men held out for another 24 hours inside the building they now shared with the Germans. On the 20th they received word from a civilian that the Germans were preparing a tank assault. The attack came on the morning of 21 September – 'the darkest day'. Dragan's battalion was pushed right back from the station square. The men retreated in groups down the street that led towards the Volga, less than a mile away, but 'the soldiers would crawl back from their positions only when the ground was burning beneath them and their clothes were beginning to smoulder.'

By the afternoon of the 21st, separate bands of Russians were fighting inside the Univermag department store building, a quarter of a mile east of the railway station. (This building was destined to play its own part in the battle some months later, at the very end of the drama.) Dragan himself was in a building one street away to the right, no more than 600 yards (550m) from the river. The supply of ammunition was now so low that the men in Dragan's group had pulled bricks from the walls and laid them in rows, ready to throw at the Germans.

There were now only 12 men left with Dragan, but they held out in this new redoubt for five days. One young officer lost his nerve and sneaked away at night. He was sure that all his comrades were going to be killed, so when he reached HQ, having floated across the Volga on a log, he announced that he personally had buried Dragan. So now no one at headquarters knew that the 1st battalion of the 42nd regiment was still in action.

The Germans were still well aware of it, though, and Dragan thought it would be a good thing to rub their noses in it.

We decided to hang out a red flag on the building, so the Nazis wouldn't think we had given up the fight. But we had no red material. What could we do? One of the wounded heard of the plan and took off his bloody vest. He wiped it on his bleeding wounds and handed it to me. The Nazis called out at us through loudspeakers: 'Rus! Give up! You are going to die anyway!' At that moment our red flag was raised over the building. My radio operator Kozhushko shouted back: 'Bark all you want, you scurvy dogs. We still have a long time to live!'

A German tank appeared at the rear of the building, and Dragan sent an anti-tank man named Berdyshev to deal with it. Berdyshev took the last three anti-tank shells with him but did not manage to fire them because he was grabbed by some Germans and dragged out through a window as he got into position. An hour later, the Germans launched an attack at exactly the point where Dragan had put his last emergency machinegun. Dragan guessed that the Germans had asked Berdyshev to tell them the weakest point in the defence, and that he had told them the opposite. This guess was confirmed in the afternoon when the Germans led Berdyshev on to a hillock of rubble in sight of the Russians and executed him with a bullet to the head.

The finale came later that day: another attack with tanks. The Russians knew their lives were at an end. They fired off the last of their ammunition as one man scratched a message on the wall: 'Rodimtsev's guardsmen fought and died for their country here.' Tank shells slammed into the building at point-blank range, and it collapsed on top of the defenders.

The Russians were buried in the rubble, but not all of them were dead. Some time after dark Dragan gained consciousness to find Kozhushko tugging him from the wreckage: 'You're alive!' The survivors were now stranded behind enemy lines. The Germans had advanced past them, but were still a few hundred yards short of the Volga. So Dragan and the handful of men he had left crept through the streets towards the river and their own lines. They killed two sentries along the way. They slipped into the cold water and drifted across to the safety of the left bank.

> Towards morning we washed up on a sandy spit, where there was an anti-aircraft battery. The artillerymen looked in amazement at our rags and our hollow, unshaven faces. We were barely recognizable as fellow soldiers. They fed us with some astonishingly tasty crusts of bread and fish soup – I have never eaten anything more delicious in my life. It was the first food we had seen in three days. Later that day, the artillerymen sent us on to a field hospital.

ON MAMAYEV KURGAN

While Dragan's men fought a losing battle for the station, a larger detachment of the 13th Guards was headed for Mamayev Kurgan. Their commander was Colonel Ivan Yelin. When he arrived at Height 102, as it was designated on the military maps of both sides, he saw a small chink in the Germans' armour.

> The Germans were slow to organize a system of fire between their different units. The infantry and the artillery were not operating in tandem. That fact meant that we of the 13th Guards had some success at first. The 13th Division arrived just in time. A day, or even twelve hours later, and the Germans would have entrenched themselves in the centre of the city and we would never have made it across the river.

Constant pressure from the guards kept the Germans off balance, and made it impossible for them to set up artillery on the peak of the hill. This was a triumph in itself, though it cost the guards all their available ammunition and a full third of their entire fighting force: 3,000 men died in the first battle for the kurgan. But according to the cruel economy of those days, the sacrifice of so many lives was worth it because it meant reinforcements and supplies still had some chance of making it across the river. It kept the Russians in the game.

Some of the new reinforcements were themselves destined for the kurgan. Nikolai Maznitsa of the 95th Rifle Division arrived there on 19 September, and almost became a witness at his own funeral.

An attack began in the morning and lasted 48 hours. The enemy was moving inexorably towards the summit in six files. At times it seemed to us that they were invincible. But the sixth file did not hold out under our fire, and we rushed into the attack, and dug in on a new line to prepare for the next advance. Then came the planes once again, along with the artillery fire, the iron columns of soldiers, the renewed attacks.

Most of the German soldiers appeared to be drunk, and threw themselves in a frenzy at the summit. After each round of bombing there would be a moment of dead silence – and that was when you would get afraid. But then the hill would come alive again like a volcano, and we would crawl out of the shell holes and put our machineguns to work. The barrels of the guns were red-hot, and the water boiled inside them. Our men attacked without waiting for orders. I don't know of a single case where someone committed an act of cowardice. It was mass heroism.

We lost many men as a result of direct hits on shell-holes. On September 23rd I was buried in my foxhole during an attack, and was unconscious under the earth for several hours. When they dug me out they took my documents away as evidence of my death, and they were about to bury me in a different hole when a bomb blast threw me several metres and somehow brought me round from the concussion. I re-took command of my company that same day.

The slopes of the kurgan were completely covered in corpses. In some places you had to move two or three bodies aside to lie down. They quickly began to decompose, and the stench was appalling, but you just had to lie down and pay no attention.

The dead were buried, if at all, where they fell. But sometimes, if there was time, they were put in big shell holes – as nearly happened to me. It wasn't always possible to report the names of the dead, and sometimes the courier with the casualty report was himself killed along the way.

Sometimes it seemed that we were all condemned to death – but we despised death all the same, and wanted only to sell our lives as dearly as we could.

Maznitsa's division fought on the hill for 11 days, and was then relieved by the 284th Rifle Division, a fresh unit from Siberia. Captain Viktor Popov was among them.

At the end of September our HQ moved to the west bank of the river. It was set up in the big concrete pipes that carried waste water to the Volga. Here the cliffs rise about 50 metres above the river, and are about 800 metres from the foot of Mamayev Kurgan. Our main positions on the right flank were the southern and western slopes of the kurgan, and on the left flank the building of the Metiz factory, where the railway lines and tram lines ran from the south to the north of the city.

The highest point of the kurgan was crowned with two huge concrete cisterns, which were the main water reservoir for the city. These cisterns had no water in them, and had been that way since August.

The empty cisterns were, however, a real prize. They were a ready-made bunker right at the most strategically important point in the city. Both armies wanted to possess the cisterns, and so they played at dog-in-the-manger, trying to prevent the other side from getting any protection from them. The Germans won out – for a while at least.

The German attacks were vicious, especially on the right-hand side of Mamayev Kurgan, continued Popov. Here the

Germans made use of tanks and self-propelled guns. They
knew that from the top they would be able to fire on our
gun emplacements over open sights. The Germans attacked
without success for a long time, but eventually our battalion
on the right flank had to move back, and took up a new
position at the foot of the kurgan.

The battle for the kurgan reached a murderous stalemate that was not
broken for months. The Germans held on to the western slope, and
the Russians never quite left the eastern one. At nights the Russians
would creep forward a few metres, literally clawing back the hill,
repossessing it by tiny increments. In the daytime, soldiers fought
separate battles in ones and twos, like gladiators in the ring. The
opposing sides were close enough to each other to thrash it out using
grenades, sharpened spades and bayonets. Neither side could claim
undisputed ownership of the summit and its precious cisterns. And
the constant bombing and shelling warmed the punished earth to the
extent that no snow settled on the kurgan throughout the long cold
winter of 1942.

FIGHTING IN THE RUBBLE

By the end of September the Germans had wrested most of the city
centre from Russian control, and in several places had gained a
foothold on the riverside. In the sector defended by the 13th Guards,
the territory held by the Russians was little more than a ribbon of
bombed-out wasteland barely a quarter of a mile (400m) deep. If the
Germans, who had travelled hundreds of miles to get this far, could
just take this last little strip of land, then Stalingrad would be theirs.
But the fighting in Stalingrad was unlike anything any of the
combatants – the Germans or the Russians – had experienced before.
General Hans Doerr described the nature of the fighting inside the
city, where a hyperinflationary price had to be paid for every gain.

> The time for conducting large-scale operations was gone
> forever. From the wide expanses of steppe-land the war

moved to the jagged gullies of the Volga hills with their copses and ravines, into the factory area of Stalingrad, spread out over uneven, pitted, rugged country, covered with iron, concrete and stone buildings. The mile as a measure of distance was replaced by the yard. Headquarters' map was the map of the city.

For every house, workshop, water tower, railway embankment, wall, cellar and every pile of ruins a bitter battle was waged – one without equal even in the First World War with its great expenditure of munitions. The distance between the enemy's arms and ours was as small as it could possibly be. Despite the concentrated air and artillery power, it was impossible to break out of the area of close fighting. The Russians surpassed the Germans in their use of the terrain and in camouflage, and were more experienced in barricade warfare for individual buildings.

Doerr's grudging tribute to the Russians' fighting skills was right in all but one respect. It was not so much experience that told for the Russians, but verve and imagination. Before Stalingrad, the Russians knew no more about urban warfare than their opponents. But the fact that they had their backs to the wall – or rather to the water – and that they had to make the very best of the small resources available to them, meant Russian commanders were forced to come up with a new way of defending the town. They needed a method that made the most of their strengths.

The first and most vital element of the Russian tactic was to stay close to the enemy. Every Russian strived never to be further than a grenade's throw from a German. This meant the enemy was constantly unnerved, and it also neutralized the Germans' single greatest advantage – air power – because the Luftwaffe could not bomb the Russian vanguard without risking dropping their payload on their own men. The Germans tried to counter this by sending up white signal flares to show the position of their own front line, but the Russians took to sending up flares of their own to confuse the enemy pilots. Whenever the Germans changed the signal, the Russians soon caught on and spoiled it.

Bombing was in any case an irrelevance. After August, all the bombs ever did was reconfigure the rubble, resculpt the desolate cityscape. The Russians would tuck themselves away in basements while the raids went on, then emerge to continue the battle on the same blasted terrain. Aerial bombardment merely created new hiding places and fresh opportunities.

The total destruction of the city had another unfortunate effect from the German point of view. It rendered much of the city all but impassable to tanks. The German method right from the start of the war was to send a tank or two in first to blast the opposition's strongpoints, then to have the infantry come up in their wake, mopping up the enemy and digging in at a new forward line. But the Russians would hide in buildings and allow the German tanks and infantry to advance past them, then emerge and spray the infantry with machinegun fire from behind (this was precisely the *modus operandi* that Willi Hoffman found so unfair). The tanks would then have to back up to escape the ambush. Even if they could turn their gun turrets around, their engine grilles would be exposed and vulnerable to attack with anti-tank guns.

Molotov cocktails were also used to great effect against tanks. The Russian tactic was to hurl them down from the upper storeys of buildings. The Russians, incidentally, never used the term 'Molotov cocktails', which was a Western coinage; they always called them by the prosaic and long-winded expression 'bottles of inflammable liquid'. But they produced these simple weapons on an industrial scale and to a variety of designs. Some contained chemical mixes that ignited on contact with the air when the bottle broke; some had percussive caps that set light to the liquid in the bottle on impact; some were entirely homemade – vodka bottle, petrol from a can, rag stuffed in the top and lit with a match – and no less deadly for that.

A favoured Russian technique in Stalingrad, one at which the Red Army became very adept, was to lure the Germans into the narrow canyon of a street, then to get behind them by moving along the sewers (dry now that the town had ceased to function) or through the attics of buildings. Basements were also used for this purpose, and the Russians often went to the trouble of breaking down the connecting walls between buildings at cellar level in anticipation of an attack. This allowed them to move swiftly and invisibly to the rear of the enemy even as the German tanks rolled forwards (with the infantry creeping along behind) at street level. The Germans were constantly amazed and dismayed at how the Russians popped up in unexpected places above and behind them. They called this unhappy experience *Rattenkrieg* – 'rat war' – and they never got the hang of practising it themselves. And so the battle became a constant game of cat-and-mouse in the wreckage of the town, a kind of hide-and-seek in which the loser got a bullet to the forehead or a bayonet to the ribs.

PAVLOV'S HOUSE
The Russians' clever defensive tactics were complemented by offensive methods that were just as troubling to the Germans. Soviet commanders in the city quickly saw that frontal assaults with large numbers of troops were too expensive in terms of manpower, and often failed in any case. So they evolved a method in which small heavily armed 'shock groups' would take houses one at a time. These units were broken down into three sections. The first group would carry out the initial storming of a house, usually using grenades; the moment they were inside, the second group would follow and mop up, or set up a defence perimeter to prevent immediate counter-attacks; the third group was a reserve, which could also be used for covering fire. Once a house was taken, the storm group would set up an 'active defence' – which meant fortifying it in such a way that it became a link in the general defence of the sector, a small and integral addition to the sum of Soviet territory. Shock groups were equipped to withstand siege for long periods without significant backup. They took several days' food with them whenever they carried out an attack.

In the annals of Stalingrad, the most celebrated instance of active defence is the long siege of a four-storey apartment block known as

'Pavlov's House'. In this building a small group of Russians held out for two months under constant attack. The house was taken without a fight in the last week of September by four men under the command of a Sergeant Yakov Pavlov, a man who turned out to have a real talent for stubborn defence. 'He was quite a short fellow with a thin face,' recalled his commanding officer. 'He used to wear a rather dandyish fur cap in the Kuban style, and his tunic was faded and covered with dust.' As soon as the four men were settled into the building, Pavlov sent one of them back to report. The scout told HQ that 'all was well in Pavlov's house,' – a remark that was overheard by an army newspaper reporter. The journalist published an article, headlined 'The House of Sergeant Pavlov'. After that, the designation Pavlov's House became common currency in the 62nd Army, even among men who had no idea why it was so called.

> I could see why our commanders had felt that this building was so significant, said one of the men who fought with Pavlov. From the fourth floor you could observe not only the whole of Ninth of January Square, but also all the ruins beyond. It stuck out into the German defences. To the left and to the right of us were Germans. Only to the rear of us, towards the Mill, was there an area that was occupied by our men, and that too was under constant fire.

In other words, the long oblong of Pavlov's House protruded into German-occupied territory like a headland into the sea. (For radio purposes, the Russians gave the house the appropriate code name *mayak* – 'lighthouse'). Not only could Pavlov and his comrades watch the Germans' every move, but it was also relatively easy for them to report back. The Mill mentioned by Pavlov's comrade-in-arms was a large brick grain store about 300 yards (275m) directly behind the house and about the same distance from the river. It was an important command post, and a staging post for troops coming over from the far bank. There was a constant dialogue between Pavlov's House and the Mill, so Pavlov's vital observations were quickly transmitted back to HQ. As the siege developed a long trench was dug between the two buildings to make the process less perilous for the runners.

> **The Mill was as strong as a castle,** said Georgy Potansky of the 32nd Regiment of the 13th Guards. **But neither the enemy air force nor our own bombed the area around Pavlov's House, the Mill and Ninth of January Square because the lines were too close to each other. The only thing that saved us from starving was the fact that there were large quantities of grain in the basement of the Mill. We slept on it, and we fed ourselves with it. We often had to grab our guns and grenades and beat off German attacks. Many of our soldiers were put out of commission – some killed, some wounded. The wounded often died because we did not know how to give them first aid, how to bind their wounds. No one had taught us.**

At Pavlov's House the danger was ten times greater. The Russians sent reinforcements up from the Mill to create a 'garrison' in the block. One of the newcomers was Lieutenant Ivan Afanasyev, who outranked Pavlov and so took command of the incipient siege.

> I told Pavlov my name and why I was there, recalled Afanasyev. 'Excellent,' he said. 'We could use a bit of help. This is a big old house and there is just the four of us. The more, the merrier.' Pavlov led me down a narrow corridor and into the basement. A kerosene lamp was burning. In the middle of the room stood a table, like a carpenter's bench. On it lay a box of shells and about a dozen grenades. In one corner there was an iron bedstead, on which there was an untidy pile of blankets and pillows. On the floor there were lots of spent cartridges.
> We selected the best spots for our machineguns and for our anti-tank gun. As soon as we set up the guns, all the fighters began to block up the windows and doors with bricks and

boxes of sand. The basement was divided into four sections which were separated by thick supporting walls. Up above, the attic windows commanded a wide field of fire. The men who built this house probably never dreamed that their work would be judged from a military standpoint.

The Germans soon spotted the activity in the house, and realized they had made a tactical error by letting the Russians take it. Repeated attacks were made across the square. They came swarming over 'like bees from a rattled hive,' said one soldier. As in the wider battle for the city, the defenders were kept going by a small but steady influx of men and matériel.

Though the beam end of the house was gradually destroyed by artillery fire, and the floors flopped down like the pages of a discarded old book, the defences of Pavlov's House actually grew stronger as the weeks wore on. A minefield was sown all around it, and supplementary firing points were set up in foxholes and metal bins around the house. The men in Pavlov's House could not be budged – even when, in the first days of November, their resources were almost nil.

Our guns merrily hammered away at the enemy, continued Afanasyev. The Nazis reeled back, but almost immediately threw themselves into the attack once more. This happened time after time. Alexandrov and Sabgaida were wounded. Ammunition was running out. Pavlov would hurl a grenade at anyone who dared come close to the house. His usual spot at the gun emplacement was inherited by Svirin, who took occasional potshots: he had one magazine left. Our captured German machine gun had now fallen silent. The only weapon left was the one tommygun in the basement. We were nearly out of grenades, and started throwing bricks instead. There were two girls – Nina and Natasha – who had been with us the whole time. They crawled around the floor looking for bullets that may have been dropped, and they bandaged the wounded.

The defenders were preparing to fight the Germans inside Pavlov's House when the general counter-attack rescued them. By that time Pavlov and his house were famous – in part, perhaps, because it represented a kind of microcosm of the battle for the city, of the Great Patriotic War in general. 'We'll die before we let the Germans pass us,' scribbled one soldier on the wall of the house – and this was exactly the attitude that the Soviet High Command wanted to inculcate into every Red Army man. For the Germans, Pavlov's House was just a profligate waste of effort and of lives. Ninth of January Square was littered with German corpses, and General Chuikov relished the knowledge that more enemy soldiers died trying to take Pavlov's House than were killed in the conquest of Paris.

CULT OF THE SNIPER

Chuikov had said that every German must be made to feel that he was living under the barrel of a gun, and at the height of the battle this was almost literally true. Any German who lifted his head above the makeshift barricades, or showed himself at a window, or dared to take a flit across open ground, was in mortal danger of being shot. This ever-present hazard was partly a consequence of the closeness of the lines and the sheer density of the forces manning them: there was always someone watching, gun at the ready. But there was also, especially on the Russian side, widespread use of specialist snipers. These men did not take part in routine attacks, but prowled the city like lone wolves. They would sometimes be given specific tasks, but often they picked their own targets and their own nests. A good sniper could pick off more than a dozen enemy soldiers in a day, and of course they struck cold terror into the hearts of the Germans.

The Russian High Command well understood both the psychological and the military value of its freelance sharpshooters, and there was a carefully orchestrated propaganda campaign about the art of 'sniperism'. The Komsomol (Communist Youth League) devoted meetings to the theme of sniping, commissars preached on it to their units, and a constant stream of newspaper articles glorified the exploits of individual snipers. Papers such as *Red Star* and *In Defence of the Motherland* published the scores of the leading shooters, as if killing Germans one at a time were a sporting endeavour, a little light relief from the war.

Perhaps the most celebrated sniper of all was 19-year-old Anatoly Chekhov. General Chuikov called him a 'hunter of two-legged animals', and he was the subject of a hagiographic article by Vasily Grossman, the most gifted and prolific chronicler of Stalingrad. Grossman's piece was entitled 'Through Chekhov's Eyes', and was a kind of wartime fairytale – an exercise in myth-making as much as a piece of reportage. This is how Grossman describes the unpromising ugly duckling Chekhov, and his transformation into a killer swan:

> In March 1942, he was drafted into the Army, where he put in a request to train as a sniper. 'As I child I could not even use a catapult right, and I didn't like hurting live things. The first time I did target practice at sniper school I made a complete fool of myself – nine marks out of a possible fifty. My lieutenant said to me: 'You study well but shoot badly. You will come to nothing.' But Chekhov did not get downhearted. Instead he began working at his lessons through the long nights as well as in the daytime. For hours at a time he read the theory, and studied the weaponry. He had a great respect for books and learning, and in the end he knew the principles of optics backwards; with his eyes shut he could sketch a diagram of a ray of light on its complex path through the nine lenses of an optical sight. He understood the deep theoretical principles behind every part of his equipment. When he looked at the image magnified fourfold in his sights Chekhov saw it not just with the eyes of a rifleman, but also with the eyes of a physicist. The lieutenant was mistaken. When Chekhov was tested in his ability to hit a moving object he put all three of his bullets in the dead centre of the frisky little targets.

Such smoothly didactic writing was designed to encourage other proven good-shots to volunteer for sniper training, but it proved almost too successful. The cult of the sniper began to get out of hand because every unit suddenly felt obliged to furnish sharpshooters. Soon there was a glut of undertrained, inexperienced soldiers wandering the city with telescopic sights. The induction of Private Stepan Vernigora was fairly typical. He was writing late in the war.

> I was in an infantry company, and after reading in the newspapers about the exploits of Chekhov and other snipers I decided to become a sniper too. When I told my platoon commander, Second Lieutenant Ignatov, that I wanted to be a sniper, he granted my request and straight away fetched me a sniper's rifle, serial number 3165, from the armoury. I immediately set about sending Nazis to their deaths. They were very close by, so I got to kill a lot of them. Instead of drinking water from the Volga I made them drink lead. By the time the rout of the Germans in the Stalingrad region was complete, I had sent 142 fritzes to their deaths, and the rest will remember me and know what to expect if they ever try messing with our 13th Guards' Division again. But I'm not going to stop now. I'll carry on killing them until they have been completely smashed.

If Vernigora's tally is true, then he was an outstandingly talented amateur. Most of the novice snipers did not live for long, and while they lasted they were a downright hindrance for the professionals. There were, for example, incidents in which a newcomer occupied the carefully prepared firing position of a trained sniper while the 'owner' was away. The interloper would bang off a few rounds, and move on. By the time the real sharpshooter came back, the Germans had zeroed in on the used lair, and were ready to blast it with their artillery. Several top-flight Russian snipers were killed by German fire because some goldilocks with a gun had recently been sleeping in his bed.

Accidents of this sort became such a problem that *Red Star* had to cool down the whole sniperist movement by condemning the practice of issuing telescopic sights to anyone with a hankering to become the next Anatoly Chekhov. But in the meantime, the propaganda-driven cult of the sniper spawned one of the enduring legends of Stalingrad. It concerned a sniper named Vasily Zaitsev, a Siberian sheep-herder who first came to the attention of the Soviet authorities after he had made a hundred kills. Like Chekhov, his achievements were made the subject of a little personality cult. He became a folk hero, a star of Stalingrad, and his big grinning face was often seen on the pages of the newspapers.

The Zaitsev legend tells how a German major, the head of a sniper school in Berlin, was sent from Germany especially to kill him. The tale was given credence by General Chuikov in his memoir of the battle, but to this day it is not clear how much truth there is in it. There are no German records of any such sniper being despatched from Berlin (his name is usually given as Major Konings or König, or sometimes as Heinz Thorwald), and the idea may well have been cooked up by the Russian propaganda machine. Certainly there are tell-tale signs that the story of their duel in the ruins of the city is a Soviet invention. The simple struggle between good and evil seems designed to appeal to an unsophisticated Soviet public; moreover, the major of the story is an intellectual, a bourgeois academic in a way, so there are overtones of classic Marxist class conflict in his struggle with the working-class peasant. And there is a deeper David-and-Goliath element of myth in the tale – the honest shepherd-boy takes on the champion of a mighty enemy, and beats him. What seems clear is that Zaitsev himself was told that a German hitman had been sent with the specific task of assassinating him, that he believed it, and that he was convinced that he killed that man.

Zaitsev himself was later wounded in the eyes, which put an end to his sniping career. But he continued to teach his special skill to others. He and another veteran named Viktor Medvedev set up their own sniper schools. Since Zaitsev means 'hare' in Russian and Medvedev 'bear', their graduates were known respectively as 'the leverets' and 'the bear cubs'.

Mikhail Mamekov was one of this second generation. Unusually, he was not a loner, but hunted in a pack. This is his matter-of-fact account of his time as a killer, written when he was still on active service. He joined the battle in December and his first job, in the Zaitsev tradition, was to snipe back at German snipers.

I am a Kazakh, born in Alma-Ata. Before joining the Red Army I was a sailor with the Pacific Fleet. I served as a gun-aimer on a destroyer. Before that I was a hunter. I joined the Party in 1942.

My sniper group consisted of seven men. I was the leader of the group. We began our work in the region of the Red October housing estate. The Germans were about twenty-five or thirty metres away at that time – and were laying down a constant barrage of accurate fire: they would not let us lift our heads. At night we crept closer to the enemy, and found spots for ourselves in attics, near the windows. From there we began to take out German snipers. We would put out a decoy target, and when the Germans shot at it we would use the direction of the bullet hole to pinpoint the shooter's hiding place. In our first five days we killed four lone snipers and three machinegun teams.

Sometimes we had to seek out the enemy by more complicated means. One time we put a sniper in the centre of town, knowing that his shots would attract the attention of the enemy to a dressed dummy which we placed not far from our man's foxhole. To the sides were two observers whose job was to spot the German when he shot. Once we knew where the fritz was located, we closed in on him secretly and took him out. Over the course of six weeks, we killed eighteen snipers, thirteen tommygunners, six machinegun teams and seven anti-tank teams.

I gave each sniper in my group a kill sector of his own – an area of anything from 50 to 1,200 metres. Every one of us had reserve firing positions, at least four, so if we thought that we had been spotted at one location we could move unnoticed to another. As a rule you would always be spotted by the time you had killed five or six fritzes from the same lair. The Germans would then usually try to flush you out with mortar or artillery fire.

Proximity to the enemy was a necessary environmental condition for a sniper. The nearer the enemy the richer the pickings – but there was also such a thing as being too close.

In the last days of the battle for Stalingrad we were surrounded by Germans. They were very nearby, and more than once we had to stand up and fight them face to face or attack with hand grenades. In these skirmishes, four of my comrades were killed, and I too was wounded by shrapnel. The battalion commander ordered me to the field hospital in the rear, but my wounds were light so I didn't go. I could still shoot. In the next three days my team wiped out 165 fascists.

Altogether my sniper group killed 1,002 enemy soldiers and officers during the time it was active. I was awarded the Order of the Red Star and I was recommended for the Order of the Red Banner. My personal total was 261 fritzes killed.

I am now training to be an officer, but I still have a burning desire to go into battle, to kill and destroy the damned German-fascist dogs. I shan't waste a single cartridge. One bullet will be enough for each fritz.

Of course, the German snipers that Mamekov sought out were just as resolute as he was, and just as coldly parsimonious with their ammunition. Vasily Sokolov was a lieutenant in the naval infantry, the same brigade of fighting sailors as Mamekov. At the end of September Sokolov was sent on an errand by his commander, and found out what it was like to know that you were the image in a sniper's cross-sights.

It was the 26th or 27th and three of us had to go from the command post of the 62nd Army back to our own 92nd Brigade. There was me, Lieutenant Zhurba who was the adjutant of the brigade commander, and one soldier who was accompanying us. Before we reached the sector of the 13th Guards, we caught sight of a sergeant sitting on the ground some distance away. He was wounded. We asked him: where are you hit, and what is your unit? He made a gesture with his hand and said: 'I was crossing this open patch of ground about half an hour ago when I was hit in the leg by a German sniper.' The area in question was about fifty metres long, and had a steep bank at either end. The patch of ground was not being defended by our side, but had not been occupied by the Germans either. There were lots of artillery shells lying around, as well as ammunition for rifles and machineguns still in its boxes.

The sergeant told us that he was from the 92nd Brigade. A short time ago, he had seen the German sniper kill two of our men, even though the sergeant had shouted to them not to come over as there was a sniper in the building nearby. Sure enough, there were a couple of bodies lying not far from us. We spoke to the sergeant and advised him to try and drag himself in the direction of 62nd Army HQ, so that he could be ferried across to a hospital on the left bank. He said: 'If I find I can't move or get to a safer place, and if the Germans come this way, then I will try to blow them up with a grenade – and myself too.'

As for us, we still had to get across the area controlled by the sniper, as we could not go back without having carried out our orders. I decided to make a run for it first. I hunched up, thought to myself 'what will be will be', and dashed across the square and down the steep bank.

The German didn't shoot. Lieutenant Zhurba made his run next, and then the soldier who was with us. Again the sniper didn't shoot. Either he was taking a nap, or he didn't get us in his sights quickly enough.

We found ourselves lying in the midst of fifteen or so corpses, our people. There was one woman among them –

most likely a medic. Only the torso was there: her head, arms and legs had been torn off, probably by the blast of a bomb or a shell. Three of the bodies were in a sitting position, leaning against the high bank, almost as if they were asleep.

There is that famous remark of Dolores Ibarruri's – better to die on your feet than live on your knees. Now I have never seen anyone die on their feet: usually they fall over first and then die. But to die sitting down – that I have seen.

Two signallers now came our way. They were dragging a drum of cable with them. I advised them to run across the sniper's field as quickly as they possibly could ('Fly like a bullet!' I said). I thought they had got my meaning, but they didn't seem to go any faster for it. Maybe the drum of cable slowed them down. While they were on their way across the square, two or three shots rang out. They were dum-dum bullets – I knew because you always get a puff of smoke with an explosive bullet. Both soldiers went down. They looked to be dead, but we didn't go near them because we would certainly have been killed ourselves. We went on our way to Brigade HQ.

This was perhaps the best anti-sniper tactic of all, whether you were German or Russian: to keep out of their way as far as possible, and to trust to your luck. Because the chances of coming out of the battle alive were growing slimmer with each passing day.

4
CONQUEST OF THE FACTORIES

A steady drip-drip-drip of reinforcements percolated through to Stalingrad from the east. Many of the Russian fighters who came to the city in the autumn were Siberians, like those who had held Moscow the previous year. These men were as fresh and as hard as an overnight frost, and they were keen to get at the enemy. Sometimes, however, the enemy found them first. Viktor Kartashev was a young military cadet who, along with his classmates, had been drafted into General Smekhotvorov's 193rd Rifle Division. In the last week of September he was travelling towards Stalingrad across the hot and dusty steppe of Kazakhstan.

Beyond Saratov we were greeted by fascist planes which made several attempts to bomb and strafe our train. We had to jump out of the carriages and dig in. One night, a plane came at us from behind. I was in the last carriage. The bullets only punctured the roof of our carriage, but in the neighbouring carriages the strafing killed three men and wounded another three. The train stopped somewhere in the steppe. We buried our dead comrades. We lined the inside of the grave with planks that we took from the bunks in the carriages.

The train stopped outside Leninsk, about 50 kilometres from Stalingrad. We got out of the carriages and proceeded on foot. We only moved after dark. It was tough going. It was hot, and we were dying of thirst, but we didn't come across any water along the route. The tramping of so many soldiers' feet brought a cloud of dust up into the air. It was becoming

difficult to breathe. On the horizon ahead of us, there was
a continuous glow. It was Stalingrad burning. By day it
smouldered and smoked, and by night it blazed brightly.

Kartashev was about to be thrown into the new epicentre of the battle.
General Paulus had decided to suspend the struggle for the possession
of the city centre and switch the focus to the factory district north of
Mamayev Kurgan. Perhaps here, he thought, he could smash through
to the river and roll up the right flank of Chuikov's tired army. The
Russians were well aware of Paulus's intentions – cocky Wehrmacht
soldiers in that sector had for some days been shouting out the same
piece of pidgin Russian at their adversaries: *Russ! Zavtra Volga bul-bul!*
– 'Hey Russian! Tomorrow it's glug-glug in the Volga!'

Mamayev Kurgan, pitted and pockmarked and sown with the dead
of both sides, was a tactically important spot for an attack on this part
of town. Its summit looked straight down on the roofs of the factories.
Shelling the Russians from here would be as easy as dropping pebbles
in a bucket, so it was worth the Germans' while trying again to take
the highest point of the hill. Consequently, the planes of the Luftwaffe
circled over Mamayev Kurgan like vultures. The bombing and strafing
from above all but annihilated the men of Soviet 95th Rifle Division,
who clung to the eastern slopes like doomed mountaineers. Vasily
Burguchev, a young officer with the Russian 112th Rifle Division, was
sent on an errand to 62nd Army HQ from the factory district, which
took him past the kurgan. He saw it at night, when it looked like
something out of one of Hieronymus Bosch's gruesome fantasies.

The German planes dropped burning fuel. All of Mamayev
Kurgan was enveloped with fire. The ground was on fire,
and everywhere dead bodies were burning too. We tried to
find a way through it, but we had to make a detour. We ran
through trenches hunched up to avoid the flames.

The HQ that Burguchev sought was located in the cliffside beside the
Volga. It seemed like a relatively safe spot, because it was dug deep into

the bank like a rabbit warren and it faced the left bank, and so was unbombable from the west. But in the first week of October the entire staff of the 62nd Army, including General Chuikov himself, came close to being killed by a fluke shell. Mikhail Balebanov, a staff officer, was in Chuikov's bunker when it happened.

> The problem was that, on top of the bank where the staff was quartered, there were many oil tanks, which exploded as a result of enemy shellfire, starting four huge fires. These fires posed a great danger to the staff, as the burning oil, spilling downhill, was setting everything in its path alight, including the staff's dugouts.

Observers on the left bank, seeing the immense clouds of smoke rising from the riverbank, were sure that Chuikov and his staff were dead. But they had escaped, and were standing watching the HQ go up in smoke. Oily flakes were drifting down on their heads like malevolent black snow. Balebanov turned to look at the river.

> The burning oil flowed out to the Volga, where it spread over almost the entire surface of the water, just as it had done on land, burning boats, barges and other floating assets that had been used to bring provisions to the army headquarters from the left bank. The Volga looked like it had been turned into a huge flow of molten lava whose flames had been blown to the bank by the wind, setting fire to our dugouts.
>   So the staff had to up and leave in a hurry and move to the section of the bank by the Barricades factory, where they remained until October 17th.

FIGHTING FOR RED OCTOBER

It made sense for Chuikov to be in the factory district at this time. For the past week the Germans had been advancing across the ruins of the Red October workers' settlement, and the entire industrial quarter was under threat. The German offensive had begun on 26 September.

Viktor Kartashev arrived at the Volga the following morning. It had been a hard forced march from Leninsk, so he and his comrades snatched a couple of hours' relaxation before embarking on the terrifying rite of passage that welcomed all Russian newcomers to Stalingrad: the river crossing.

Along the edges of the road, from the village all the way to the Volga, banners and posters calling for Stalingrad to be defended were hanging from posts and trees. September 27th was a sunny day, and we decided to take a dip in the Volga. The water was clear, and looked greenish from the reflections of the trees growing on the banks. Much refreshed, we put on the clean underwear that our sergeant had handed out to us. At around eight o'clock in the evening our battalion got into formation and the field order was read out: we were to dislodge the enemy from the Red October housing estate. The command was given to prepare to move out, and about 15 minutes later we were already heading towards the crossing. The infantry was moving, and vehicles were dragging the guns and carrying the munitions. The horses harnessed to the carts were snorting from the unbearable dust. The road was covered in pot-holes, in places a flooring of thin poles had been laid, and the surface was strewn with bundles of brushwood. We arrived at the crossing. Smashed boats were lying on the bank beneath some bushes, and people were sitting in ditches and trenches awaiting their turn to cross over to the right bank of the Volga, to Stalingrad.

The city was burning, and was lit by one continuous glow. The whole ground seemed to be burning and there was nothing to breathe, but the order was given to cross over to the right bank. While we were waiting to cross over, we sat looking at burning Stalingrad. The night was dark. Neither the moon nor the stars could be seen, only the bright lines of tracer bullets rising up into the sky, looking like some sort of weird fan made of multicoloured fireflies. Searchlights swept the sky, looking for their victims. Over the course of several hours, five planes were caught in their beams and shot down. We had not yet been under fire, and did not know enough to tell whether these were our planes or German ones. Only later did we discover that they were ours – U-2s – and that they had been bombing the German forward positions. Stalingrad was ablaze, the flames turning now white, now yellow, now red. Light and dark chased one another around in a merry dance. All of a sudden, it became as bright as day. Dozens of parachute flares were shining in the night sky, illuminating the whole of Stalingrad and the crossing.

We went up to the water's edge, one platoon at a time. Four or five men climbed into each boat. Each one went 30 or 40 metres upstream, and then crossed quickly to the opposite bank of the river, propelled by the powerful strokes of the experienced army ferrymen. Several mortar shells plopped into the water behind us, bringing up a huge column of water. As soon as the boats reached the bank, we jumped into the water. We disembarked onto a small island covered with tall, slender willows.

Kartashev crossed from the midstream island to the right bank that same night. By morning he was in the heart of the factory district.

We took up a defensive position in a large two-storey building, in the basement of which we found the families of workers from the Red October factory. The children were crying, asking their parents for something to eat, but they had no food to give them. They had chanced upon two freight cars full of rye on the factory's railway tracks, which had caught fire from the bombing. They had gathered up the burnt grain and cooked flat bread from it, but the bread had an unpleasant taste of ashes. One of the old women treated us to some of this bread. Those of

us who were in the basement gave the children our
emergency rations.

How the children had survived for nearly two months in the factories
until this point is beyond comprehension. One hopes that someone
found the time and opportunity to evacuate them that night, because
some of the fiercest fighting of the entire war was about to begin
precisely where they were taking shelter. The German 24th Panzer
Division was rolling towards the gap between the Red October and
Barricades complexes, to the right of Kartashev's position.

The first battles of this offensive were fought in the crazy forest of
chimneystacks west of the factory buildings, all that remained of the
workers' homes. The Germans were intending to make use of a deep
balka that ran due east into the river between the two factories. This
weak spot was held by two fresh but understrength Soviet divisions:
General Guriev's 39th Guards and General Batyuk's 284th Rifle
Division (another largely Siberian unit). The Germans, for their part,
brought up the 14th Panzer and the 94th Infantry Division from the
quieter southern suburbs of Stalingrad to support the 24th Panzer.
This redeployment was a bitter disappointment for Willi Hoffman. On
the 28th he had been told that his division was being withdrawn for a
rest; on 2 October he was informed of a depressing change of plan.

We have new orders, he wrote bitterly in his diary. Tonight
we are being transferred to somewhere in the north of
the city. Our battalion will be the first into the attack.
In Stalingrad, anyone can die at any moment.

The next few days were a torment, made all the worse by the fact that
the Red Army – like the hydra of Greek myth – seemed to grow many
new heads each time one was cut down.

3rd October. After marching through the night we have
taken up position in a balka filled with bushes. They say we
are going to attack the factories, the chimneys of which we

can clearly see. Beyond them is the Volga. We are in a new part of town for us. Though it is night, I can see many crosses with our helmets on top of them. Can we really have lost so many men? God damn this Stalingrad.

4th October. Our regiment is attacking the Barricades settlement. The Russians seem to have many machinegunners. Where are they getting them from?

5th October. Our battalion has gone into the attack four times, and each time has had to hit the ground. Russian snipers hit anyone who is so careless as to show a glimpse of himself from behind his shelter.

In fact there was nothing mysterious about the growing number of Russian opponents. The failure of the Germans to cut off the Russian supply lines across the Volga meant that every night new men were coming over and fortifying the line in the factories. The 37th Guards crossed on the night of 2 October, and took up a forward position west of the Tractor Factory. The 84th Tank Brigade was shipped over the river a couple of days later. Sergeant VA Shishkin was with them.

I was born on the banks of the Volga in Stalingrad, at the spot where the Mill still stands close to Pavlov's House, so it was especially painful for me to look at the river which I loved and where I had spent my childhood.

It was in October 1942 that our independent 84th Tank Brigade came up to the left bank of the Volga near the village of Burkovsky. It was dusk, and Stalingrad was in flames. The men were standing in a circle waiting for orders. General Novikov arrived, and delivered a short speech. He turned round towards the burning city and with a noticeable gleam in his eye he said: 'Comrades! In a few hours' time you'll be on the right bank of the Volga. Remember, there's no way back. Before us lies either death or victory, and we will be victorious!'

That night, under heavy enemy fire, our brigade started crossing over to the city, into the area by the Red October factory. It's difficult for me to describe everything that happened that night, when we were up against an enemy with superior forces. All I can say is that, if we had not had any weapons, we would still have killed the people who had come to take our Volga from us with our bare hands – which at one point is exactly what we had to do.

The desperate character of the fighting in these days was reflected in a rash of self-sacrificial acts by Russian fighters. On 28 September, a Red Army soldier named Mikhail Panikakha caught fire when a bullet hit the Molotov cocktail he was about to throw. Engulfed in flame he rushed at a German tank and threw himself on its engine grille, so that it burned with him. A week later, a soldier of the 124th Rifle Division, NF Averyanov, ran up to an enemy pillbox and covered the gun slit with his own body, thus blocking the view of its occupants for a few moments and buying his comrades enough time to attack it. Averyanov's feat was emulated several times once news of it spread. To the Russians, such deeds were pure, undiluted heroism. To the Germans they looked like a form of madness, the fruit of a diseased Bolshevist mentality. Though most of them killed without a qualm, the men of the Sixth Army never understood how individual Russians could sell their lives so very cheaply.

KARTASHEV'S WEEK

By the end of September Viktor Kartashev was ensconced inside the grounds of the Red October factory – doing his best to stay alive. The advancing Germans had not yet reached him, but he continued to have strange encounters with civilians who had made homes for themselves in the factory workshops and labs.

The shop buildings were still intact, and the machinery was still standing except for the building which housed the chemical laboratory. That had several shell holes in its walls

and roof. On the ground floor, there were metal-cutting
lathes. There was a store-room of metal samples, each of
them wrapped in paper in its own separate cubicle of the
rack. A wooden staircase led to the first floor, where there
were rooms filled with bottles of various different acids.
The laboratory faced onto the Volga.

Not far from the factory was the factory's club-house.
A railway line ran past the club-house. On the tracks, there
stood two tanks of oil. I remember that on the afternoon of
September 30th, three German planes dive-bombed these
tanks. The tanks caught fire, when I was standing only
about 30 or 40 metres away. It got extremely hot.

A trench had been dug between the buildings to the
south-west of the club-house, and on the parapet of
the trench we mounted one of our heavy machineguns.
While the Junkers were dive-bombing the tanks, I managed
to jump into the trench and reach the machinegun.
The trench was deep and narrow, and was covered by an
iron sheet weighed down by a metal bar. Bombs fell so close
by that the iron sheet was blown off. The Maxim gun was
turned into a heap of metal.

I then ran over to the brick building that stood to the
south-west of the club-house. An anti-tank gun was
mounted in a ground-floor window. Beneath the ground-
floor staircase I came across an old man, who had
gathered his belongings – pillows and a blanket – in a
corner. Next to him there was an enamel teapot, but he
didn't have any water or food. That night, I was sitting
in the trench again when a girl came down into the trench
looking for water, but I didn't have any water either.
The only water was in the casing of the machinegun.
I remember that I advised her to go down to the Volga,
but she didn't manage to reach it and came back with tears
in her eyes. The girl said that a blocking battalion had
refused to let her through to the Volga.

The girl was fortunate not to have been shot. Had she been in uniform, the blocking battalion would almost certainly have taken her for a deserter and executed her on the spot. Kartashev could not look after her, because the next day he engaged the advancing Germans on the factory grounds. This is his long account of the first ten days of October, within the walls of Red October, where he fought to hold a single building – the factory canteen.

Our company moved up to an attack line north of the factory canteen. On our left flank, the boiler-house was on fire. When the riflemen went into the attack, we covered them with machinegun fire. But whenever we changed our firing positions the machineguns in the pits and shell-holes nearly fell over. The Maxim is a heavy machinegun, but you don't feel its weight. It manoeuvres with incredible power and speed. But our tunics were soaked in sweat and clinging to our backs. The grit was crunching in our teeth. Our mouths were completely dry.

We had to sling our guns over our shoulders when we moved, and that made it difficult for us to run. Bullets were whistling past, mortars were exploding, but we couldn't see the Germans at all. They had taken cover behind piles of rubble in wrecked buildings. I came across a trench in which a machinegun had been mounted, and started feeding a cartridge belt into the bandolier. It seemed to take forever, but in fact it can't have been more than a minute. I squeezed the trigger: the machinegun was working fine.

Our machinegun crew consisted of Alexei Bochkaryov, Sergei Kobelyov, Shulakov, and myself. Bochkaryov and Kobelyov were lying on the ground with their rifles not far from me. Bochkaryov didn't like carrying around anything more than was strictly necessary. He didn't even have a kit-bag, but would always simply stuff cartridges into his coat and trouser pockets. Whenever we moved to new positions I would immediately set about digging in, and since he didn't have a sapper spade he had to share mine. But after this battle Bochkaryov got himself a small spade, which he would never let out of his sight.

He quickly learned to smoke. He smoked a lot and often. I remember one time he clambered up some crates to me while I was manning my machinegun, which was mounted in a basement window. He was so dirty that his eyes and teeth seemed to sparkle against the grime which covered the rest of him, and his eyes had become sunken from too many sleepless nights. We didn't have any water, so we had to make do without washing.

The soldiers were frantically digging in; every minute counted. The deeper you dig in, the better you'll be able to repulse enemy attacks and hold on to your position. A cloud of dust soon appeared from the west. Fascist tanks were coming, and behind the tanks, infantry. Several of the tanks turned and started heading straight towards us.

It's difficult to describe a man's feelings at moments like this. There's a continuous rumble in the air, the ground seems to be alive and groaning. The tanks were firing as they went, from every gun they had. Shells and mines were exploding close to us, bringing huge quantities of earth up into the air. All around there was hissing, roaring and wailing. Thousands of splinters and bullets were flying through the air.

I remember the belt in our machinegun ran out, so a new one had to be put in fast. I went down into the trench for another box, but at that instant a mortar shell exploded close to my Maxim, piercing its casing with splinters, bending its barrel and jamming its breechlock. The stench from the exploded shell was overpowering. There was only one thing to do: shoot at the fascists with my rifle and hurl grenades at them. The thought suddenly occurred to me that the smashed machinegun would only draw attention to itself, so I shoved it into a bomb crater.

The battle lasted for about two hours. Two tanks were
burning in front of us, but the rest of them were continuing
to fire on our trenches. Behind us, there stood an anti-tank
gun. It managed to disable one tank before being smashed.
A second gun was firing at point-blank range. It was
mounted in a window on the ground floor of the brick
building. Things had reached the stage where we were using
anti-tank grenades, though we didn't have many of them.
Someone not far from me disabled a tank with a grenade.
The tank turned around on one caterpillar track, revolved
its turret, and started firing at our right flank. Anti-tank
riflemen from the 184th Independent Machinegun
Battalion came to our aid, and we held our positions.
There were a lot of dead and wounded men. We stayed there
until nightfall, when we moved out and took up a defensive
position in the building of the factory canteen.

The canteen stood in a complex of buildings in various stages of
collapse. Kartashev cast his eye over the shattered outhouses and
edifices. They were a mixed blessing: they could be used by the Russians
for the defence of the canteen, or by the Germans for a stealthy attack.

The factory canteen was a T-shaped, single-storey building,
with large windows facing north and south. The boiler-
house was about 15 metres to the west. Only two of its
boilers were still intact, with the remains of their water.
There was no roof or ceiling, and the walls had been
destroyed. Gunner Karpov's heavy machinegun was
mounted in a hole in the boiler-house wall, from where it
could rake the area in front of the boiler-house. To the right,
that is to the north, you could see a three-storey building.
They said it was School No. 35 – I saw this building in
flames. There was a bath-house 200 metres to the west of
the factory canteen. Around the canteen, there were brick
buildings only on the western side. On the eastern side, that

is, towards the Volga, and to the north-east on both sides of the cutting, it was mostly wooden houses.

Another heavy machinegun and a Degtyarev light machinegun were dragged over to us from somewhere or other. The heavy machinegun was mounted in one of the basement windows, from where it could rake the north-western side. This job was entrusted to me. That night, though, we covered up the window with beams and bricks and piled earth up around it, turning it into a sort of earth-and-timber pillbox. When our lads went out of the basement and started building the pillbox, I stayed behind with my machinegun. I was ordered to keep watch over our forward position.

It was a dark night, and I was only able to keep watch over the forward position by lying down and looking at the horizon: against the background of the sky you could make out any movement. But I couldn't stay lying in that position for long. It was hard to stay awake: the sleepless nights were really taking their toll. My eyelids were getting heavier and heavier with every minute. I couldn't keep my eyes open any longer, so I had to report this to the commander of our platoon, who gave me permission to keep crawling around rather than stay lying on the same spot. One of the lads made sure I didn't fall asleep by whispering loudly to me from time to time.

In the basement, a narrow corridor led up to the window. The machinegun was mounted quite high up, and since we didn't have a ladder I had to use some beer and vodka crates that were in the basement to climb up to it. There was a vat in the corridor, which we were using as a place to sleep. It was too short, you had to bend your legs, but you could sleep in it.

All the men at Stalingrad, German and Russian, longed for the sweet luxury of sleep. But the nights were never silent and never comfortable, and sleep was rationed like everything else. An hour or two of fitful oblivion was the most anybody had for weeks on end.

We never took off our boots, and would take it in turns
to get some sleep, which we did with our weapons in our
hands. We would put our helmets on and rest our heads
against a brick. One day we were brought an accordion,
a samovar and a whole sack of various different items.
Someone said that a shell had blown a whole load of things
out of the ground not far from the factory canteen. There
was everything from women's shoes to red velvet and some
sort of white material. The white material came in handy
for bandaging the wounded, and the samovar really hit the
spot. In the basement there was some sort of half-collapsed
pit with water in it. None of us knew what kind of water it
was, but we were thirsty, so we had no choice but to drink it.
The samovar came to our rescue, though many of us got
stomach upsets from drinking this water. It was very
difficult getting food to us. Hot food rarely reached us.
Bread was sent to us in sacks, so we got only crusts and
crumbs. We could make do with the food we were given,
but ammunition was another matter entirely. We needed
grenades and cartridges. We all realized that without
ammunition it might be the end for us.

The Germans opened up with heavy artillery fire again.
It felt like they were going to turn the factory canteen to dust.
In the basement, we were able to sit tight behind the thick
brick walls. It looked as though the ceiling was going to come
crashing down at any moment. The air in the basement was
filled with dust from all the collapsed plaster. As soon as the
artillery bombardment stopped, the Germans attacked. We
dispersed to the windows. Bochkaryov lay down with the
light machinegun in the ruins of the boiler-house, Karpov
manned the other heavy machinegun, and I went to my own.
This time the Germans' main effort was directed at the right-
hand side of the factory canteen. Ten or so Nazi tanks were
moving along the hollow and towards School No. 35. We
could hear the roar of their engines, even though they were

not moving towards us. But we had to ward off some sub-machinegunners who were coming at us, shrieking as they came. We could hear the yells of the officers and the shouting of the men. There were so many of them, they just kept coming and coming. But our fire forced them to the ground and they stayed there. I was firing until the water in the casing got so hot that it was boiling. I remember that we used up nearly all our cartridge belts. But the battle was over for now, and we had managed to hold on to our position.

Kartashev's battle may have come to a temporary stop, but the larger struggle for the factories was still in full flow. The Germans were about to make a supreme effort to break through the factory grounds and get to the river. Before that, there was a little time in which to count the new crop of dead, and to put a name to each of them.

Toporkov and Mukhin had been killed. Toporkov was a thin, middle-aged man. In quiet moments, he used to talk about his home, his family and his friends. Mukhin was a stocky lad of nineteen with thick stubble. He didn't say much, but he was always cursing that fast-growing beard of his. Sergeant Shaposhnik was lightly wounded in the leg, and several other solders were put out of commission. There were fewer and fewer of us left. Arkady Myshkin had taken up a fire position with his heavy machinegun about 50 metres to the north of the factory canteen. In this battle his machinegun was smashed, and he was killed. I was later told by Sergeant Kuzmin, who had been with Myshkin at the time, that a Nazi tank had crushed him to death along with his machinegun.

Traitors appeared in our ranks. Bondarenko, Bychok and Mironenko ran over to the Germans. I didn't want to mention their names but, as the Russian saying goes, every family has its freak.

... In 1952, I was working as a production engineer in a factory, and prisoners who had been sentenced for betraying the Motherland were working in our shop. One of the prisoners looked like Bondarenko. So one day, during a break on my shift, I went up to a group of prisoners and asked them what the surname was of the man who looked like Bondarenko. It turned out that he was his younger brother. Later, the younger Bondarenko waited until I was alone and then asked me about his brother's disappearance, since he knew nothing about what had happened, and his family had been told only that he was missing ...

On October 8th, some fascists burst out towards the Volga. They were drunk, walking completely upright, without stooping, shooting aimlessly as they went. But these were some sort of special fritzes. Even when they got wounded, they kept crawling forward, shouting something. This time, they nearly succeeded in driving us out of the factory canteen. On October 11th, the Germans decided to deal with us once and for all. Their infantry started advancing towards us, under cover of machinegun and mortar fire. Several tanks were bearing down on us. We had been outnumbered for some time, but the order was 'Not one step back!', and we were carrying out that order. Karpov's machinegun, which had miraculously survived the attack of the drunken fascists, helped to repel this latest attack. But the wall in front of him was brought crashing down by tank shells, burying Karpov and his machinegun.

That's how machinegunner Karpov died. His family must have been told that he was missing in action, as by that time there were few of us former cadets left. Though we all knew each other, the reinforcements may not even have known his surname, and none of them displayed any interest in our fallen comrades. There was never enough time to establish how a man died, and who he was.

So Karpov and his Maxim remained under a pile of rubble on the soil of Stalingrad. That left only my machinegun still operational, but that same day it was damaged by some shell or mine fragments. This is how it happened. A shell exploded about two metres away, badly damaging the Maxim. I was lucky, I got only a light contusion, though I still had to lie down in the basement for a while until the noise in my head went away. Then we patched up the Maxim. At first we covered the holes with bread and bound them with rags, but water was still seeping through, so we cut up some sticks and jammed them in with the rags; the machinegun could then fire in short bursts.

The wounded men and the patched-up guns had held out just long enough. The first German assault on the factories had burned itself out. Like punch-drunk boxers, the two armies staggered back to their own corners and slumped down in exhaustion. The fighting never ceased completely, but now, for the first time since August, something like a lull descended on Stalingrad. It was to last for four days – an illusion of calm before the next homicidal storm.

THE FATAL FOURTEENTH

Stalingrad was fast becoming an obsession for Hitler. The original aim of the 1942 campaign – to get Soviet oil – was forgotten. Capturing Stalingrad had in Hitler's eyes become a matter of personal prestige and national honour – for the eyes of the world were on the city, and the progress of the battle was being reported around the globe. Hitler was now like the petitioner in Kafka's tale *The Trial* who, denied entry to court by a gatekeeper, comes to believe that getting through the gate is the only obstacle to his winning the case. The Führer convinced himself that if he could only take Stalingrad, then the morale of the Red Army and of the Soviet people would quickly collapse too – and then the whole Soviet edifice would fall down and he would win the war. Everything depended on this one battle.

On 14 October Hitler formally suspended all operations on the eastern front apart from the battle for Stalingrad. The same day, Paulus relaunched the onslaught on the factories. His attack force was bolstered by four battalions of fresh combat engineers, experts in demolition shipped in from the western front. In total, 90,000 men and 300 tanks were assigned to the assault, which had the same aim as the previous attack: to drive a wedge between the Barricades and Red October factories, and so to split the 62nd Army in two.

Hans S——, the soldier who two months before had so cheerily threatened to shoot a Russian who asked him for a smoke, was now crouched in a bunker, watching the Luftwaffe bombardment of the Russian lines as he waited to go in himself.

> Today an almighty air battle raged overhead. The whole sky was full of planes, flak firing from every gun barrel, bombs hurtling down, planes crashing, a tremendous spectacle that we followed from our dug-outs with mixed feelings.

The unit that bore the brunt of the air raid and the subsequent land attack was General Zholudev's 37th Guards Division. Dmitry Bakanov, an observation officer, was at his post – inside a large pipe in the foundry. He watched the Germans advance into the factory and join battle over a slagheap in the yard. Soldiers clambered and scrambled on the manmade hummock, firing their guns and jabbing at each other with bayonets. It was like Mamayev Kurgan in miniature.

> This great mound had grown up over a number of years as slag from the furnaces was dumped here while it was still hot. It had sort of cooked down into one solid mass. There was no way you could dig foxholes in it. But the soldiers would grab big lumps of the slag and use them to build dugouts, along with sheets of metal which they found in the factory.

The 37th Guards lost ownership of the slagheap in the course of the morning. German tanks were pushing them further and further back, into the labyrinthine depths of the factory grounds. Separate battles were fought inside the 19th-century factory halls amid the industrial machinery. The Russians climbed inside the dead blast furnaces: they were as bullet-proof as any purpose-built pillbox and they still retained some residual warmth, so were good places to sleep in as well as to shoot from. Germans used concrete troughs in the floors as shallow trenches. They fought over tables and chairs. Though the Germans were making inexorable progress there was no sense of elation, still less of victory, even when the Volga came in sight. This is how one German tankman described the fighting:

> It was a ghastly, wearisome battle both on the ground and below the ground, amid the ruins and in the basements of that large city, in its industrial quarter. The tanks tottered over mountains of rubble and broken bricks, they screeched as they picked their way through the factory workshops, shooting at short range down blocked streets and in crowded factory yards. Once in a while one of these armoured giants would shudder and suddenly fly apart with a great booming noise as it ran over an enemy mine. But all that would have been bearable. Ahead of us there was still the steep cliff edge of the Volga bank, like a bottomless pit. That was where the worst fighting happened.

The Germans had not reached the Volga yet, but they were getting dangerously close. Some units were near enough to bring the landing stage behind the factory under small-arms fire. The Russians were already so short of ammunition that they had to grab it from dead men – comrades or enemies – in order to continue fighting amid what one Red Army man described as 'the smell of smoke, the grinding of twisted iron, the stink of cordite and fresh blood'. Viktor Kartashev was still holding out in the Red October canteen, but he was on the point of losing the foothold he had occupied for two weeks.

> The Germans were firing mostly explosive bullets, which made a peculiar clicking sound when they exploded upon impact with the ruins. You could hear groans and individual cries, including some good old-fashioned Russian swearing. I remember that Sergei Kobelyov killed

a fascist in this battle. When he saw the fascist drop dead, he let out a joyful yell and shouted: 'That's one more fritz down!' And he added that if he was killed it wouldn't have been in vain, and carried on firing.

I was firing from my rifle for so long that it became impossible to touch its barrel. Even the hand guard couldn't stop my hands from getting scalded, and the palm of my right hand was hurting from all the opening and shutting of the breechblock. I was having to use a brick to open the breechblock, as the plaster and sand that had got into it were preventing it from shutting properly. My shoulder was in constant pain, battered by the rifle butt from all the shooting.

Towards midday on October 14th, the Germans took the boiler-house. Only one soldier managed to get out of it alive. There were wounded men in the basement with us, but there was no way to get them across the Volga. The battalion commander sent a messenger to the regimental command post to report this, and he must also have asked for reinforcements, since about two hours later dozens of sub-machinegunners arrived. The sub-machinegunners brought us cartridges, grenades, and bottles of inflammable fluid – excellent reinforcements indeed!

We immediately set about retaking the boiler-house. Shouting 'Hurrah!' we rushed the ruins. After a brief engagement, the Germans retreated. All around lay the bodies of dead Germans, and of some of our lads, too. Two disabled tanks were still smoking. They had probably been hit by our anti-tank riflemen. I heard the rumble of tank engines coming from behind the ruins of the boiler-house. On our right flank, the fascists had taken our trenches, but the battle was still raging, albeit not as intensely as it had been that morning.

Five or so of our men surrendered. I saw them running towards the Germans with their hands in the air. I fired at them several times from my rifle, but didn't hit any of them. There's nothing more painful than when your own comrades betray you to save their own skins!

The loss of the boiler-house meant our left flank was exposed to the enemy. The battalion commander telephoned the regiment's command post to report the situation, but at almost exactly the same time the communications broke off. The battalion commander sent a messenger, but he was killed. There was no way of getting through. So those of us who were still alive were stuck in the basement of the factory canteen. Only then did we realize how difficult it would be to escape from the basement by day, so we decided to wait until nightfall. We gathered up the last cartridges and grenades. We didn't have any food or water left, and the pit of water was full of debris from the ceiling, which had finally fallen in. We tried to dig it out, but the water was now an undrinkable gruel of soil and lime.

Meanwhile the Germans had overrun the divisional command post of the 37th Guards. It was at this point that General Zholudev, commander-in-chief of the 37th, had a brush with death almost as horrible as the river of flame that so nearly carried off Chuikov the week before. Petr Shcherbina, a staff officer who was with General Zholudev at the time, tells the story of their shared ordeal, and how they were rescued by a soldier whose name – Vyruchkin – means 'help out' in Russian.

A large group of tanks broke through into the tractor plant's yard, and individual tanks advanced on the command posts of the regiments and divisions. They were destroyed by assault teams from headquarters sub-units. At twelve o'clock, heavy aerial bombing commenced. Major Pustavgar was wounded, and his place was taken by Regimental Commissar Nikitin. Bombs smashed several of the divisional command post's dugouts, and the General Zholudev, Senior Battalion Commissar Flyagin and myself were trapped inside our dugout.

Imagine what it was like, after being subjected to the relentless roaring of dozens of aeroplane engines, and constant explosions, to be suddenly surrounded by a deathly silence! We were cut off from the outside world. Were we staring an agonizing death in the face? A single thought filled our minds: we mustn't suffocate, we have to hold on. Then someone started singing:

> 'It's a lovely thing, my brothers,
> To live the life we've had.
> And when our general's with us
> There's no reason to be sad.'

The three of us started singing this little rhyme together. Time dragged on slowly; we had given up all hope of being rescued. The deathly silence was oppressive. All of a sudden, we heard a rustle. We instinctively hunched our shoulders, as if to brace ourselves against the tons of earth that could come crashing down on us at any moment.

It was soldiers from a signals company. One of the signallers was a sergeant by the name of Vyruchkin. A few days earlier, he had run to a burning vehicle carrying munitions and put out the fire. He was the first to break through to us in the collapsed dugout, and it was he who freed us from our dungeon using a crowbar. We later related this incident to the writer Vasily Grossman when he visited the division, and he remarked: 'Perhaps this soldierly valour – rushing to the assistance of those in trouble, heedless of the danger – is in his blood, passed down to him from his forebears; perhaps that's how the Vyruchkins got their name!' It's a real shame that this brave man, this hard worker and lover of life, was killed later the same day. General Zholudev and I were deeply affected by the death of our saviour, Sergeant Vyruchkin who helped us out.

It was an affecting day for Zholudev in many ways. Even before he was buried alive he saw most of his guardsmen wiped out. The Germans swept past him and reached the river, occupying almost all of the Tractor Factory and the Barricades plant in the process. Late that night, after he was exhumed from his collapsed dugout, Zholudev was summoned to give a report to General Chuikov at 62nd Army HQ. General Yeremenko, commander-in-chief of the Stalingrad Front, was there too. Zholudev, a veteran of many battles, recounted the day's events to his two superiors. As he spoke the horror of it all crowded in on him – and he burst into tears.

TEACHING GRENADE STUDIES

Chuikov later said that 14 October was the darkest day of the battle, that one more day like that and the struggle for Stalingrad would have been lost. But in fact the next few days were no less bleak. The fighting was just as furious in the factories, and the Russians continued to retreat stride by painful stride. Dmitry Lutsenko was with the 39th Guards, what was left of them, in the Red October plant. He was told by his officer, a lieutenant named Miroshnichenko, that they were up against fresh Germans just arrived from France. The officer decided that it would be good to give the new boys a crash course in Stalingrad fighting methods.

> Lieutenant Miroshnichenko had been studying to be a teacher before the war, said Lutsenko. As we went into battle he turned to me and said jokingly 'Now those fritzes are all lovely and fresh from their time in Paris, so I think I'll give them a little lecture in grenade studies. I'll let you know how it went in the morning.' The lecture took place at night. There was a house in which the lecturer, with the help of his able assistants, brought to bear his immense talent. Comrade Miroshnichenko personally conducted a demonstration of grenade-throwing and machinegun shooting, as a result of which fifty-three fritzes received an education. By the time dawn came round,

Miroshnichenko and I were sitting having a quiet smoke
and discussing the impression which our lecture had made
on the new students.

Most Red Army men were too busy in these days for jokes, however
brief. The Russians were holding the Germans off in the Red October
plant, the southernmost part of the factory district, but to the north
all seemed lost. The tractor plant was entirely in German hands and
the neighbouring Barricades factory was slowly succumbing. The men
of the 308th Division were manning the factory gates, like archers on
the battlements of a castle. They were supported by the newly arrived
138th Division under General Ivan Lyudnikov – and by a scratch
regiment, the 178th NKVD, made up of civilian workers from the
Barricades factory itself.

Ivan Burlakov was an officer with this regiment of enthusiastic
amateurs. His job was to arrange supplies for his fighters, an
impossible task made just about feasible by the circumstance that his
armed factory workers were defending familiar turf.

We were feeling the effect of being cut off from any means
of getting food or ammo. Steps had to be taken to deal
with this. Nearly all of the factory's buildings had been
destroyed. The plumbing was not working, and water had to
be supplied from the Volga, which was full of planks from
smashed rafts, islets of burning oil, and other objects.

A search of the concrete installations beneath the factory's
power station revealed three settling tanks full of water.
This was a marvellous stroke of luck. We made use of this
water, and also supplied the neighbouring units that were
fighting in this sector. Later, a huge water tank was
discovered in the ground close to the factory's offices,
which probably used to serve as the factory's reserve supply.
I set up a 24-hour guard around it, so as to prevent any
possibility of its being spoiled or contaminated, since the
basement of the factory's offices housed the dressing

station where the wounded were sent. This reserve of water proved invaluable, as it supplied all the units in that combat sector, including the 308th Siberian Division.

The workers knew the factory's storage facilities and found 50 sacks of flour, 38 vats of melted butter and several boxes of expensive cigarettes in the ruins of the stores. When the supplies situation became dire, I gave the 308th Siberian Division over 35 sacks of flour and a large half-vat of butter.

This is how the regiment was kept supplied with munitions: we would pick up any rifle rounds, sub-machinegun rounds and mortar shells that we found and store them in the boiler room. When provisions were low, the soldiers would make butter-and-flour pancakes in the cellars, and would joke: 'It's Shrove Tuesday for us, but the Germans are on a Lenten fast.'

In the course of the relentless battles of October 15th to 17th, the Germans started to drive a wedge into our neighbours' right flank. A lieutenant ran up to me (I don't recall his surname) and asked me to give him as many cartridges as I could spare, as the Germans were starting to encircle them from the flank. I recalled Suvorov's dictum: 'Though you perish in the attempt, come to the aid of your comrade-in-arms!' I handed over seven boxes of cartridges and poured some more into some kit-bags.

Day and night, embrasures were made in every building, connecting trenches and concrete underground passages were dug between all sectors and the shops, and trenches, machinegun foxholes and so forth were dug. I shall never forget the 2nd company's battle by the Maritime workshop. On the 16th or 17th the Germans launched several attacks against the factory and managed to break through to the main gates with tanks, disabling our two anti-tank guns outside the power station. The 2nd company fought for over four hours. Contact with the Siberians to our right was lost,

the Germans were breaching the line of defence in the area
of the boiler room and main gates, there was a high risk of
our being surrounded by the Germans as they had more men
and weapons than us. The company therefore fell back to the
next line of resistance (I don't recall which shop it was),
repulsing the enemy as it went with sub-machinegun fire
and grenades. The shop was strewn with German corpses.

   On the evening of the 18th, the factory's defensive line
had gone as far back as the southern edge of the factory.
On this line, there was continuous fire for several days.
By the last days of October the Germans were attacking the
Red October factory at several points. The wail of sirens and
dive-bombers, the blasts of bombs and grenades and the
crackle of machineguns never let up. The area was veiled in
smoke and dust, which covered the buildings. By the 27th
the situation was grave. The Germans' superior forces had
driven a wedge into the area between factory No. 221 and
the Red October factory.

All the soldiers at Stalingrad, German and Russian, had become
familiar with the strange phenomenon, unique to this battle, whereby
the fighting grew ever more intense as the area of territory fought for
grew smaller and smaller. It was a process of distillation of the horror
of war until all that remained was a toxic compound of fear, pain, hate
and blood. The Sixth Army had once seen itself as the conqueror of
entire countries. Earlier in the struggle for Stalingrad they had had to
adjust their expectations to the point where they saw it as a victory if
they could take and hold a suburb. Then the measure became a single
street, then an individual building, then half a building. Now, at the
climax of the battle for the factories, they fought and died to gain or
hold the space behind a lathe, or a stretch of wall one side of a
drainpipe, or a corner of a washroom.

   The Germans were forced to fight like this because the Russians,
with the river only a few hundred yards behind them, took an entirely
literal view of the two slogans that they repeated like a mantra: 'Not

one step back' and 'No land beyond the Volga'. Though they had been on the retreat through the factories for a month, they saw every yard lost as a small but shameful defeat, and in their bitterness they made the enemy pay. And they did not surrender. Inside the Barricades factory, the 138th Rifle Division under General Ivan Lyudnikov found itself completely surrounded. The Division set up an all-round defence that the Germans could not break, try as they might. Pavel Tyupa was with Lyudnikov, and he describes an uncompromising and cramped tussle in the first days of the unit's isolation.

The Germans took the 14th workshop of the Barricades factory, which was being defended by the 2nd battalion of our regiment. The commander and the commissar were both killed, and since we in the 1st battalion still had both a commander and a political instructor, I took command of the 2nd battalion.

The Germans were dug in behind a wall and between the machines. It was going to be hard to shift them from there, so we decided to dig underneath the wall of Workshop No. 14 on the right-hand side. This meant we would not have to attack through the hole in the wall that was already there. We put explosives in the trench, hoping to get at the Germans from another angle. Many of them were killed or buried when the charge exploded, and we killed the rest of them in hand-to-hand fighting.

Here is how one German soldier described this indoor war:

The front is a corridor between burned-out rooms. It is the thin ceiling between two floors. Help comes from nearby buildings via fire escapes and chimneys. There is ceaseless struggle from morning until night. From floor to floor, we bombard each other with grenades amid explosions, clouds of dust and smoke, heaps of mortar, floods of blood, fragments of furniture and fragments of human beings.

Hans S——, now just one more hapless Landser adrift in the carnage, was more laconic. 'Stalingrad can only be described as hell,' he said.

THE RIVER IN WINTER

Mother Volga – *Volga-Matushka* – was the Russians' single biggest asset in the battle. The presence of the river meant that it was never enough for the Germans to occupy the greater part of Stalingrad: to win, they had to have it all. At the end of November Paulus's men held nine-tenths of the city, but the Russian tenth was at the water's edge, and that meant reserves could still be brought up from the east and ferried over. So long as the Russians held a stretch of the riverbank, however slim that sliver, the battle was not lost.

Moreover, the immense breadth of the river – a mile (1.6km) wide at the point where the city stands – allowed the mass of Russian artillery to be ranged on the far bank, where it was relatively safe from attack but could pound the German positions inside the city. Russian gunners soon learned to do this with pinpoint accuracy – there was even a dedicated sniperist movement for artillerymen. The soldiers in the city held the artillery in the highest regard, as this Red Army man testifies.

Our gunners made a huge contribution to the battle for Stalingrad. It was often the case that one side of a street would be in our hands and the other in the enemy's, or even that one half of a building would be in our hands and the other half in the enemy's. In such situations our gunners really showed their skill. I remember one time when the commander of an infantry battalion telephoned the artillery to ask for some help. He explained that his lads had dislodged the enemy from one half of a hotel, but could not drive them out of the other half. He told them what part of the building they needed to aim at. Our gunners were wary at first, worried that they could end up firing at our own lads. But they still said they'd give it a go, and asked him to observe a test shell. The test shell slammed straight into the section of the building where the fascists were holed up, and once the gunners received the signal 'Good shot!' they fired off two salvoes and a column of smoke and dust rose up above the hotel. A little later, the battalion commander thanked the gunners for their excellent shooting. Our soldiers had dislodged the enemy from the building without sustaining any losses.

There were no permanent bridges across the river, but during the battle several pontoons were built. These connected the islands opposite the factory district to the riverbank. Some soldiers walked part of the way across the river, others made a waterborne dash for the right bank. It was hard to say which was more hazardous.

We crossed the Volga on a shaky footbridge in the form of a wooden ladder attached to steel cables. The footbridge was swaying on the waves, our feet were slipping on the sodden planks, and if you lost your balance even for a second you could find yourself taking a dip. That's what happened to one soldier in our company. He was pulled out and helped to wring the water out of his sodden clothes. Crossing over the footbridge was even more difficult for those of us who were carrying the barrels for the Maxim machinegun. It was hard not to fall in.

Aron Shifrin was the engineer in charge of bridge building during the battle. It was heavy construction work, but he knew his edifices were as fragile and vulnerable as a tent in a whirlwind.

The 119th motorized engineering battalion built three footbridges in the area of the Tractor Plant and the Barricades factory, each of them around 270 metres long. The footbridge in the area of the Barricades factory, at the southern end of Zaitsev Island, was built from rafts and barrels fastened together with steel cable and flat-steel plates. Planking was laid lengthwise along the cross-pieces.

This bridge, despite being susceptible to the slightest choppiness, lasted for more than a month. In that time, it was crossed by several thousand men. Attacks by German dive bombers and relentless artillery and mortar fire caused only slight damage to the bridge – and that was easily repaired.

The footbridge that was built at the southern edge of the Stalingrad Tractor Plant lasted only three days. A bomb fragment broke the cable, and the bridge was carried downstream by the current. In the area of the northern edge of the Stalingrad Tractor Plant, a footbridge of iron barrels was built. Attempts to build a footbridge from fishing boats and log rafts were unsuccessful. The enemy was firing ceaselessly on the area where the bridge was being built, causing destruction that made it impossible to carry on building.

The bridges would not have lasted much longer, because in late October and early November began the annual *ledokhod*, the drifting of the ice. This is the time when large ice floes as big as ships float down the river from the north – coming in ones or twos at first, and then by the dozen. They are unstoppable, and they make the river totally unnavigable. The ledokhod ends when the haphazard platforms of ice become so numerous that they form a huge jam. By that time the temperature has usually fallen well below zero, and the river soon freezes over completely. Shipping then comes to a complete standstill until the spring.

Russian commanders in the city had been dreading the ledokhod, because they knew that while it lasted the river would be working for the enemy: no supplies would be coming in across the river until the ice was solid, and thick enough to support the weight of men and (better yet) trucks. Grigory Gulko, a sapper with the 13th Guards, was on one of the last river transports to make the crossing before the menacing ice closed in. The boat he was about to board had been nicknamed the 'barge of death' for reasons he was soon to discover.

Hundreds of soldiers were silently and hurriedly loading boxes of munitions: mines, shells, grenades, bottles of flammable liquid. They were being tidily stacked right at the bottom of the barge. Vehicles kept arriving with more cargo. After the munitions, they started loading chemicals, medical supplies, provisions and other goods. The frost was getting harder and harder.

From time to time the Germans hurled shells; they were landing ever closer to the 62nd crossing, and suddenly one of them hit a vehicle loaded with munitions. A column of fire rose up into the sky, and shells started exploding. The Germans must have thought they'd hit a munitions depot, and intensified their fire in that direction, firing shell after shell. In the meantime, the loading of the barge had been completed. The reinforcements were embarked – 500 Siberians.

The sappers were manning their posts on the barge, checking the cargo. There is a saying: a sapper slips up only once in his life. They checked everything on the barge, prepared the backup tow-rope, checked that the boat-hooks were in position. The tug did not hang around. Silently cutting through the thin layer of ice, it set off upstream. A heavy-duty tow-rope had been attached to the barge. The tug strained with all its might to move forward, but the barge refused to budge. They made another attempt, but once again the barge stayed put. It was clear that the barge was overloaded and had got stuck in the sand at the bottom of the Volga. But nothing could be unloaded from the barge, since the longer we stayed there the more chance there was of the enemy's detecting us. In any case, everything that had been loaded onto the barge was urgently needed in Stalingrad.

So the soldiers were commanded to push the barge away from the bank. Immediately, hundreds of hands were pushing against the barge in the icy water, helping the tug to shift it from the sandbank. At the tug's third attempt the barge moved, and started following the tug at a snail's pace, leaving in its wake a wide trail in the thick, grey, broken ice. For a short time, they proceeded under cover of night undetected by the Germans, but before they had gone 500 metres towards the central crossing the tug turned sharply around, in full view of the enemy, and headed across the Volga towards the burning city of Stalingrad. More and more of the Volga was getting covered in ice. The gaps between the blocks of ice were getting ever narrower. In places, the blocks of ice were scraping against each other, making a sickening crunching sound.

The tug's engine was roaring under the strain, its prow was lifted high above the water. The tug was searching for unfrozen patches of water, and was trying to avoid large blocks of ice and ice-jams. The tug was literally gnawing a path through the thick floating ice. It often ran onto a large block of ice, where it would remain, helpless; try as it might, it would not be able to reverse off the block of ice, and with its prow lying on the ice it would start floating with the current, taking the barge with it. But when this happened soldiers would immediately rush to its assistance. They would grab the tow rope and pull the tug off the block of ice, and the tug's captain would resume his search for a passage through the unfrozen water.

The tug's struggle with the congealing river was perilous enough, but a greater danger was about to make itself felt.

Loud explosions shook the night air: the barge had been spotted by the Germans. Enemy batteries rained fire down on the barge, lines of tracer bullets were cutting through the sky towards the barge. You could see them being slightly blown off course by the gusting wind. The Volga was seething from all the exploding shells and mines. The barge was rocking, huge leaden columns were rising up into the sky, shards of icy water were pouring over the soldiers, freezing their clothes, and cold drops were rolling down inside their collars. One direct hit, and the barge would be blown up by its own shells.

Then our artillery opened up from the left bank of the Volga, sending shells whistling over our heads. Salvoes from the right and left banks of the Volga blended into a single, mighty rumble. We were clearly visible to the enemy. Shells were falling ever closer to the barge. All of a sudden, one exploded next to the stern, bringing up plumes of water filled with small grains of ice. The blast wave blew the sapper Voronko over the starboard side. He landed on a block of ice and was knocked unconscious by the impact. Before our eyes he started slowly slipping into the Volga. His heavy, sodden boots started dragging him down, and his swollen overcoat was frozen rigid. He was brought round with a start by the icy water, and with great difficulty managed to cling on to the edge of the block of ice. He tried to get his legs out of the water, but his strength deserted him. At any moment, the block of ice could turn upside down and cover him, and it would all be over.

One of his comrades, Sergeant Grin, threw off his overcoat and was about to jump into the icy water to help his drowning friend when someone shouted imperiously 'Stop!' It would have been pointless for him to jump into the water, as they would both have been covered by the creeping block of ice. 'Boat-hooks, *now*!' I shouted. Moments later, two boat-hooks were stuck into sapper Voronko's swollen overcoat. He grabbed one of the hooks and at the same time his legs went into spasm. The huge block of ice, as if offended that he had been snatched away, was slowly following him towards the barge. 'Lift him up onto the deck, *quickly*!' shouted several voices at once. Dozens of hands stretched over the side of the barge to help

pull Private Voronko onto the deck. The block of ice was
still creeping towards him, and was on the point of pinning
its victim against the side of the barge. 'Lift him faster,
faster!' the soldiers were shouting. Then Voronko cried out,
in an unrecognizable voice: 'My legs, my legs!' 'Hoist him
onto the deck!' I shouted, and his bare feet were lifted into
the air, though his boots ... his boots remained, pinned to
the side of the barge by the block of ice. 'One more second',
said the sergeant to his friend, 'and both your legs would
have been crushed like a nut.'

Many Russians died in the embrace of Mother Volga that autumn.
Valentin Orlyankin, a newsreel cameraman, narrowly escaped with his
life on almost the same spot in the river – but this was a week or two
later, and by now the river was crossable on foot.

One night, after shooting combat operations in the city, I
was taking the material I had filmed across the frozen Volga
to Akhtuba on the left bank, from where it was to be sent by
plane to Moscow. I was escorted on the way back by three
soldiers from Rodimtsev's division. At dawn we were in the
middle of the Volga. The Germans suddenly started
shooting at us. They were in wrecked buildings that had
a good view over the Volga. We scattered in different
directions, lay down on the ice and crawled forward.
A second salvo landed close to me, throwing up splinters
of ice. When the machinegun stopped shooting, we leapt
up and ran further. And again bullets started landing in
front of me and behind me. 'What the hell's going on?'
I thought to myself. 'Why are they all shooting at me?'
My companions were about fifty metres to the side of
me. Suddenly I heard one of the soldiers sharply saying:
'Hide your camera under your camouflage suit!' Of course:
the black Aimo camera, which never left my side, was giving
me away – even though, like my soldiers, I was wearing

white overalls. The camera stood out against the white snow on the river as clearly as a full stop. When I hid the camera, the shooting ceased.

In the afternoon I was filming again, and I forgot about the morning's episode. Imagine how surprised I was when, that evening, a soldier came up to me in the dugout with a piece of white material and an order from General Rodimtsev to sew a camouflage cover onto the camera, which I immediately did.

Alexander Rodimtsev, hero of Spain, commander of the celebrated 13th Guards, had found the time to worry about a cameraman's kit. That white cover soon became grey and dirty, but it always reminded me of the general's big heart.

THE LEADERS SPEAK

Both Germany and the USSR celebrated national days during the weekend of 7 and 8 November 1942. In Germany it was the 19th anniversary of Hitler's failed *coup d'état*, the so-called 'beer-hall putsch'; in Russia it was the 25th anniversary of the Bolsheviks' more successful coup, the October Revolution. To mark his special day, Hitler addressed an invited audience of Nazi party veterans at the cavernous Löwenbräukeller in Munich. He used part of his speech to talk about Stalingrad. This is what he said:

I wanted to reach the Volga, and I wanted to get there at a particular spot, at a particular city. It just so happened that the city bore the name of Stalin himself. But do not think that this is the reason I marched there. I went there for a very different reason, namely, that it is a very important strategic point. I could cut off 30 million tons of river traffic at that point, including nine million tons of oil traffic. All the grain from the vast open spaces of the Ukraine and the Kuban flows through there on its way to the north. That is where all the manganese ore is taken, because it is a gigantic transport hub. That's why I wanted

it, and – do you know – we shall certainly have it. All there is
left to take is a couple of little scraps of land. Why can't they
capture it a little more quickly? Because I do not want to
have a second Verdun there. I would rather take it with
small bands of troops. Time is of no importance.

The most striking thing about this justification is its mendacity. The strategic reasons for taking Stalingrad had long since been eclipsed by Hitler's personal fixation with the city – hence, perhaps, his coyness about mentioning it by name. It was not true that time was of no importance: Hitler was constantly badgering Paulus for a date by which the battle would be won. As for the reference to Verdun – the fortress where in the Great War thousands of German soldiers had died in the attempt to annihilate the entrenched defenders – Stalingrad was already something far more costly in men and far more horrible in character. The mention of 'small bands of troops' will have raised eyebrows in the ranks of the Sixth Army, which was losing the equivalent of five divisions a week in the factory district. The nearest thing to a truthful remark is the observation that the city was almost totally in German hands. Looking at the situation map, it would have seemed to anybody that the battle was all but over. A week, two at most, and Stalingrad would surely be finished.

Hitler and his generals did not know what the Russians had planned for the next two weeks, but they might have been a little alarmed if they had listened closely to Stalin's Revolution Day speech. At the end of his broadcast address this most secretive of men dropped a small hint that there was something big in the pipeline: 'There'll be a party on our street too,' he said, and all over the Soviet Union people wondered what he meant. The event that Stalin was referring to was the counter-offensive that General Zhukov had mooted six weeks before, at the night-time meeting in the Kremlin. Even now, the general was in the steppeland near Stalingrad, putting the finishing touches to the arrangements. The operation had been given the code name 'Uranus' – the father of Lightning and Thunder.

5
URAN – THE COUNTER-ATTACK

Operation Uranus, the long-awaited counterstrike, was set in motion at dawn on 19 November. The Russian word *uran* – 'Uranus' – is reminiscent of the word *uragan* – 'hurricane', and the counter-attack began with a storm of artillery fire the like of which had never been seen on the eastern front. Three and a half thousand big guns and mortars, the 'gods of war' as the Russians liked to call them, roared without ceasing for 80 minutes. Above their thunder the whistle and screech of katyusha rockets could be heard as they arched across the sky like a furious meteor shower. High-explosive shells fell so thickly on the frozen steppe that they created a solid wall of smoke, flame, noise and flying earth.

The Russian barrage was directed in such a way that this wall of fire crept remorselessly forwards. Ahead of it, the ground was covered with a level blanket of snow. Behind it, the earth was dark and uneven like a newly ploughed field. The men of the Romanian Third Army, who were in the front line of defence, cowered and trembled in their trenches. They watched the terrain change from white to black as the barrage moved towards them, and they waited to die.

Theodor Plievier, in his novel *Stalingrad*, described how it felt to be a German soldier of the line at this moment.

> Had there been a forest there, the trees would have been mowed down like grass under the strokes of a mighty scythe. But there was no forest; it was flat, treeless terrain and looked now like the surface of a lake beaten by plump raindrops. Only here it was not rain but glowing metal

tearing into the earth, and what was thrown up was not spray but sand and mud; what remained were yawning shell holes. Where snow had lain, the fierce heat laid bare the scarred grass, and a moment later grass and topsoil as well disappeared. A landscape like the mountains of the moon was created; it drew closer and closer to the German lines and took over a terrain where there was not only sand and mud, but bunkers and corridors, and pillboxes with built-in battery positions, machine-gun nests, and mortars; a terrain where munitions dumps, command posts with map tables, stables, bedrooms and living rooms were embedded under heavy layers of soil, and where the crowded German crews fought – eyes glued to sights, hands on firing levers, dragging up shells and mortar ammunition. The muzzles of the guns flashed; shell after shell shot up out of the mortars. Brown smoke rolled over the earthworks. Where machine guns and riflemen began firing, it was a sign of incipient panic, for there were as yet no recognizable targets.

Along the whole front death stalked the German positions. Foreground and background were a billowing mass of smoke, dust, and fiery vapours bursting toward the sky and sinking down again. A hill spitting fire appeared – a heavy battery had blown up in the shape of an inverted pyramid. The dark fragments in the glare were pieces of metal and bodies. Black, cloudy masses spurted upward. Darts of fire, balls of smoke. Beams and props clattering to earth. A horse falling from the sky, legs and hoofs pointed upward. A barbed-wire entanglement with posts attached floated through the air. An infantry regiment with its divisional artillery was blown up, fell back to earth, and was again thrown up, turned over, and reduced to dust.

The human figures that bounded out of a crater and moved over the ground like dry leaves swept before the wind, that stumbled over one another, fell and remained

OPERATION URANUS

ENCIRCLING THE SIXTH ARMY

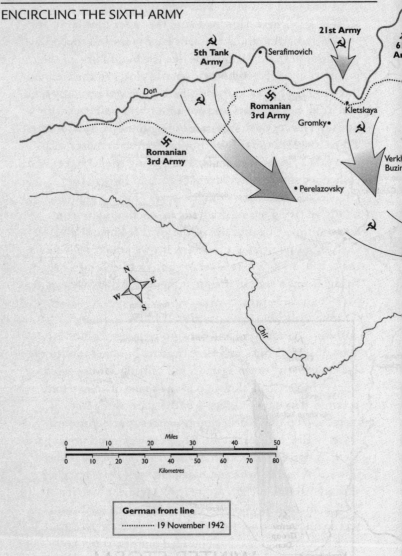

German front line
.... 19 November 1942

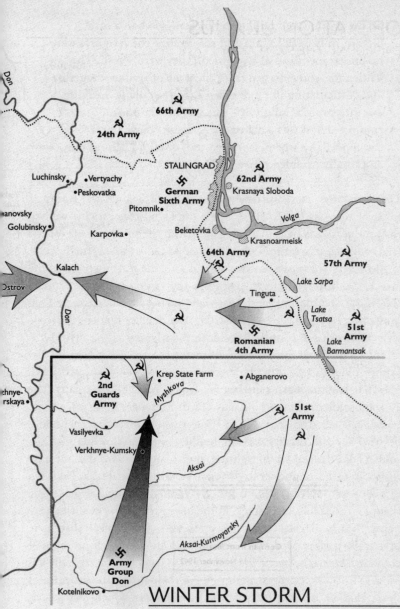

66th Army

24th Army

Luchinsky

Vertyachy

Peskovatka

STALINGRAD

German
Sixth Army

62nd Army
Krasnaya Sloboda

Pitomnik

anovsky

Golubinsky

Karpovka

Beketovka

Volga

Krasnoarmeisk

Kalach

64th Army

57th Army

Ostrov

Lake Sarpa

Tinguta

Lake
Tsatsa

51st
Army

Romanian
4th Army

Lake
Barmantsak

Krep State Farm

Abganerovo

2nd
Guards
Army

Myshkova

51st
Army

khnye-
rskaya

Vasilyevka

Verkhnye-Kumsky

Aksai

Aksai-Kurmoyarsky

Army
Group
Don

Kotelnikovo

WINTER STORM

THE RELIEF COLUMN DECEMBER 1942

on the ground or stood up again, struggled on a little
farther, only to fall again and run again – these figures were
no longer members of a regiment; they were 'chaff'. The tall
lieutenant who emerged from the zone of smoke staggering
and gesticulating like a drunkard, and suddenly breaking
out into peals of laughter – this was no platoon
commander; it was a madman. A figure crawled over
the snow like a worm, leaving a trail of blood behind him,
and finally tumbled into a hollow.

This first blow of the offensive was directed against the northern
flank of the Axis forces. Here, where the Don flows roughly west to
east, the Russians held two bridgeheads on the southern side of the
river: one was at Serafimovich, the other 25 miles (40km) further east
at Kletskaya. These two patches of land were the starting point of the
attack. Launching the offensive from the largely German-occupied
side of the river meant that the Russians did not have to cross the Don
in the first hours of the counterstrike. And the fact that the Russians
went in two-fisted confused the enemy – where was the main blow
falling? Which way should reinforcements be sent? Each blow looked
as threatening as the other.

What is more, both punches fell largely on the Romanians. The
170,000 soldiers of the Romanian Third Army were in an unenviable
position. Their strategic value to Hitler lay in the fact that they could
be used for the donkeywork of holding the flanks while German
soldiers did the real job of fighting. But the Romanians did not have
the tools or the manpower to perform even this menial task. Their ten
divisions were spread over a front of 100 miles (160km), which made
them far too feeble an obstacle in the open steppe: the defences were
paper thin, and their anti-tank guns were so obsolete they were
practically useless. Moreover, most Romanian troops felt no sense of
commitment to the battle for Stalingrad anyway. Their only political
interest in the war against Stalin was in taking back the province of
Bessarabia, on the east bank of the river Dniestr, which they saw as
historically and culturally Romanian territory. They could not

understand how they were serving their country by freezing to death on the wind-blown Russian steppe. Most galling of all for the Romanian rank and file, they were treated with disdain by their own officers – and they were viewed with unconcealed contempt by their German allies, for whom they were only one step up the racial ladder from the Slavs.

These demoralized, unhappy, badly equipped, homesick men were no match for resurgent cohorts of the Red Army. As soon as the opening artillery barrage ceased, Russian tanks came trundling out of the mist towards the dazed and deafened survivors of General Dumitrescu's Third Army. About a thousand T-34s poured through the gap at Serafimovich, and almost as many rushed into the breach at Kletskaya. Riding on the back of tanks, or plodding along in their wake, were the teeming masses of the Russian infantry – about half a million men in total. And then there was the Russian cavalry. They galloped into battle holding their swords aloft, a curiously anachronistic sight alongside the steel hardware of tanks and self-propelled guns. These riders did what cavalrymen everywhere have done to shattering effect since medieval times: they hacked the enemy's footsoldiers to pieces. Pulat Ganiyev was one of the Soviet horsemen. He was an Uzbek, from the ancient Muslim city of Samarkand on the Silk Road, and he gave his account in the manner of a tale from *The Arabian Nights*. Pulat himself is the Sinbad-like hero of his own story.

> The cavalry of Pulat Ganiyev was riding out of the north-west, when suddenly it came upon the Germans, wrote Ganiyev, after the war. Pulat and his fellows charged the German column and cut into them. Some of us were on horses, others were on wheels. It was a cruel battle. Not only were there Germans, but also Italians, Hungarians and Romanians. We fought hand to hand. Pulat and his fellows used their swords, their bayonets and their knives. Blades flashed in the frosty air and down went the enemy. The day was cold and foggy too. It took a strong spirit and a strong body to win through.

OF MICE AND MEN

German commanders behind the front line could tell by the sheer din of the Russian artillery that something ominous and spectacular was under way. Berlin was informed, and Hitler was told the 'alarming news' at the Wolf's Lair. He nodded sagely and declared that he had long foreseen this development. From 1,200 miles (2,000km) away, he decided to take control of the battlefield. After taking a look at the situation map, he issued orders to activate the 48th Panzer Corps under General Ferdinand Heim. The 48th Panzer had been sitting behind the Romanians for months. The unit had been given no fuel, because all available resources went to fighting units, and so the Panzers had gone into hibernation. Pits were dug and lined with straw, and the tanks had been driven into these burrows to protect their engines from the Russian frost. Unfortunately, field mice had snuggled down in the straw too, where they nibbled into the insulation of the tanks' wiring. When the men of the 48th Panzer rushed to man their tanks, like fighter pilots scrambling for a dogfight, they found that many of the machines wouldn't start because the mice had eaten through ignition cables. In some cases the gun turrets didn't work. One or two tanks short-circuited and burst into flames.

Less than half of Heim's 102 tanks turned out to be battleworthy – or even roadworthy. But this much reduced yet still formidable force set out north-east towards Kletskaya, as ordered by Hitler. They were already on their way when new orders came. Hitler was suddenly worried that the more dangerous prong of the attack was the one spearheaded by the Russian Fifth Tank Army, heading south from Serafimovich. He sent new instructions to Heim via Berlin: 48th Panzer was to make a sharp left turn and engage Romanenko's Fifth Tank. Heim's men did as they were told, but somewhere along the way Heim lost touch with the Romanian tank units that were accompanying him. When Heim eventually encountered Russian tanks, the only Romanians he could see were fleeing infantrymen. Nevertheless he joined battle, and destroyed a couple of dozen T-34s with his force of 42 machines. He then withdrew before he was caught between the two streams of Soviet armour flowing to the left and right.

Heim's engagement was a gallant and businesslike piece of soldiery. He had made the best of a bad job and inflicted damage on the enemy. But the Führer did not see it that way. He interpreted the withdrawal of the 48th Tank as an act of cowardice, and had Heim arrested in the field. The unfortunate general was flown back to Germany, court-martialled, and thrown into jail. Between them, Hitler's temper and Russian mice had destroyed a capable commander at the very moment when his skills were most sorely needed in battle.

While Heim was careering across the steppe looking for someone to fight, General Paulus was trying to establish the extent of the Russian offensive. A staff officer sent to make an assessment found himself in the midst of a rout before he got anywhere near the front line. Thousands of Romanians were fleeing south, away from the flashing blades and the roaming T-34s of the Russian strike force.

An unrestrained, disorderly crowd flows past me. Soldiers trudging along in groups or alone. A field kitchen heads towards us. Wounded soldiers hang off it, as it is dragged along by horses. A few more field kitchens, and then three small trucks. They are also packed to the roof with men. Unhappy, dumbfounded faces. Men looking like ghosts cling to the sides with hooked fingers. They trudge along, moving their legs robotically. Their tall sheepskin hats are pulled down to the bridge of their noses, the collars of their greatcoats are turned up to cover their mouths, so all you can see is a band of their unshaven faces, which they try to hide from the burning-cold wind. Almost all of them, apart from a few yowling drunks, are marching in silence. Nobody reacts when I try to speak to them. I am glad when this nightmare passes by me, but a little further on I encounter another group. And once again this barely moving trail of ghosts winds past, some with open eyes, others with eyes shut. They don't care where this road leads. They are running away from war and want only to save their own lives. Nothing else means a thing. A Romanian colonel tells me frankly, as he straightens the pus-soaked bandage on his head: 'You'll get nothing more out of my soldiers. They are not obeying any of my commands.'

Another German officer saw a similar sight: frightened, shell-shocked Romanians who in the space of an hour had lost all their will to wage war. He felt little pity – only anger at his feckless allies.

They all had an expression of horror which seemed to be frozen on their faces. You would have thought the very devil was snapping at their heels. They had thrown everything away as they made their escape. And as they ran for it they added to the number of withdrawing troops, which was huge enough without them. It all added up to a picture which was reminiscent of the retreat of Napoleon from Moscow.

As in 1812, the avenging Russians were not far behind. Petr Zhulyev was with an artillery battery of the 21st Army, which had pummelled the Romanian line at Kletskaya from the far bank of the Don. As soon as the bombardment was over, it was time to pack up and move forward. But Zhulyev advanced a little further than was good for him.

After the artillery barrage our forces headed towards the river crossing. We had to climb the steep right bank. Thousands of soldiers clambered to the top, ripping their fingernails and cutting their palms on the jagged, frost-hardened ground. It was hard to imagine how the expanse of earth ahead of us, encrusted with ice and churned up by bombs and shells, could be peaceful or fruitful ever again. But it was the desire to see it flourish, covered with grass or wheat, that gave us strength.

As we moved towards Kletskaya we saw German defensive positions half-buried in the earth, as well as guns and tanks turned inside out by our artillery fire. More and more often we came across Romanian soldiers with white flags.

They were a laughable sight. They went along singing our song: 'Little Katya went out to the riverbank ...' It seems our famous katyusha rockets had made an impression. I have to say that the Romanians did not look much like proper soldiers. They were like one big gypsy caravan, and their uniforms were a strange mish-mash: battered sheepskin hats, all sorts of rags around their necks and on their feet. They weren't enjoying the Russian frosts.

We crossed back over the Don, from the right bank to the left, near Golubinsky. Around that time I was called to HQ and ordered to drive the divisional commissar to the battery. We set off in a half-track. It was the middle of the night by now. A ferocious frost had formed a crust on the fallen snow. There was a monotonous white nothing every way you looked. We somehow went past our own guard post and didn't even notice when we crossed the little Chervlenaya river. Completely unexpectedly we came upon a sentry who must have been half-asleep or half-frozen, because too late he shouted out in German 'Halt!'

I instantly jumped out of the cabin and shoulder-barged him as I hit the ground. He went headfirst into a dugout. I tossed a few grenades behind him. This alerted the other Germans with him, and they began shooting wildly. A volley from a machinegun made a string of holes in our half-track and mortally wounded the commissar. I jumped back in and drove off, steering with one arm while trying to support the commissar with the other. I could feel him getting heavier and heavier. He was dead by the time we found our way back to the division.

THE SECOND ARM OF THE PINCER

The Germans did not yet suspect that the attack on the upper Don was merely the first stage of the Russian plan, that it represented only one half of a giant pincer movement. The Russians had done a fine job of keeping the Germans in the dark. They had hidden their build-up by moving men and matériel only at night, and by disguising the hardware. It is not easy to hide a fleet of tanks on the open steppe, but there were special units dedicated to the magician's art of camouflage – *maskirovka*, in Russian. Ivan Dovbishchuk was second-in-command of the First Guards Army's Chemical Section, and he used his scientific knowledge to keep German reconnaissance away. He was learning all the time.

An example of the importance of camouflage and basic cover was the stationing of a tank corps in the jump-off zone. To the south of Kotluban station there stretched deep ravines, and the units of the tank corps had parked their tanks right up against the sides of one of them and camouflaged them to blend in with the colour of the terrain, which was clay.

The decision had already been taken to use obscuring smoke. We selected a site for the smoke machines, which were fairly cumbersome things, and during the night we earthed them up well and camouflaged them with branches of wormwood. These machines stayed on the forward rim for several days while we were waiting for the right wind direction, and despite repeated enemy bombings and artillery raids there were no losses of men or equipment.

Using smoke machines on the forward rim proved inexpedient. So we deployed smoke charges to produce a smokescreen that concealed this wing of the army. It also became clear that it was not a good idea to use planes fitted with smoke devices to produce smokescreens, as the attack planes had to fly at such low altitudes that many of them were brought down by anti-aircraft fire. Later, planes were routinely used to drop smoke bombs and blind the enemy.

Similar measures disguised the stealthy preparations of the three armies that made up the southern pincer. The Russian 64th Army lay in wait south of Stalingrad in the bulbous salient dubbed the

'Beketovka Bell'. On its left flank, behind the archipelago of frozen water known as the Sarpa lakes, were the massed ranks of the 57th and 51st Armies. The Russian intention was to strike once again at the thinnest point in the Axis chain of defence. Here, as in the north, the unfortunate weaklings were deemed to be the Romanians: General Constantinescu's Fourth Army. The second attack was scheduled to take place on 20 November, a day after the northern offensive. The force was to dash to the north-west and link up with the armies heading south-east towards them. The two pincers were to meet and close the trap at Kalach, just east of the Don.

The southern arm had less distance to cover and fewer rivers to cross. This is why it was scheduled to set off 24 hours later. The timing of the attack was crucial, but on the morning of the 20th conditions did not look good. At six o'clock, two hours before the opening artillery barrage was due to begin, a fog as thick as milk obscured the entire attack zone. The Russian aimers could not see the ends of their gun barrels, let alone the enemy's positions.

General Andrei Yeremenko – the stocky, pudding-faced commander of the Stalingrad front – was on hand. He set out for his forward command post at precisely seven o'clock in the morning. The fog was looking a little thinner as he made his way, but he could see it was still not nearly clear enough to shoot by. He had already had one phone call from the Kremlin that morning, asking him if he was quite sure that the offensive was going to begin on time. He had managed to fob off the functionary on the other end of the phone, but he knew that Stalin himself was wanting to hear some good news. And Stalin did not like his generals to keep him waiting.

By 07.30 I was at the forwardmost observation post of the 57th Army on Height 114.3, said Yeremenko. On a day with good visibility you had a remarkable view of a broad landscape from this point. You could certainly see the entire area of our attack. But the fog was still thick, and visibility was nowhere more than 200 metres. The artillery men were anxious. The Stavka called me to demand that I 'get on with it'. I was forced to explain to the members of the general staff (not entirely tactfully) that I was not sitting on my backside in an office, but was on the battlefield, and so was in a better position to see when it was right to begin.

It got to nine o'clock. Everybody was nervously awaiting the signal. The infantry were hugging the ground, ready to go in. The gunners loaded their cannon and stood to, holding the cord. From somewhere behind us came the growl of tanks as their engines were warmed up.

Then the fog started to lift and scatter. Visibility was approaching normal. At 09.30 the order was given to start the barrage at ten. So in the end, the start of the counterattack on the Stalingrad front was held up by fog for two hours. The katyushas played their music first. Then the artillery and the mortars began their noisy work. It is hard to express in words what one feels listening to the many-voiced choir of an artillery cannonade before the start of an offensive. But what one feels above all is pride in the might of one's homeland and faith in victory. Only the day before our slogan, which we spoke through gritted teeth, had been 'Not one step back'. And now the Motherland urged us forward. The day that the people of Stalingrad had been waiting for had arrived.

A few minutes before the tanks and the infantry were due to go in, we laid down some mortar and machine-gun fire. And right before the attack we let off the powerful M-30 mortars. That was the signal. Out of their foxholes rose the endless lines of our soldiers. I could hear the long, continuous cries of 'hurrah!' and the workmanlike clatter of the tanks.

Right at the beginning of the attack, a strange thing happened. We had decided that the use of the big mortars would be a signal for the start of the artillery attack, and that the second time they were used would signal the start of the infantry and tank attack. A simple system which, one might think, everyone would understand. But no. I was scanning

the whole front with my binoculars during the artillery bombardment when – oh no! – I saw that the infantry on the left flank were already rushing towards the first enemy trenches while the red-tailed heavy katyushas were still firing on their lines. I came out in a cold sweat. Once an attack has started it is impossible to stop. It seems that the commander of the 143rd naval infantry brigade, Colonel Ivan Russkikh, had got mixed up and gone in straight after the first signal. Fortunately it was on the flank and not in the centre.
I decided to call off the artillery bombardment in this sector and to do something to help the 143rd brigade, who seemed to be doing well. Twenty minutes into the attack they had already reached the second line of trenches and were starting to disappear beyond the horizon. Near to me was the commander of the 13th Mechanized Corps. I ordered him to send his first brigade into the breach. He tried tactfully to point out that according to my own plan the 13th Corps was due to go in on a different sector, and in two-and-a-half hours' time. 'I know that, comrade Tanaschishin', but the situation demands changes. Send in the brigade.' I said.

Twenty minutes later, they too disappeared over the horizon without encountering any resistance. A second brigade followed. Even before the barrage finished, we had two brigades in the rear of the enemy, then the entire 13th Mechanized Corps went in after them. By manoeuvring quickly deep behind the enemy defences, they made a great contribution to the success of the attack. So sometimes in war you can make use of an unforeseen and chance event to keep things right, or even to strengthen your position – so long as you do not lose your head and don't stick too closely to the rulebook.

One soldier who needed no lordly lessons in improvisation from the commander of the front was Pulat Ganiyev, the sheherezade of the Soviet Fourth Cavalry Corps. Soon after the counter-offensive began he found himself in a tricky spot that Ali Baba himself would have recognized. He had been sent to catch a 'tongue' – a German who could be interrogated for information about enemy dispositions.

Ganiyev was a courageous scout, and a clever one too, wrote Pulat Ganiyev. His commanders valued him not only for his boldness and valour, but also for his ability to solve problems and understand events. It sometimes happened that several scouts would be sent out to catch a tongue, but would not come back – because they had been killed. No such thing ever happened to Pulat Ganiyev. Of course it was not easy, indeed there were many difficulties along the way, and Pulat risked his life hour after hour. But Pulat knew that he always had to do his duty as a soldier.

So it was that one day Pulat Ganiyev came to a village. He went to look for some hay for his horse. But this happened in the depths of the frosty winter, and here in the steppe by the River Don, there was no hay to be found. Ganiyev went to one farmyard, then to another, and nowhere was there so much as a single straw. Then Ganiyev went to the very last yard, on the edge of the village. He climbed into the mow, because he knew where peasants kept their hay in wintertime.

And lo and behold, there was plenty of hay. Pulat grabbed one armful, then another, so that he could tie them and take them to his horse. Then he heard something rustle, and it seemed to him that there was someone in the big pile of hay – perhaps none other than a German. So pointing his gun, Ganiyev shouted loud, telling them to come out. Imagine his surprise when out of the pile of hay came four armed Germans.

'Throw down your guns,' commanded Ganiyev. And though the fascists did not know the Russian language, they knew well enough that this tall, strapping soldier was telling them to drop their weapons. What they didn't know was that Pulat was all alone; they were sure that there were other Soviet soldiers in the yard. What was Pulat to do? Because as soon as these fritzes realized that he was on his own, they would surely attack him. But they did drop their guns. Ganiyev ordered them to approach one at a time, and he kept his gun pointed at them all the while. As he was doing this, a Russian soldier happened by, and with his help the fascists were delivered to the proper place.

One of the Germans, by the way, had indeed hidden a pistol, and could have shot Pulat Ganiyev had Pulat not been so watchful. Bold Pulat was recommended for a medal for his actions that day.

THE TRAP BEGINS TO CLOSE

The Germans had known that some kind of an offensive was coming, but they were completely taken aback by the scale of it. Hitler had managed to convince his General Staff that the Russians had bled themselves white inside Stalingrad, and that any counter-attack would be a feeble gesture at most. This wishful thinking had filtered down to all levels of the Sixth Army, but certain precautions were taken nevertheless. As the Russians attacked, some valuable German units were withdrawn to the west, beyond the reach of the approaching enemy, and they were replaced with regular infantry. Wilhelm Beyer was unfortunate to belong to one of the units that were heading east, towards Stalingrad.

We marched in across the Don. There was an emergency bridge, built by the pioneers, narrow, only two lanes wide. SS troops were on the second lane, pulling out from the unformed pocket. Some were thinking to themselves that these were elite troops that needed to be 'spared'. We marched eastwards in close formation, namely into the all-round hedgehog defence position that was forming. Long columns three abreast. I'd been detailed a position right up in front. We became increasingly aware that these special units going in the opposite direction were hurrying out with their baggage convoys and guns. We poor buggers, the privates, were going to take their place. Our none too cheerful mood sank even further.

Some troops had a rather more dramatic awakening. Corporal Heinrich Simonmeier was sent to a supply dump at a German airfield on the Don steppe to get a new uniform. 'But instead of the expected Junkers,' he said, 'Russian tanks came and closed the pocket.' Gunter Toepke, quartermaster for the Sixth Army, was near Pitomnik airfield on 21 November, far from the prongs of the Russian attack. But in the course of a couple of days' hectic travel, he felt a growing sense of claustrophobia. The Russians were closing in: it was like watching the steel doors slam shut on a bank vault – knowing that you are on the inside.

I was on my way to Chir from my main supply dump at Karpovskaya. I was going to supervise the loading of our horses. On the way through Kalach I heard all sorts of rumours from the supply troops stationed there: talk of a Russian offensive from the Kremenskaya bridgehead. It was said that the Russians had already broken deep into our lines. Things were supposed to be looking particularly nasty for the Romanians, our neighbours to the left. In the distance I could hear the rumble of a battle. There was nothing more to be learned for now.

I had no difficulty getting over the Don High Road from Kalach to Chir. I spent the night there. But the next day I couldn't cross the High Road: it had already been taken by Russian tanks. To get back I had to drive back to the southern bridge over the Don, at Chirskaya. I was not in the best of moods as I bounced along in my car, heading east over a dull tract of steppeland. Suddenly some of our soldiers jumped out of a bush and frantically waved me down. They asked me where I had come from. And then they told me: 'Four Russian tanks came up that road a quarter of an hour ago. We fired at them with our anti-tank gun, then they turned around and headed into the steppe.'

'You've been seeing ghosts. How could there be Russian tanks here. There might be some up in the north, on the other bank of the Don, but surely not here in the south?'

The anti-tank team knew nothing of the Russian offensive in the north. 'They must have come from over there,' they said, pointing away to the south. 'We've been hearing sounds of battle from there all day.'

'From over there. That's the way to Tinguta.'

'Yes, the noise is coming from Tinguta.'

Suddenly it dawned on me. Damn it all, it looked like the Russians were attempting a large-scale pincer movement to box the Sixth Army into Stalingrad. Kalach was the meeting point.

Ever more worried by the growing sound of battle from the south, I drove on to Karpovskaya. I knew that there were no troops there in the south apart from the Romanians. So the Russians had gone for the Romanians both in the north and the south, and had apparently broken through.

That same night I telephoned my divisional commander and told him of my concerns. The divisions inside Stalingrad had no idea of what was going on, of what was being played out deep in their rear. Around that time I put my supply units on alert: bakers, butchers, mechanics, horse grooms and drivers were formed up into battle units and made to man a line around our headquarters. There was no more I could do for now.

While Toepke's bakers and candlestick-makers waited, combat units were fighting to keep a corridor open to the west, to prevent the Sixth Army from becoming completely surrounded. Lieutenant Hans-Erdmann Schönbeck, 22 years old, was a tank commander. Two days earlier he had been idly thinking that at this time of year he usually went pheasant-hunting with his father, back home in Silesia. Now, out in the eerie steppe, the Russians were the hunters, and he was the prey.

Drifts of dense fog that seldom parted turned the steppe into a wonderland. But it was an evil kind of magic. You could no longer tell friend from foe, or often not until it was too late. And now it suddenly turned cold. In the space of a few days, bitterly cold. I'd already lived through the previous winter outside Moscow, but here there was no cover, no forest, no trees, no shrubs, just this constant biting wind.

And with the cold came the great catastrophe. The Russians advanced from the north and the south. On the 19th November, the first day of this offensive, we already seemed to be largely encircled. Once again the Panzer men had to chase around like firemen. We were immediately turned round 180 degrees and then moved westward for a counterattack. But the forces that were massed against us were enormous!

During my years in Russia I had developed very keen antennae for the strength or weakness of my own situation. I was just a *Frontschwein*, so I was hardly ever aware of the overall picture. For me it was always just a matter of carrying out the current order. And the orders were coming thick and fast at this time. At this point we were already worn down and exhausted from attacking the city. The number of our operational Panzers had shrunk by a half, we had little fuel and only enough ammunition for a few days' fighting. We fought moving westwards with our remaining Panzers – but firing back eastwards as we went!

As the Germans and Romanians reeled back, the Russians seemed to gain confidence. For Grigory Onishchenko, a staff officer with the 51st Army, the early successes were a natural consequence of the careful planning that had gone into the operation.

About two weeks before the offensive we already knew what units we were going to be given, which elements of the air force were going to support our attack. As the operation got closer we could see how the strength and the power of our armed forces was growing – we could feel it. All of us who knew about the operation or took part in devising it were impatiently looking forward to H-Hour. On the day, the breakthrough was so swift that by 11 o'clock the General Staff of the Army broke camp and continued its work while moving forward. As we followed in the traces of the forward units we saw many curious sights. For example, as we drove towards one village, we saw a huge column consisting of many regiments, complete with horse-drawn artillery, field kitchens, vehicles, food trucks. It was moving towards the rear, and it seemed strange for a moment that such a large force of our men was heading backwards. When we got closer we saw that regiment after regiment was being escorted by a few machine-gunners, one of whom had a note asking for someone somewhere to disarm these Romanians and take them prisoner. It was the Romanian 9th Army, utterly demoralized.

There were other eye-opening sights to be seen during the advance of the southern pincer. Konstantin Artashkevich was with the 13th Tank Corps, the unit that General Yeremenko had wilfully tossed into the gap in the line during the first hour of the attack. From his gun turret he saw a clever piece of improvisation that testified to the Russians' growing skill.

After a tank battle on our sector three German aircraft came flying in and began to bomb our forwardmost line. The planes came in very low, no more than 300 metres above the ground, and at that moment one of our soldiers lay down on his back and shot upwards at the planes. One of them crashed into the ground not far away. The others, seeing that one of their number had been killed, turned tail and flew away. That soldier was given a medal for bringing down a plane with just his rifle.

THE FLIGHT OF THE NIGHT WITCHES

The Luftwaffe had enough problems without that kind of bad luck. Their superiority in the air was diminishing rapidly, and Russian air power was growing at the same rate. Germans who had looked to the skies for reassurance in the summer and autumn months now feared the worst every time they heard the sound of an approaching plane. Stories circulated about *Nachthexen* – 'night witches' – fanatical Russian women pilots who bombed bridges and forward airfields at night. It was said that German pilots automatically received the Iron Cross for shooting one down. The tale of the night witches played to all the German fears about the unnaturally aggressive nature of Russian womanhood. Many of them had seen the female corpses in the ack-ack emplacements and pillboxes on the approaches to Stalingrad in August. Perhaps that was where the rumours originated. Or perhaps not – because the stories were true.

The night witches were the women of the 46th Guards Night Bomber Regiment. All the pilots in this unit were female, and so were the ground crew. The pilots flew tiny two-seater aircraft called the Polikarpov U-2. This obsolete biplane was slow, but it was very quiet. The Germans called it the *Nähmaschine*, the 'sewing machine', because of the homely clickety-clack of its engine, while the Russians affectionately christened it the maize-cutter – *kukuruznik* – for its dinky little propeller.

Notwithstanding its old-fashioned profile and its cosy domestic nicknames, the U-2 was an effective aerial weapon – one of the surprise successes of the war. Beneath its small undercarriage it could carry a payload of 520 pounds (240kg) of bombs. It was used almost exclusively at night because the darkness made it less vulnerable to attack by faster aircraft, and in the general cacophony of battle it was hard to hear it coming. So the U-2 was almost undetectable, and the falling bombs of the night witches materialized as if from nowhere, like a curse.

Zhenya Zhigulenko was a pilot with the 46th Night Bombers. She flew almost a thousand missions, and was awarded her country's highest military honour – Hero of the Soviet Union – at the age of 24.

Flying was very frightening, said Zhigulenko. We would take off ten or more times a night. During some flights we'd have to tear free with our hands the bombs that had got stuck under the ice-covered wings. The problem was that sometimes we used bombs that had been captured from the Germans and their lugs didn't properly fit our bomb-carriers.

When all is said and done, one can reconcile oneself to many things: to being blinded by searchlights and shot at by anti-aircraft guns, to seeing bullet-holes in the wings of one's plane, to being unable to speak and to feeling one's knees quaking after a touchdown, and even to missing a friend after a mission and hoping against hope that she will return.

The 46th were not the only female pilots on the Stalingrad front. There were also two all-woman squadrons in the 586th Fighter Regiment. Colonel AI Gridnev was their (male) commander.

The girls acquitted themselves with great honour on the severe testing-ground of the Stalingrad front, said Gridnev. As flyers they were no less skilful than the men, they were also just as fearless and full of valour. They made a worthy contribution to the destruction of the fascist forces at Stalingrad. The girls fulfilled all kinds of combat missions. They attacked enemy bombing formations, covered ground troops from air attack, and carried out raids on the enemy's ground forces.

I cannot help but feel emotional when I recall the self-sacrifice of Raya Belyayeva, Katya Budanova, Anya Demchenko, Klava Nechayeva, Inna Lebedeva and others. These girls knew no fear. There was one time when Raya Belyayeva and Anya Demchenko were patrolling above a railway junction near Stalingrad. They spotted forty enemy bombers heading towards them. Two girls against forty of those damn vultures! There was no time to think or to wait for help. They used their advantage of height and speed and went into the attack. They sent two Junkers down in flames, and at the same time disturbed the attack formation of the enemy, who consequently dropped their bombs early and missed their target.

Then there was Katya Budanova, one of the most courageous of my fighter pilots. On one occasion she was returning from a mission, and her fuel and ammo were already low. Katya came upon twelve German bombers heading for our front line. Like Belyayeva and Demchenko, she had no hesitation about going into the attack. But she only had sufficient ammunition for one pass. She fired off the last of her cannon at the lead plane, which broke up in the air. She could now have broken off the attack. But she thought: they don't know I have no guns left. She dived into the formation of bombers again and again – imitating an attack but without shooting. The heavy bombers knew that they could not manoeuvre out of the way of an attack by a Soviet fighter. They would have been worried about colliding with each other in the air. So they jettisoned their bombs onto the heads of their own men.

There were times when the pilots carried out seven missions in a day. Sometimes my girl-pilots went without sleep for two or three days at a time. And there were days when the joy of our victories was tempered by grief. Klavdiya Nechayeva and Inna Lebedeva, gallant flyers both of them, died over Stalingrad.

The women of the 586th Fighter Regiment flew Yak-1s, an aircraft with the same dash and elegance as the Hawker Hurricane. But there were also actual British Hurricanes on the Stalingrad front, part of the mass of hardware given to the Soviet Union under the lend-lease arrangement with the USA and Britain. Some Russian pilots had an opinion of the Hurricane that would have surprised their British counterparts, but which bears out the offhand and disparaging remarks made by Stalin about the plane on the day he met with Zhukov and Vasilievsky.

We were told that we had to get to know the English Hawker Hurricane in a hurry, said I Stepanenko, a Russian flyer. These aircraft, or rather the bits that made them up, lay in huge wooden crates. We had to unpack them and put them together ourselves – and that was part of our education. We already knew that these planes were of an obsolescent design, and we knew their weaknesses.

But what we subsequently discovered went beyond the low expectations we had of them. The planes had a water-cooled Rolls-Royce engine with a honeycomb-style radiator. In our winter, the radiator often froze up and the engine broke down. Moreover, the planes had very inadequate firepower – and a wooden propeller which broke too easily. The centre of gravity of the plane was too far forward, so on soft ground or on snow the tail would seesaw upwards and the nose would go into the ground. When that happened the propeller would break off. We were given very few spare props, because the English had not thought about the 'behaviour' of their product.

The lack of spares was overcome when Hurricane propellers began to be produced locally. As for the perceived tendency of the Hurricane to tip on to its nose, a very Russian solution was found to that problem. Stepanenko tells the story.

'I have a very simple idea,' said engineer-lieutenant Aleksei Melnikov. 'When you taxi out onto the runway for take-off, I'll sit on the tail of the plane. My weight will be enough to move the centre of gravity to the back. That will stop the plane nodding forwards.'

We tried it out. Melnikov rode around the airfield a couple of times. The aeroplane speeded up and slowed down, got to the point of take-off and set back down. And the prop did not plough into the ground. 'Well then, lads, you'll have to learn to saddle the Hurricane,' joked the senior engineer, Captain Aivazov. 'Those of you who have never mounted an Orel trotter can ride on the back of an English filly instead.'

It was a risky business. There was one time when the pilot forgot that he had a member of the ground crew sitting on the back and he accelerated and took off. He soon realized what he had done and landed. No harm came to the 'horseman', except that his hands were frozen and he had turned blue.

THE BRIDGE AT KALACH

The southern arm of the pincer made good progress on the first day and a half. By 21 November, it had got as far as the village of Buzinovka, halfway to Kalach. The forces of the northern arm, meanwhile, had covered 60 miles (96km) and were on the Liska River, 25 miles (40km) from the west bank of the Don. It was imperative to gain control of the bridge near Kalach. If the Germans could retreat across it and blow it up, then the trap could not be properly closed. And if the Germans could hold the bridge, then their supply line would still be viable. It had to be taken, and taken intact.

The capture of the Kalach bridge is one of the legends of the battle of Stalingrad. Like all legends it has been altered in the telling and now exists in many different versions – some of which are closer to the truth than others. Here is the story of that *coup de main* as recounted by the man who pulled it off: Colonel Grigory Filippov, commander of the 19th Tank Brigade. His account begins on the night of the 21st. He had been ordered to push ahead of the main advance with a column of tanks and armoured cars. Along the way he had already blundered into some German armour and taken a battering. Now it was first light, and he was heading towards the river. It was a race against the clock, a mad dash full of frustration and firefights.

We were left with five tanks, an armoured car with a communications officer, and five trucks of a motorized brigade carrying fifty or so soldiers. We continued along the road to the crossing and a kilometre further along, about two or three hundred metres to the right of the road I saw a platoon of Germans getting up from the ground on the edge of a copse. They had been asleep and now they were washing themselves with snow. Of course, with the advantage of surprise we could easily have killed them all. But that would have meant losing time. And the noise would surely alert the Germans at the crossing. I decided to move on without engaging, and gave the necessary order to the commander of the tank company, who was riding with his turret open in the tank ahead of me. But further along we did have to take out two or three enemy trucks which were coming down the road towards us. We were risking giving ourselves away, but if we hadn't done it they would have alerted the combat units behind us.

Continuing down the road, we caught up with a cart being pulled by an old Russian man by the name of Gusev. Sitting on the cart was a German. We killed him because, according to Gusev, he liked to torment prisoners. We asked Gusev where the crossing was, and he told us that the Germans had blown up the old bridge, but built a new wooden one a little further upstream. To get there you had to take a different road.

From Gusev's directions it became clear that the right road led off a crossroads that we had already passed. What were we to do? Returning to the crossroads would mean going back past the Germans we had seen earlier, only now they would be battle-ready. It also meant wasting more precious time fighting them, and losing the element of surprise. Then Gusev remembered that there was another road somewhere nearby that led to the crossing.

We spent a long time looking for it, and had to go quite a way back. I was already starting to wonder whether this Gusev was perhaps a traitor. I sat him on a tank next to Nikulin. Things were getting difficult. I was thinking that it was now going to be hard to take the bridge by surprise. There was nothing but bare steppe all around. I couldn't help thinking about my brother and his three children, all of whom had died in the siege of Leningrad. I hated the fascists so much that I was determined to make them pay somehow. I began to look for some place to stop and take up a defensive position. To the right was a deep ravine – it was better than nothing. Then Gusev said that he had found the road.

Now we turned off onto the new road. The right bank of the Don was high at this point, but the road led gently downwards. Along the way we took out an SS-man, a sentry. I thought, there goes the surprise once again – there must surely be a guard post around here somewhere. We descended towards the Don, and saw that the road did indeed lead along the bank. We turned left along the river, but could see no crossing. Then I was told that the trucks had run out of fuel.

Damn our luck! I looked around and there I saw a middle-aged man, Russian, in civilian clothes. I asked him if he knew where there might be some fuel around here. He said that there was a German fuel dump nearby, that it was dug into the steep side of the riverbank just at the point where we turned left along the Don. The trucks could only get at the fuel dump one at a time, and then they had to reverse out before the next one could go in. I only let my men take a bucketful each. We dare not dawdle, as we had lost enough time as it was.

Finally we were once more on the road leading upstream. But there was no bridge to be seen. But then beyond a little bend in the road, to the right of us, there it was. A little further on and we were close enough to see the guards on the bridge. We got quite close before we stopped, and then a machine-gun opened up on us from a long way behind. That meant that the Germans had spotted us. Possibly we had passed by a guard post when we killed the sentry, and someone had telephoned ahead.

There was not a moment to lose. I ordered the infantrymen from one of the trucks to head out across the ice of the river (it was quite thick near the bank) and take up positions on an island in the middle of the flow. This island hid part of the crossing from view. I lay down on the left side of the lead tank and got ready to shoot. The other trucks and tanks followed me. We drove up level with the island. There was no shooting from the other bank of the river. As we passed the island we could see that most of the defenders on the bridge were standing in clumps at the far end, on the left bank of the Don. On this bank there was just one pillbox and a sentry.

The thought popped into my head: they are not ready for a battle, they haven't reacted to the gunfire coming from behind us. We drove onto the bridge. The Germans did not sound the alarm until we got to the left bank. There was a short skirmish, and the guards were dead.

That is how the only crossing in this area was taken, the only escape route for the Germans. The capture of the bridge was an important event. If we had not succeeded in taking it, then we would have had to force the Don, and much time and many men would have been lost.

The tanks adopted a circular defence on the bridge at the left bank. The tanks added steel to the defence, and allowed the motorized infantry to manoeuvre in any direction from which a threat might come. The Germans were terrified of our tanks. The explosive charges on the bridge were disabled. We used an axe to cut through the thick cable which ran all along it.

With the capture of the bridge the trap was shut. The Germans at Stalingrad were surrounded. Filippov's men proceeded into the town of Kalach, where they liberated a POW camp. Most of the inmates were on the point of starvation. One of them was Anna Andreyevskaya, the nurse who had so manfully stood up to the Germans on the day of her capture in September. She had not expected to get out alive.

> There were about 2,000 people in the camp, said Andreyevskaya. Every day, thirty or so dead bodies were carted away and buried somewhere. On November 23rd, before the Soviet forces arrived, the Germans took ten of us – nine men and me – and put us before a firing squad. They shot me, but by some fluke I was only wounded in the shoulder. So I consider November 23rd to be the day when I was born for a second time.

For all the attacking forces, 23 November was a memorable day. On that day, the two pincers linked up at the village of Sovetsky, not far from Kalach. Operation Uran had succeeded, and the Russians were jubilant. They had scooped up thousands of Germans and Romanians like fish in a giant net. The Soviet High Command immediately invited the press to come and admire their catch. Western journalists were offered a visit to General Chistyakov of the 21st Army at his new front-line HQ. Henry Shapiro, the Moscow correspondent of the United Press, was one of the party. He started his exploration of the battlefield at Serafimovich, the jump-off point for Chistyakov's army.

> Well behind the fighting-line there were now thousands of Romanians wandering about the steppes, cursing the Germans and desperately looking for Russian feeding-points, and anxious to be formally taken over as war prisoners. Some individual stragglers would throw themselves on the mercy of the local peasants, who treated them charitably, if only because they were not Germans. The Russians thought they were 'just poor peasants like ourselves'.
> Except for small groups of Iron Guard men who, here and there, put up a stiff fight, the Romanian soldiers were sick and tired of the war; the prisoners I saw all said roughly the

same thing – that this was Hitler's war, and that the Romanians had nothing to do on the Don.

The closer I moved to Stalingrad, the more numerous were the German prisoners. The steppe was a fantastic sight; it was full of dead horses, while some horses were only half-dead, standing on three frozen legs, and shaking the remaining broken one. It was pathetic. Ten thousand horses had been killed during the Russian breakthrough. The whole steppe was strewn with these dead horses and wrecked gun-carriages and tanks and guns – Germans, French, Czech, even British (no doubt captured at Dunkirk), and no end of corpses, Romanian and German. The Russian bodies were the first to be buried. Civilians were coming back to the villages, most of them wrecked. Kalach was a shambles: only one house was standing.

General Chistyakov, whose HQ I finally located in a village south of Kalach, said that, only a few days before, the Germans could still fairly easily have broken out of Stalingrad, but Hitler had forbidden it. Now they had missed their chance. He was certain that Stalingrad would be taken by the end of December.

German transport planes, Chistyakov said, were being shot down by the dozen, and the Germans inside the Stalingrad pocket were already short of food. The German prisoners I saw were mostly young fellows, and very miserable. I did not see any officers. In thirty degrees of frost they wore ordinary coats, and had blankets tied round their necks. They had hardly any winter clothing at all. The Russians, on the other hand, were very well-equipped—with *valenki*, sheepskin coats, warm gloves, et cetera. Morally, the Germans seemed completely stunned, unable to understand what the devil had happened.

6
INSIDE THE CAULDRON

The Germans had been beaten at their own game. They were supposed to be the experts at surrounding large groups of the enemy and cutting them off. In German military manuals this mode of advance was called a *Kesselschlacht*, a 'cauldron battle', and was a standard manoeuvre. The Germans had used it to great effect in the conquest of Europe, and the Sixth Army had employed it repeatedly in their advance across the Ukraine. But creating a cauldron was no use unless you could then keep the lid tightly on it. The Wehrmacht knew it was just as good at breaking out of encirclement as it was at imposing it. So no one inside the newly formed *Kessel* was unduly worried just yet.

> The Russians tried to break the inner spirit and morale of us
> German soldiers by dropping leaflets showing a picture of the
> Kessel, said a Corporal Jödicke. I need hardly spell out the use
> to which this paper was put. Well into December we remained
> hopeful that we would be plucked out of the cauldron.

In these first days, as the encirclement was consolidated, the German chain of command was chaotic (though this too was at first seen as nothing more than a little local difficulty). Even after the trap snapped shut, some tank units were issued a series of hasty, contradictory orders that had them stampeding hither and thither across the steppe – just as General Heim's 48th Panzer had been made to do on the vital first day of Operation Uranus. Sergeant Roemer of the 16th Panzer Division was inside Stalingrad when the Russian attack was launched; for him, the next 72 hours were a wild-goose chase on ice.

On our return from the attack on Rynok, we learn that the Russians have broken through on the Don bend in large numbers. The division is put on alert for immediate departure. At daybreak on November 21st we set out at top speed towards the Don bend. We cross the Don at Peskovatka and arrive back at our earlier battle position.

We are making for Sukhanov, and intend to intercept the Russians there. The Don High Road is completely iced over. We haven't yet been fitted with anti-skid chains. Our Panzer slithers around as never before. During the following night our drivers perform the unimaginable. Armoured cars continuously slide right across the road or into a ditch. There were times when we managed to climb several metres uphill, but the slightest touch on the steering wheel had the Panzer sliding all the way down to the bottom again.

News from the front informs us that the Russians are already in Sukhanov. Our marching plans are changed. On the way we come across straggles of Romanians and lost German units. They're all flooding back across the Don bridge towards Stalingrad. We hear the craziest rumours: the Russians are supposed to have reached the Chir and Kalach already.

At about five in the morning we're ordered to take a short break in a village. The crews thaw out their frozen limbs. The whole village is crammed with stranded German and Romanian soldiers. At the local headquarters, where I'm warming up with my crew, we discover that the Russians were ten kilometres from here yesterday evening.

At daybreak we drive on again southwards. It takes several hours for the section to get out of the village as the roads are so icy. Meanwhile we've reached a German airfield. All the Panzers fill up, as we'd almost run out of fuel. Then the airfield is abandoned, and all the aircraft blown up.

In the early afternoon we receive orders to drive the Russians out of the village again. 'F' Company is in the lead. At the northern end we encounter the first Russians. They are very tough and won't budge. We're left with no alternative but to wipe them all out. In the evening the section turns back along the same road we had come down earlier. A platoon from 'F' Company stays behind to secure the northern exit from the village. I stay here as well with my Panzer. Towards 21.00 hours we drive back with our platoon to catch up with the section. We pass very many wrecked German vehicles on the way, indicating that the Russians had been here ahead of us. It's panic stations all round, no one knows what's going on.

In the evening of the 23rd we form a hedgehog defence. At about 20.00 hours we receive the order for all Panzers to cross back over the Don and halt the Russian tanks that have apparently broken through south of Stalingrad. 'F' Company is again out front. It is an unusually bright night. We approach, I'm the second vehicle, left of the road. Just 400 metres further on we come under heavy tank fire. All the tanks leave the road and drive off to the right. We land right in the middle of a field full of infantry and do heavy damage to them.

At night we reach our base. At last there's something warm to eat, and coffee. Our ammunition and fuel is replenished, and off again across the Don back to the Stalingrad area. It's a long time since we had any sleep, we can hardly keep our eyes open, but rest is out of the question. Together with the section we proceed southwards along the road towards Stalingrad.

At the end of his account Roemer notes that 'Lieutenant F. summons the crews and informs us that we are encircled. But no one takes this very seriously or hangs their heads. This is nothing new to us, after all it's not the first time.' Such insouciance was commonplace. News of the encirclement gradually filtered down to all ranks, and was often greeted with a shrug of the shoulders. It took a few days for the news to reach everyone, but all Paulus's men were in the picture before he addressed the troops on the morning of the 27th. He sent this message, to be read out by commanders to all troops. 'Soldiers of the Sixth Army ...' wrote Paulus,

> ... the Army is surrounded. That is not your fault. You have conducted yourselves with great tenacity until the enemy was at our backs. We have held him here. He will not achieve his aim, which is to annihilate us. There is much more that I must ask of you: to go through exertion and privation in the cold and snow; to stand fast and to hit back against greatly superior forces. The Führer has promised us help. We must hold on until it gets here. If the whole army stands as one man, then we can do it. Have no doubt, the Führer will get us out. Commander-in-chief, Paulus.

The slightly odd tone of this address must have troubled some of the more thoughtful men. Behind the sub-Churchillian call to hardship there is a weary note of resignation in the words, as well an implied criticism of the higher powers that allowed this dangerous situation to come about. And why was he telling them that it was not their fault? Who had said it was? Then there was that clunking rhyme in the last sentence. Clearly it was hoped that the men would take it up as a morale-boosting catchphrase. But soon enough it was being muttered with bitter, bitter irony: *Drum haltet aus, der Führer haut uns raus.*

THE STORMING OF THE L-SHAPED HOUSE

The encirclement of the Germans took some of the pressure off Chuikov's men, who were still thoroughly besieged inside the city. The fighting within Stalingrad was no less deadly now, but as one soldier remarked: 'After November 19th we knew that it wouldn't get any harder.' The Germans naturally turned their attention away from the city and began to contemplate the problem of the Kessel. The 62nd Army used the enemy's distraction to push the front line away from the banks of the river, so winning themselves a little breathing space.

The slow reconquest of Stalingrad was about to begin. It was a matter of attacking one building at a time, then using it as a base to move on to the next enemy strongpoint. In this way, house by broken house, the city would be liberated. One major objective of the Russian fight-back was the building known as the 'L-shaped house', a little to the north of Pavlov's House. This huge, solid, five-storey building had been a thorn in the left flank of the 62nd Army for ten weeks. Ivan Glazkov was a sergeant with the 34th regiment of the 13th Guards' Division, in whose sector the L-shaped house was located.

Why was this house so terrifying to us? Because it had a field of vision over the whole Volga from the 62nd crossing to the point where it bends, downstream towards Beketovka. The Germans had moved into it before we forced a crossing of the Volga on the night of the 14th September. If we, the 34th Regiment, had managed to get there sooner, then this house, standing a mere thirty or forty metres from the precipice overlooking the Volga, would have been ours. Right from the outset, the L-shaped house caused problems in the 2nd battalion's sector on the regiment's left flank – by day and especially by night. We regimental scouts under the command of Lieutenant Sorokin stormed this fortification more than once, only to retreat with heavy losses, having failed in our mission of capturing a tongue. Other sub-units stormed this damned building, too. A lot of men were deployed, but none of them were able to achieve anything.

The place where the L-shaped house stood was the Germans' closest point to the Volga in the 34th Regiment's sector. Indeed, it was probably the closest point to the Volga for the entire 13th Division, which was protecting the 62nd Army's left flank all the way from the brewery to the Dolgaya Balka. We called this the 'Mitiz factory sector'.

The scout Vyacheslav Belov often used to say that a tank would drive up to the house at night and start firing at the crossing, but he was mistaken. The sound was, indeed, similar to that of a tank shot. But after the house was captured we discovered that there was a gun in the angle of the letter 'L' on the ground floor. By day, the window was bricked up. The gun had a brake on the mouthpiece of its barrel, and the noise it made after the gun was fired was amplified by being trapped in the corner of the house, and so sounded to us like a tank shot.

Now, in the last weeks of November, the time had come to take back the L-shaped house once and for all. The planning was meticulous. The whole operation was an object lesson in urban warfare, and demonstrated just how much the Russians had learned in the smoke and rubble of Stalingrad. It needed something more cunning than the usual three-team shock group. Nikolai Alexenko of 13th Guards was involved in the attack. He explains the nature of the problem.

> The house was 150 metres from our trenches, dugouts and pillboxes. The Germans had turned it into one of their best observation posts and strongpoints. From its upper stories they were able to look down on the Volga as if it were on the palm of their hand. But more than that: they had a view of the left bank and of the village of Krasnaya Sloboda where our divisional artillery was located, as well as our support units such as supply and the cookhouse.
>
> The stone cellar of the L-shaped house had ferro-concrete walls dividing it into separate rooms: the Germans had turned it into a real fortress. On the ground floor they had placed artillery pieces, and on the upper floors there were mortars and machinegun nests. Anything that moved on the Volga in the hours of daylight was instantly subjected to a storm of gunfire. Consequently, the Volga was dead in our sector during the hours of daylight.
>
> So the house had to be taken. There had already been some rushed, ill-prepared attempts, but they had all failed. Our company did not have any part in these attempts to take the house by frontal assault, but from our gun-ports we could see separate shock groups coming under machinegun fire and

rolling back or being cut to bits where they were. Our men died before they could even get near the house. It growled and snapped at us like an angry, wounded wolf. The commanders came to the conclusion that it could not be captured at a running jump.

And so on December 1st a large storm group was formed to take the house. The group consisted of a team of machinegunners and sub-machinegunners, riflemen, two flamethrowers and a platoon of anti-tank men.

Our own commander, Lieutenant Dorosh, was in Moscow at some kind of seminar or conference at the time, so our company was not included in the attack force. But that evening Dorosh arrived back from Moscow (it had taken him ten days), and as soon as he heard about the planned attack he went to the regimental commander and asked that our anti-tank platoon replace the one that had been slated for the job. 'If I have earned a trip to Moscow at a time when blood is being spilt all around,' he said 'Then how is it that I have not earned the right to take part in the attack on the L-shaped house?' The regimental commander agreed with him and acceded to his request.

Dorosh was a young Leninist as well as a guardsman. He was well-built, disciplined, neat, smart. The men in our company were constantly amazed that his leather boots were never dirty, that he could keep his tunic-collar white, and he was always clean-shaven. Lieutenant Dorosh made the same demands on us as he did on himself. He was both straightforward and approachable.

Lieutenant Sidelnikov was appointed commander of the storm group, Lieutenant Isayev was his deputy. During the night of December 1st, we went on parade on the banks of the Volga, at the HQ of the 34th Guards Rifle Regiment. The order to attack the house was read out to us by the regimental commander, Major V.K. Kotsarenko. Here, at the HQ, we ate our supper and received our 100 grams of *narkom* vodka.

The Russian acronym *narkom* is short for *narodny kommissariat* – 'people's commissariat', or government ministry. At the start of the war, all Red Army soldiers had been entitled to a ration of 100 grams of vodka a day. But in May 1942 this sizeable dose of Dutch courage was restricted to front-line soldiers. The new ruling came from the People's Commissariat of Defence, hence the soldiers' name for a tipple that was the perk of a man about to go into the fray.

> Dorosh spent a long time giving a thorough inspection to every member of the anti-tank platoon, continued Alexenko. Is everything tucked in and strapped up? No loose equipment that might make a noise? Nothing's been forgotten?
>   Lieutenant Dorosh had gone off to Moscow in his summer uniform. While he was away, we had all been issued with our winter uniforms. Now our commander had his on too: big felt *valenki* on his feet instead of those polished boots; fur hat with earflaps instead of his officer's forage cap. We could hardly recognize him as he walked up and down in front of us. What had become of his soldierly bearing? He walked like a big bear cub now. 'Comrade guards lieutenant,' piped up one of the men. 'Tell us about Moscow.' 'First we'll take the house, then I'll tell you all there is to know about Moscow,' replied the lieutenant.
>   About two o'clock in the morning, when all was set for the attack, it suddenly started to snow. This was the first big snowfall in Stalingrad that cold winter. It fell in great, even flakes and soon covered the ground in a thick layer. Winter had truly come – and that changed the situation. Now we needed white overalls as well as white cloths to camouflage our guns. We knew from previous failures that we had to be able to crawl all the way up to the house unobserved.
>   We began our crawl towards the L-shaped house a short way downriver from the pillboxes of our anti-tank unit, on the cusp between the 34th and 42nd Regiments. The sappers had managed to make a path through the minefield

and to cut the barbed wire before the snow began to fall. Sidelnikov and Isayev went first, crawling on their stomachs, and behind them came the tommygunners and riflemen, the machinegunners and the flamethrowers. We, the anti-tank men, were bringing up the rear. I crawled along second-to-last, behind my number one, a Tatar from Kazan called Gabdurakhman. I was dragging a gas-mask bag containing shells for the anti-tank gun, and I was carrying my rifle without its bayonet. Right next to me was Lieutenant Dorosh. In one hand he held his TT pistol, and in the other he had a grenade. Everybody was in brand-new camouflage suits, and all the guns were wrapped in broad white bandages.

Back in September our anti-tank unit had received some reinforcements. Our company got a sergeant named Dubov (who at this moment was advancing at the head of the unit) and two privates – Kalinin and Stepanov. All three had come to us from the prison camps: they were 'enemies of the people'. Rather than sit in prison, they had been sent to the front. They were all strong and brave lads. In the very first battle with us, they had shown themselves to be devoted patriots who loved their motherland.

Thousands of men – victims of the purges of the 1930s – were released from prison camps and fed into the war effort at times when things were looking bad for the Russians. Among them were many military specialists arrested during the great purge of the armed forces in 1937–38. They were not pardoned or officially rehabilitated, but most were only too glad to be allowed to put their skills at the service of their country. Their comrades-in-arms knew this, and they knew well enough that the camps were full of innocent citizens.

We came to the end of barbed wire, and stopped about thirty metres from the house, said Alexenko. Noiselessly we crawled into position, then we lay low. Softly-softly now. From time to time a German tracer bullet would arc towards

the Volga or a flare would fizz away to the side of us, but
then deathly quiet would fall again. I didn't even notice
Lieutenant Dorosh come crawling up to me.

Your heart beats hard when you are waiting for the signal
to attack. Snow was still falling in fat flakes. As dawn drew
near there was a little mist. The L-shaped house was all
quiet. But from beyond the Volga we could hear
loudspeakers playing music. The sound of a Russian song
wafted over: 'Out on the steppe, the wide Don steppe, a
young lad went a-walking ...'

At this time Sergeant Ivan Glazkov was in a trench not far away.
He was among the scouts who had cleared a path for the main attack
force, and so had been waiting in the cold for longer than Alexenko.
In the dark before dawn he made his final preparations for the attack,
and got a piece of advice from one of his men.

Our regimental scouts huddled in the trench, said Glazkov.
I remember, as if it were yesterday, Lyosha Burba whispering
to me: 'Vanya, you may be the sergeant and section
commander, and this may be the last time we storm the
house, but a bullet could find you too, so you'd better put
your helmet on.' I had gone on reconnaissance many times
before without a helmet. Mishchenko would follow my
example; he was from Rostov-on-Don, and we saw him as a
bit of a reckless character. Vanya Proshchenko, on the other
hand, from the Kuban, was the most composed and level-
headed man in our team, and putting on his helmet he said:
'Well lads, even if we don't take the house today, we'll at
least manage to get a foothold on the ground and first
floors, and others will storm the rest of it later.'

At six o'clock a series of red rockets was launched from the command
post of the HQ of the 34th regiment. This was the signal for the attack
to begin. It was the moment Alexenko had been waiting for.

'For motherland and for Stalin!' called Sidelnikov, jumping up. 'Hurrah!' shouted Dorosh. He too leaped up and bounded forward with great tigerish steps. He overtook the entire storm group and was one of the first to reach the house. We were right behind him and charged through the window holes and the gaps in the walls. We were in the house before we fired a shot. Now we were fighting hand-to-hand. It was fiercest at the entrance to the cellar, where groups of sleepy fascists were spilling out through the doors. Dubov and Kalinin were doing a good job blocking the way out of the basement. They were using the butts of their rifles, and sticking the fascists with their bayonets, while the flamethrower men sent streams of fire through the doorway.

At dawn Lieutenant Dorosh went down wounded. He toppled over backwards, dropping his pistol. His lower jaw was smashed. I was right by him at that moment. I lifted him up and Sergeant Dubov pulled a field dressing out of his tunic and bandaged him. Then a worse thing happened: a German on the next floor up dropped a grenade through a gap in the ceiling. It fell at our feet and exploded. Dubov was thrown to the side, and I was slightly wounded in the hand by shrapnel. Lieutenant Dorosh slipped out of my grasp and fell dead to the floor.

Lieutenants Sidelnikov and Isayev were wounded too, and had been carried out of the house. So the sun was not yet up, and we did not have an officer left. Sergeant Marchenko, who was a machinegunner, took command of the entire storm group upon himself. So far we had occupied only a few rooms on the ground floor. We could not get any further because ahead of us was a solid wall without windows or doors.

Glazkov and his men now joined the first wave of the storm group inside the house. Skirmishing was still going on.

We had all been waiting in the trench for our gunners to fire off a volley. As soon as they did, two of them were killed by the fascists' bullets, even though the fascists were shooting more or less at random. We were all wearing camouflage suits and it would have been almost impossible for them to spot us against the snow. Nevertheless, the others immediately fired another volley at the house.

This time they hit their target so we, firing from our sub-machineguns, took the ground floor of the house. The spot that had been hit was already in ruins, and there were no fascists left alive there. We had killed them all with grenades or sub-machinegun fire. So we had seized a bridgehead in the house – but what next? Forty or fifty metres of the house, including the bend of the house, were still in German hands. They regrouped and started a counter-attack. Fascists were holed up in the cellar beneath us and the neighbouring room. We had to drive them out, so we started taking it in turns to hack away at the wall with a crowbar and a pickaxe, which warmed us up nicely. A hole was soon made. We threw bottles of flammable liquid through it and, firing our sub-machineguns continuously, we hacked at the wall until the hole was big enough to climb through.

Part of the house was now in our hands – but only a part of it. We spent the whole day stubbornly defending the house from the fascists' counter-attacks. There were few of us left. Lyosha Burba was injured, as was Mishchenko, and there remained only myself, Vanya Proshchenko, and another two men who had only arrived the day before: Sergeant Chernushchenko and Gyena Kuklyov.

The operation was precariously close to becoming another costly failure. 'There were Germans all around,' said Alexenko. 'Behind the wall, in the cellars, on the upper storeys, and on three sides of us outside the house.' But it was the Russians' move. Sergeant Marchenko, the self-appointed commander, decided that brute force might work.

Marchenko assessed the situation and decided to wait for darkness, withdraw the storm group from the house back towards the Volga, then blow up the blank wall together with the fascists and continue the attack from there.

Late in the evening, sappers crawled up to the house. They laid several charges of TNT at the base of the blank wall, and as soon as they lit the fuse we all withdrew.

Not quite all the Russians left the building. The suggestible Sergeant Glazkov was persuaded by one of his subordinates to hang around and watch the demolition job close up:

Vanya Proshchenko then said to me: 'Comrade Sergeant, let's not leave!' So we climbed into the cellar, which we had just retaken from the Germans, and hid there waiting for the explosion to come. At around three in the morning there was the roar of an explosion, followed by shouts of 'Hurrah!' and the lads who had been mustering in the newly dug trench threw themselves at the remaining section of the house and took it by storm. Vanya Proshchenko and I joined in the assault, firing from our sub-machineguns and throwing grenades. Picking our way through the ruins to the bend of the house, we came across the following scene: a fascist was lying beside a banner with a knife in his belly and a sub-machinegun around his neck. It was a large fascist banner; we tore it down, and later I took it to Major Kotsarenko at headquarters.

Nikolai Alexenko was also looking for a dead body in the ruins.

I went to the place where my commander Lieutenant Dorosh had been lying, along with the others who had fallen. But they were all buried deep below the broken wall of that five-storey house. By four o'clock in the afternoon on December 3rd, the L-shaped house was entirely in our hands. In one section of the basement there were still some Germans. They were shouting out, but the way in to them was completely blocked up with the wreckage of the wall we had blown up.

From the upper floors you could look out across the tortured, spoiled centre of the city. 'Can you see Pavlov's House from here?' asked some fellow in a rather unmilitary sheepskin coat with no insignia on it. 'They are on the attack too, you know.' He had a camera and some flashbulbs. He clicked and clicked away with it, taking lots of photographs of the town, of Mamayev Kurgan and of the Volga.

Our first anti-tank company took heavy losses in the storming of the L-shaped house. My friend Nikolai Karpenko was seriously wounded that day. He and I had been chums since we were boys. He was my neighbour, and my comrade in battle. For three months we ate together from the same pot. He was hit in the head by shrapnel. He whispered something to me as he lay bleeding, but I couldn't make it out. The only bit I could get was this: he was calling to his mother. She had been ill for a very long time. When he left for the war she was bedridden, and could not even get up to see him off at the gate. Now he was bleeding to death, and feeling sorry that he had to die without seeing his mother one last time.

Only four of our 16 men came out alive from the L-shaped house. Stepanov and Kalinin 'atoned for their guilt with their blood', as the saying went. Stepanov was killed by machinegun fire; Kalinin was seriously wounded in the stomach and sent across the Volga ...

With the capture of the L-shaped house, the front line moved forwards 300 metres. The German invaders lost an important observation post and strongpoint. Two regiments of our division could now move freely in daylight and maintain contact with the left bank. These were the first steps on the journey of our guards division from the Volga to the Elbe.

ON LYUDNIKOV'S ISLAND

The grand offensive out on the cold steppe subtly altered the nature of the fighting inside Stalingrad. It was as if every German in the city now had to look over his shoulder, to keep an ear open for the enemy approaching from behind. The very chatter of the machineguns acquired a nervous note. The reporter Vasily Grossman noticed a change in the music of the urban battle, a new motif in the noisy opera of war. His keen ear picked this up when listening to the sounds coming from the factory district.

> The battle continues in the factories, where the dark, tattered walls are suddenly illuminated by the white and pink lights of gunfire. Cannons peal and boom; mines go off with a clear, dry, resounding bang; the precise enunciation of tommyguns and machineguns is heard. The sounds of battle in the factories at night speak of a new page in the struggle for Stalingrad. The sounds are no longer the elemental roar which rises high into the air, or falls from the sky in great waves, or flows unstoppably over the huge expanse of the Volga. This is now a battle of snipers. Volleys of bullets and shells fly swiftly and directly between the workshops. They are not like the slow shining hyperbolas of aerial warfare. In the short distances between the shops they resemble bright spears or arrows thrown by invisible warriors in the darkness. They suddenly appear from the stones of the walls, penetrate the cold stone of other walls, and disappear into them.

Weeks after it was first hemmed in, Colonel Ivan Lyudnikov's 138th Rifle Division was still holding a patch of ground in the Barricades factory. Now there were only 500 men left in the division, and they were surrounded on three sides by German troops. A couple of hundred yards behind them was the Volga, and the Germans were constantly threatening to slip in between them and the river and cut them off from that side too. They had little contact with the rest of the city.

Lyudnikov's predicament was, in a sense, a microcosm of the battle of Stalingrad. The Russians were aware that the 138th was fighting on, and their fight came to be seen as one of those symbolic encounters – like Pavlov's House and the Nail Factory – which defined the struggle for the Russians, and typified the grim righteousness of their fight. And as with those other mini conflicts, the soldiers' strange gift for toponymy supplied a name for this little battleground. It was dubbed 'Lyudnikov's Island', and as such it became part of the contemporary geography and the future mythology of Stalingrad. Vladimir Borisov was a supply officer for the 138th Division. His job meant that he went constantly backwards and forwards from the left bank of the river to the front line in the city. Even in the first days of November, before the 138th was cut off completely, he had his work cut out.

You see, the 'Island' itself was a territory of no more than 500 metres across. I well remember the regimental command post, which was located like a swift's nest in the high bank of the Volga. The fritzes would run up the edge of the cliff and throw grenades down at us. The work of us quartermasters was very difficult at that period. The Germans had occupied most of the bank and all the approaches to the river from the rear of the island were well covered.

I often had to take food and so forth up to the front. The enemy was laying down constant fire on our bank to stop supplies being brought across the river. Under such fire we would bring up supplies by car to an area near our front line, then unload and repack everything into a small boat. Sometimes we would get covering fire from the far bank. The boat would go right up the enemy positions at the riverbank, still under constant fire. Sometimes, to be safer, supplies such as shells and bullets would be put on a separate boat and towed along behind. In this way we tried to keep up the supply of ammunition.

On November 6th, the chief of supply Spiridonov and I decided to celebrate the anniversary of the October

Revolution with the regiment. We got a shipment together and crossed to the other side. There was drizzling rain, as always in the autumn, and the clay bank of the river was slippery and hard to climb. We got to the 'gully of death' and checked the German enfilades, and then made a run for it. In my haste I tripped over a dead body and fell straight on top of it. I got covered in mud as I kissed the face of that unknown dead comrade. But there was no time to stop and think. I jumped straight up and we ran on to the command post, where they were glad to see us. We had a good celebration of Revolution Day – and then we were cut off.

Vladimir Sokolov, a captain with the 295th artillery regiment, was on Lyudnikov's Island from the start.

It was the hardest time we went through in the whole of the Great Patriotic War. The enemy came stronger and stronger and they were more and more reckless. Drunken fascists, pushing towards the Volga, came straight at us. But the bodies just piled up at the edge of our trenches, where they formed a kind of rampart. Once they hardened in the frost they were practically impervious to bullets, which actually strengthened our defence.

On the 16th November our commander, comrade Lyudnikov, gave an order to the effect that each soldier and officer should receive 25 grammes of dried bread per day, and that each rifle and machinegun be issued 30 bullets a day. Anything else we needed we had to get from the enemy.

The daily norm of both bread and bullets could easily be consumed in a few seconds. Capturing the enemy's resources was the only means of continuing the fight. To kill a man was no longer enough: it was crawling over and taking his weapon that counted. Nevertheless, with a little imagination it was possible to make a little go a long way – as Sokolov found when he went on his rounds of the besieged island.

I was sent to check up on our 'garrisons'. I remember the garrison of Sergeant Morozov from the 344th Rifle Regiment. When I arrived, or rather crawled up, he had the following arsenal: one Maxim gun, two German machineguns, two German sub-machineguns, one of our own machineguns, one anti-tank gun, two dozen anti-tank grenades, and about three dozen 'lemons' – that is, hand grenades. Morozov's partner was asleep in the dugout, and Morozov was carrying on a conversation with himself – quite loudly and using different voices. He would shoot off a couple of rounds every now and then – first from one weapon, then another, then a third, always in different directions and from different corners of his strongpoint. Very occasionally he threw a grenade. In this way he created the impression that there was an entire platoon defending the place.

And what was most surprising for me was this: he never for one moment looked the least bit afraid. Alone, in total darkness apart from the odd flare (after which it always seemed even darker), with a cunning enemy who was armed to the teeth right in front of him. But there was Morozov with his Olympian calm, his slow, carefully calculated peregrinations around his territory, his clever use of weapons, his cool-as-a-cucumber shout-it-loud dialogues in their various voices and intonations. All this made me not just admire him, but also want to learn from him. He knew the magnificent art of valour.

You could not help but be envious of such deathless heroism. He was one person, on his own, but he had absolute faith in victory. But there were hundreds – thousands – like him at Stalingrad.

THE AIRBRIDGE TO STALINGRAD

The Germans who surrounded Lyudnikov were themselves surrounded by a much larger contingent of Russians. In the last week of November the unstable borders of the Kessel congealed and solidified like a puddle in a pothole. The cauldron acquired definite form and extent. Its front line encompassed a large lozenge of Russian earth, about 40 miles (64km) wide and 20 miles (32km) deep. The eastern end of it was anchored in the city; the tapering western end was out in the bleak and empty steppe, and reached as far as the village of Marinovka, some way short of the Don. In the north it extended to Samofalovka, and in the south to Varvarovka.

Looking at the Kessel on his operational charts, Hitler had another of his grossly self-deluding ideas: he designated Stalingrad a *Festung* – a fortress – as if by speaking the word he could conjure up the battlements and thick walls that the Sixth Army so conspicuously lacked. It was a laughable misnomer, but 'Fortress Stalingrad' is how the encirclement was described henceforth in German communiqués and press reports.

The Russians did not know it at first, but they had surrounded a quarter of a million men of the Sixth Army. This was nearly three times as many as their own intelligence services had estimated. In the first days after the encirclement, the Russians did not rush to attack the surrounded men – the first task was to strengthen their own stretched lines and prevent a rapid breakout. German commanders inside the Kessel were already planning to burst through the encirclement to the south-west before the Russians could strengthen the ring. The plans did not get far.

Early on the 24th November, while Paulus and I were preparing the necessary measures for a breakout to the south, we received a 'Führer decision' from Army Group, said General Arthur Schmidt, Paulus's chief of staff. It said that the Sixth Army was to stay in Stalingrad and wait to be relieved. We reacted to this order with astonishment, since we had expected some sort of discussion with the Army Group, and were fairly certain of the breakout. Paulus and I came separately to the same conclusion. It now seemed to us more impossible than ever to act against an order of the High Command or the Army Group.

Hitler had absolutely forbidden the army to break out of encirclement straight away. Stalingrad was not to be relinquished, and the Sixth Army was to deploy all around the edge of this territory with the barrels of their guns pointing outwards – the classic 'hedgehog' defence, writ large. Hitler's intention was to organize a relief column that could smash through from the outside. In the meantime, the army would be supplied from the air. On the 22nd, Hitler had asked Göring whether his Luftwaffe could supply the Sixth Army, to which Göring replied 'Yes, it can be done.' The Reichsmarschall then boarded his luxury train and went to France for a holiday.

While Göring was off collecting paintings in Paris, a furious row developed over the logistics of the proposed airlift to Stalingrad. The Sixth Army estimated that it needed a minimum of 550 tons of fuel, arms and food every day in order to remain fighting fit. Göring's supply experts of the Luftwaffe averred that 300 tons a day was possible, but only if aerial combat operations were scaled down and – crucially – if the Russian weather permitted.

In fact, the weather had already turned bad. There was fog and low cloud, and the temperature was diving well below zero. Consequently, in the first days of the encirclement a mere trickle of supplies made it into the Kessel – far less than the Luftwaffe's already inadequate pledge. Werner Beumelberg was a Luftwaffe major with the Fourth Air Fleet. He could see at once that the airlift was a hopeless undertaking. This is his analysis of the situation on the ground and in the air, as it deteriorated through the last days of November and into December.

On the 24th November, 47 Junker 52s carrying 80 tons flew in, 27 of which either crashed or were lost under enemy fire. On 25th November 30 Ju 52s flew in carrying 55 tons of fuel and 20 tons of munitions with a loss of 9 Jus. On the 26th November Heinkel 111 fighter planes were also diverted from their real task for the first time to bring in supplies for the Kessel. This use of these planes subsequently became commonplace, until a point was reached when combat needs became so urgent that ferrying supplies had to be set aside.

Wide-ranging measures were introduced to bring in all available Luftwaffe transport planes from the front and from back home, and also to use rail transport to bring in the necessary provisions. Both took time to organize. By the 30th November, 80 planes had been put in place, 15 of them were lost, and 40 tons of fuel and 20 tons of munitions had been landed in the Kessel.

But by now the provision of rations was becoming urgent. It was an endless process. By the time the daily provisions had been increased to 200 tons and more, the needs of the Sixth Army had increased several times over, because in between the peak achievements on a particular day, there were days when the weather prevented any flights from coming in. With the loss of some of the positions outside the fortress the fighters no longer had sufficient range to protect the planes by day.

Meanwhile the units of the Sixth Army inside were fighting for every metre of ground, at first still in the certain expectation of relief from outside. But from the very start they operated under the severest shortage of heavy weapons, fuel, munitions and, day by day, fewer rations. Russian pressure on the west and south-west front increased unremittingly. Even when 60 Russian tanks were destroyed on December 2nd, the very next day there were 100 new ones in place to attack. When German fighter planes destroyed 43 enemy planes over Stalingrad on one day, with flak destroying another nine, the very next day 100 new Russian planes were flying.

General von Richthofen himself saw Beumelberg's figures, and was well aware that his air fleet had been given a completely impossible task. He knew there was no way the Luftwaffe could ever fly in 300 tons a day, and he made frequent phone calls to highly placed Luftwaffe acquaintances in Berlin, trying to get someone to tell Hitler so. He also sent a report to Paulus urging him to break out, orders or no orders. 'The army has a clear choice,' said von Richthofen. 'It must break through to the south-west, or face destruction within days.'

Göring's own staff officers did not need von Richthofen to tell them that the assurances of their commander-in-chief were worthless, but they felt unable to undermine the Reichsmarschall by saying so officially. Instead, Army Chief of Staff Zeitzler, appalled that the Sixth Army was being condemned to starvation by the Luftwaffe's empty promises, took up the cudgel on behalf of the men on the ground. When Göring got back from Paris on the 27th, Zeitzler arranged a confrontation in Hitler's presence. First, the army man explained the impossibility of transporting the tonnage required with the aircraft available, then asked the Führer to summon Göring. Hitler did so, and then put a straight question: 'Göring, can you keep the Sixth Army supplied by air?' Göring made the Nazi salute and declared: 'Mein Führer, I assure you that the Luftwaffe can keep the Sixth Army supplied.' 'The Luftwaffe certainly cannot,' retorted Zeitzler. 'You are in no position to give an opinion on that!' shouted Göring.

But Zeitzler had done his homework. 'Herr Reichsmarschall,' he said, 'Do you know what tonnage has to be flown in every day?' Göring flushed. 'I don't, but my staff officers do,' he said lamely. This allowed Zeitzler to make his case – and the logic was overwhelming. 'Allowing for all the stocks at present with the Sixth Army, allowing for absolute minimum needs and the taking of all possible emergency measures, the Sixth Army will require delivery of 300 tons a day. But since not every day is suitable for flying, this means that about 500 tons will have to be carried to the Sixth Army on each and every flying day if the irreducible minimum average is to be maintained.'

'I can do that,' said Göring. 'That's a lie,' shouted Zeitzler. He knew that even if every plane in the Luftwaffe were brought to Stalingrad – from France, from North Africa, from the Caucasus and the Russian north – it would still not be enough to guarantee a delivery of 500 tons on flying days. He looked to Hitler, who after a moment's thought pronounced judgment: 'The Reichsmarschall has made his report to me, which I have no choice but to believe. I therefore abide by my original decision.'

Hitler's siding with Göring was a nail in the coffin of the Sixth Army. But the Führer's final decision had probably been taken days before the row between his two commanders. On the day the Kessel closed, 23 November, he had lost his temper with the turbulent Zeitzler and screamed at him: 'The Sixth Army will stay where it is. If necessary they will hold out all winter, and I shall relieve them by a spring offensive.' Tragically for the men in the Kessel, it would all be over much sooner than that.

WINTER STORM AND THUNDERCLAP

The consequences of Hitler's determination to go ahead with the airlift were immediately felt inside the cauldron.

> From the very first day of the encirclement, everything was in short supply, said Werner Beumelberg. Some divisions still had some horses, which they had to share out with others. Little by little the horses ended up in the field kitchens. There were insufficient field bakeries in the Kessel, so bread had to be flown in, and that took up a great deal of space in the aircraft. There was hardly any fuel, because the large depots were far behind lines on the other side of the Don. Ammunition had to be used sparingly from the first. Transport movements inside the Kessel were severely hampered, the road network was incomplete, snow drifts had to be cleared, and the enemy had a clear view of our men. Every day that provisions were not replenished made the situation worse. But the army's needs could never be met. It was living from hand to mouth. In fact, every day it was living beyond its means, and it was easy to calculate at what point there would be nothing left at all.

Peter Wunschel was an intelligence officer with the 384th Infantry Division, under the command of General Strecker. Before the war he had been a journalist by trade, and he had a hack's nose for a looming catastrophe. The day after the completion of the encirclement, he heard something that sounded to him like a great disaster scoop. Unfortunately for Wunschel, it looked as if the disaster was about to happen to him.

> It was probably the 24th November that the General returned from the discussion at Army HQ, following the formation of the Kessel. *We are shutting ourselves in of our own free will.* The core of this information, the full significance of this sentence, struck me like a screaming headline.

Wunschel added that 'the mass of the Sixth Army firmly believed that this Kessel would be broken through from the outside, as all others had been before,' and this remained the Sixth Army's last best hope: they could hold out for a little while, even on starvation rations, so long as they knew that help was on its way.

The task of opening what Hitler called the 'land corridor' to the Kessel fell to Field Marshal Erich von Manstein. He was admired both by Hitler and by the mass of German soldiery. He was one of the architects of the conquest of France, and he was also the man who had subjugated the Crimean peninsula earlier in the Russian campaign. Now he was brought south from Leningrad and charged with the salvation of the Sixth Army.

At Kotelnikovo, 80 miles (130km) south-west of the southern edge of the Kessel, Manstein began to assemble his forces. It was a hotchpotch army: there were two panzer corps – the 48th and the 57th – which were all that was left of General Hermann Hoth's Fourth Panzer Army; then there was the 11th Panzer Division, said to be the toughest unit on the entire eastern front, which was brought up from the Caucasus; also from the Caucasus came the 23rd Panzer Division, and the Sixth Panzer Division was on its way from France. With the additional support of infantry and Romanian cavalry, Manstein's strike force amounted to 500 tanks and about 75,000 men.

The Field Marshal had also scraped together a motley collection of 800 transport vehicles – Russian ones, German ones, Czech ones, captured American and British lend-lease trucks. These were loaded with 300 tons of food and fuel, ready to roll into the Kessel as soon as the tanks had blasted a channel through the snowbound, Russian-held flatlands. As this strike force made ready, Manstein sent a message to Paulus: 'We will do everything to get you out.'

Manstein's new command was designated Army Group Don, and the relief operation was given the name *Wintergewitter* – 'Winter Storm'. Hoth was given the key task of leading the relief column. The sole aim of Winter Storm was to resupply the Sixth Army within its 'fortress', to give it the means to fight on. But in defiance of Hitler, Manstein cannily laid plans for a second operation – code-named *Donnerschlag* – 'Thunderclap' – the goal of which was to effect the evacuation of the Sixth Army down the corridor hacked out by Army Group Don. Manstein seems to have regarded this as the real point of the exercise: carry out Winter Storm first, then invoke Thunderclap and get the Sixth Army out of Stalingrad before it was too late. Hitler would rant and rave, but by then it would be a *fait accompli*.

Winter Storm was delayed for some days by an actual winter storm, but the operation finally got under way on 12 December. The tanks were painted white for camouflage, and looked like mechanical wraiths as they moved out of Kotelnikovo and headed north-east. The Germans made reasonable progress in the first two days: their main obstacle was not the Russians but the snow-filled balkas, as dangerous and invisible as a mountain crevasse.

Meanwhile, inside the Kessel, hopes began to rise. The watchword of Paulus's cold and famished men was '*Der Manstein kommt*' – 'Manstein is coming!' Karl P——, a Landser with the 376th Infantry Division, could not contain his excitement at the thought that the Stalingrad ordeal would be coming to an end, and so rather overestimated the Field Marshal's progress. In a letter home written on the 14th, he wrote:

> The worst is over for the moment. We're all hoping to be out of the Kessel by Christmas. For the time being we're still encircled, but the Russians are again encircled by German troops. General von Manstein is still 30 kilometres away.

You'll have to forgive me for writing so badly and incoherently. If you could see where I am as I write, you'd understand. I'm down here in a bunker, that's been holed to the left and right, at the front and the rear. I've got to write fast, I've no idea when I'm going to have to run for it. It's my fourth attempt at writing this letter. Now I have to stop, rations are being served. Dear parents, the war is soon going to be over. Once this Kessel battle is over, the war in Russia will be finished.

But Manstein's good initial progress proved deceptive. On the very day that Karl P— of the 376th was jotting down his dream of a Christmas in Germany, Sixth Panzer encountered the Soviet Fourth Mechanized Corps and 13th Tank Corps, which were rushing to meet them headlong. The opposing armoured columns locked horns between the Aksai and Myshkova rivers, about 40 miles (65km) from the Kessel. A brief thaw turned the ground to a quagmire, and for three days the tanks thrashed around like mud wrestlers in the hills above the village of Verkhnye-Kumsky.

Meanwhile the Russians launched a new operation, one that would put paid to the German rescue effort. Operation Little Saturn involved a tank-led thrust to the south from the upper Don, 100 miles (160km) away to the west of Stalingrad. One aim was to prevent any reinforcements reaching Manstein. A second goal was to capture the large airfield at Tatsinskaya, which was Richthofen's main depot for supplying the Sixth Army. While this offensive was under way, elements of the Soviet 51st Army moved behind Hoth's column to cut off Kotelnikovo in the rear.

By the 19th the relief column had escaped the mudbath of Verkhnye-Kumsky and had stumbled on across the River Myshkova. But here, on the northern side of the river, the Germans met a new opponent: General Rodion Malinovsky's fresh and powerful Second Guards Army. Konstantin Glukhikh was with them, and from the ground he watched the slow disintegration of the German airbridge to Stalingrad.

Under cover of night, columns of seamen and infantrymen moved along a newly rolled snow road. Behind them, on horse-drawn trailers, moved the artillery. Bringing up the rear, with their headlights switched off, crawled our signallers' trucks.

A few hours later, we could tell we were drawing close to the front. We could hear night artillery and exchanges of machinegun fire. Soon after, we found ourselves in a sort of corridor. Shells were whistling over our heads, coming first from one side, then from the other. To both sides of us, flares were flying up into the dark sky. All our units turned to face the enemy approaching the ring. At daybreak, a fierce battle flared up around the Krep state farm and the village of Vasilyevka. It went on almost uninterruptedly for about five days.

The corridor between the ring and Manstein's attacking army had become too narrow. And the enemy was launching one attack after another. Our soldiers and commanders realized that there was nowhere to go, and fought to the death to prevent the enemy's getting through to the ring.

We observed scenes like the following many times: on the horizon you'd spot a hulking big transport plane adorned with swastikas, and no sooner had it reached territory occupied by our units than a couple of Soviet fighters would appear on its tail. One turn, and the transport plane would start to break up, and boxes, packages, loaves of bread and jars of preserves would fall to the ground from it as if from a sack full of holes.

And every time, our soldiers would run out of their dugouts and trenches and shout things like 'Bravo!' and 'Well done!'

Manstein's column stalled on the Myshkova river, 30 miles (48km) short of the Kessel, on 19 December. Both sides could look up and see the German planes 'falling like apples from a tree in a gale'. That day,

Manstein sent an emissary to Paulus. This ambassador from the world of the living was a Major Eismann, and his mission was to persuade Paulus at least to attempt a breakout now that help was nearby, to meet Manstein part way. Paulus refused, saying that he had only enough fuel for 15 miles (24km), that his men were too weak, and that in any case the Führer had forbidden it.

When Eismann returned empty-handed, Manstein appealed directly to Hitler, who made the reverse case. He said that there was no point in giving the order for a breakout, because Paulus had made it clear that he did not have the means to carry it out. Neither leader would take responsibility for the final decision: they manhandled it back and forth like two men juggling with a ticking time bomb.

On 23 December, the Tatsinskaya airfield fell to the Russians. A third of the German transport fleet was destroyed on the ground: individual planes were rammed by Russian tanks as they taxied on to the runway to escape. Those that made it out would henceforth have to fly twice the distance – from the airfield of Salsk and Novocherkassk, to bring supplies to the Sixth Army. The relief column on the Myshkova river was by this time in danger of becoming surrounded. On the day of the Tatsinskaya disaster Manstein ordered it to withdraw. The attempt to rescue Paulus's beleaguered men had ended in total failure.

On 29 December, elements of General Pavel Rotmistrov's Seventh Tank Corps liberated the town of Kotelnikovo, the base from which Manstein's relief column had set out two weeks before. Here the first Russian soldiers into the town found a depot filled with delicacies that had been intended for the Sixth Army's Christmas celebrations: candied fruit, Dutch cheeses, wine from France, Danish bacon, tinned fish and vegetables. The boxes containing these riches all bore a stamp: 'FOR GERMANS ONLY'. 'But not all our tankmen can speak German,' wrote the wry Rotmistrov in his report on the find, 'so due to a lack of education they ate the stuff.'

7
COLD DAYS IN HELL

The relief column began to recede like an ebb tide. By 23 December it was clear to the Germans outside the ring that the breakthrough attempt had come to nothing: Paulus's besieged men were going to have to fight on alone. Radio contact was maintained, but what was there to say? Werner Wischnowski was a 21-year-old radio operator with a Panzer regiment outside the Kessel. From the relative safety of a communications post, he listened in silence to the radio traffic of the Sixth Army. It was like eavesdropping on drowning men:

> By day we saw the Junkers 52s flying provisions into the cauldron. But as one of the little men, you know nothing. We had no maps or anything. Once I went right to the front line in a truck. There was a unit based there with a telephone exchange. I was surprised that the driver could find his way so well without a single signpost. It was evening, and one of the men pointed out to me: 'The Russians are dug in just over there.' I couldn't see them, and no one shot at us. When I was at the apparatus we would sometimes hear things like: 'They are advancing!' or 'We need ammunition!' We didn't tell the officer, because it was forbidden to monitor conversations.

STILLE NACHT
Inside the Kessel, the mood was sombre and solemn. On Christmas Eve, the crushing news that Manstein was not coming after all seeped through to the ordinary soldiers of the Sixth Army.

The noise of battle from the relief army had been getting closer day by day, said Hans-Erdmann Schönbeck. We were geared up for the last leap westwards, to meet our liberators. But only in our minds, for we knew that we were almost out of fuel and ammo. With the first day of Christmas came the full, awful certainty. The relief troops were unable to make it, the battle sounds were getting fainter and moving to the west. Our thoughts of escape had been in vain.

On this doom-laden *Heilige Abend*, Holy Eve, Schönbeck, a 20-year-old officer with the 24th Panzer Division, took some comfort in the preparations he had made for the festivities.

On December 24th there were about fifteen men in my bunker. That morning, under fairly heavy fire, I had managed to dig up a little pine tree buried in the snow of the steppe – probably one of the very few Christmas trees in the entire Kessel. That spring, when I'd been billeted with a priest in Brittany, I'd scrounged three church candles that were just the right size to fit into my backpack. I had no idea why at the time, I just liked the look of them. It got dark very early. The candles were burning as I told the Christmas story and spoke the Lord's Prayer.

A little later, the crackly loudspeaker transmitted a Christmas message from the Forces' radio station in Germany. It was being broadcast everywhere from the North Pole to Africa. At that time an enormous part of the world belonged to us. When Stalingrad was called we began to tremble though we were indoors in the warm that evening. Then when the words '*Stille Nacht, heilige Nacht ...*' were sung, our tears started to flow. We cried for a long time. From that moment, no one said so much as a word – maybe for a whole hour.

Not all the soldiers at Stalingrad were so touched by that Christmas broadcast. The radio announcer had informed the German public that they were listening to a wireless link-up with the army on the Volga, that it was the Sixth Army themselves singing 'Silent Night'. In fact it was a choir in a Berlin studio. Some of the men, freezing and starving in their bunkers, were incensed by the attempt to cover up or at least to sentimentalize their ordeal. They were also unamused by the irony that none of them had had a silent night, or even so much as a couple of hours' uninterrupted sleep, for a matter of months.

But the goodly Schönbeck was grateful for the Christmas feast, and he did his best to spread some good cheer of his own.

> We each received an extra slice of bread, and also had some French brandy – goodness knows where from – and enough wood. I went from bunker to bunker in our balka and spoke to those on guard duty as well. Everyone's thoughts were with their loved ones back home. Meanwhile the night sky had become very clear and it turned icy cold. A very few isolated shells landed, and somewhere further off there were a few machinegun volleys. It looked as if the Russians were letting us have our Christmas Eve. Above us the heavens cleared, revealing a starry sky. At home, two thousand kilometres away, they must have been looking at the same stars as we were. That was my bridge, my link with home – the immeasurable breadth of the firmament! To this day, in good times and bad, I have sought calm and stability in the immensity of the universe – and I have always found it.

The Russians were unaware that it was a holiday for the Germans. Christmas was not celebrated in the atheistic Soviet Union, and in any case it fell on 7 January in the old calendar of Russian Orthodoxy. If the Soviet forces had realized where their enemies' thoughts were, they might have made more effort to disrupt the meagre celebrations. As it was, the everyday round of bombing and sniping was not enough to break the Germans' festive mood. 'At around 15.00 hours the

Russians started shooting randomly in various directions with heavy artillery ...' said Hans Lesko, who was having a relatively quiet Christmas Eve at the Pitomnik airfield.

'... We crept into the shelters that the privates had blown
out of the ground and shared the last of our cigarettes.
Back home they were preparing for Christmas Eve. Before
midnight, under cover of the rising mist, the Russian 'coffee
grinder' made its appearance, as on every evening for days
past. The procedure was always the same. After flying over
once, the plane turned and dropped small bombs that
looked as if they were being tipped out with a shovel, for
they scattered over the airfield in all directions. When the
bombs were finished, leaflets rained down from the sky.
They contained the usual: we should do ourselves a favour
and surrender; a pleasant life lay ahead in captivity, plenty
to eat and as much brandy as we could knock back.
But should we not wish to, we would simply be shot
on being taken prisoner.
   So far it was the same as usual. But this time the plane
with its clattering sewing-machine engine turned back a
third time. And now we were dumbstruck. They were
screaming down at us through a loudspeaker. A committee
of captive German officers had set themselves up in
Moscow. These erstwhile 'comrades-in-arms' now invited
us to break out and to shit on the oath of allegiance. For a
while we were speechless. But then the entire front line
sector around Pitomnik sprang into action. Rifles, sub-
machineguns, panzer batteries, as well as our tiny
anti-aircraft gun all fired their response into the sky.
All the fury of the German soldiers lay in every shot.
And they yelled upwards: 'Criminals! Cowards! Arse-kissers!
Bastards!' An hour later the Stalin organs started playing.
   At one o'clock in the morning, when the fireworks
had ended, carols were played over the Reich radio.

The programme ended with 'Lili Marlene', which brought tears to our eyes. Little Schick went outside on guard duty. I was supposed to relieve him two hours later with a sergeant and a lance corporal. At three in the morning when we crept across to our post, we couldn't find Schick. The sergeant told us to keep back. He went on alone. We waited under cover. After a long time we heard a shrill whistle. We rushed forwards. There was the sergeant and there was little Schick. He was standing upright in the snow trench. A bullet had got him right in the forehead. In front of him lay three empty magazines from his sub-machinegun and six dead Russians.

Such incidents were frequent enough, even on this day. But throughout the Kessel, German soldiers took advantage of the brief lull in the fighting to write letters, exchange small gifts of cigarettes or a sliver of soap, or to take part in a religious service. Alfons R——, an NCO with the 60th Infantry Division, sat down in the afternoon and wrote to his family. He tried hard to put a brave face on things, but the despair is just below the surface.

Dear parents, dear brothers and sisters,
It's Christmas Eve in the field in the Russian steppes near Stalingrad. By the time you read this letter all the Christmas excitement will be over, both here and with you too, and the harsh reality will have caught up with us again. Here the holiday doesn't make any difference to our situation and yet, in a very limited way, there is something like Christmas spirit ...
    It's just impossible to imagine all the things that happen here. What the men endure cannot be described. And now Christmas – with a simple candle and two thorny twigs from the steppe, a howling east wind, the thud of explosions and bursts of fire cracking over our bunker. Thank God, we still have wood to warm our foxholes. I'm sitting here with my platoon leader, a staff sergeant and our dispatch rider.

We've placed a few pictures from home around the candle and are thinking of you. Our rough voices have even managed to croak 'Silent Night' and another carol, but it didn't really sound right, for there was something missing – and it was you.

But I don't want to be ungrateful. I must thank God that I have been allowed to see Christmas, and to be healthy and cheerful. I hope the same goes for you. Though you're bound to be very worried, let's hope that we will soon see one another again.

I've been to see my men and sat with them a bit, trying to cheer them up. Our soldiers just amaze me, in their way they are quite unique and really unbeatable. I hope the Fatherland is aware of this, and will truly appreciate it.

Corporal Werner R— was in a similarly philosophical mood when he wrote home that same evening.

Somewhere in the front line of the German Fortress Stalingrad, in a small ravine in the steppe, where our vehicles are parked, camouflaged with white lime, and where our bunkers are located, we've put up a Christmas tree. We'd been asking ourselves what Christmas 1942 would be like. All I know is that in this defiant mood things were better and more profound than any other Christmas Eve has been or could ever be.

At 17.00 hours I went outside on watch in the driving snow, but without feeling resentful. And as the wind dropped at this hour of the night, the sky cleared, the stars appeared and a huge, serene moon rose. It seemed to me it seemed like a symbol: after the deprivation and horror of our fate, life moves on.

We passed some good time together – you could even say it was relaxing. There was a little 96 per cent schnapps, and real coffee in good supply. So we drank an amazing coffee liqueur.

Naturally, the higher ranks had a better time of it than the enlisted men. Here is an anonymous diary entry, written on Christmas Day. The celebrations of this well-connected officer were about as good as it got.

Yesterday we were expecting the Russians to disturb us, which thank God, didn't happen. At four in the afternoon I assembled most of my people to celebrate Christmas Eve. The general spoke, saying that this was a Christmas we were unlikely ever to forget: firstly, because every one of us would probably rather be in another place, back home with wife and children; secondly, because of the highly unusual situation we were in at present; thirdly, because of the really outstanding comradely solidarity produced by this situation.

We sang Christmas carols and presents were distributed. Each man received three bars of chocolate, three tubes of sweets, fifty cigarettes, half a loaf of bread, 130 grams of meat and some sandwich spread. One and all were delighted, as no one expected anything like this to happen in the present circumstances. We had conjured up a Christmas tree from a few pine branches, decorated it with silver paper from cigarette boxes, cut one of the last candles into pieces, and used the lids from empty food tins and a nail to make holders. In this way we made do. Then I went round to some people who weren't able to take part, and shortly after six o'clock I was back in our dugout, overseeing the final preparations for our evening meal.

We wanted to eat together and we set a table with a tablecloth and things to make it look nice. The presents, chocolate and so forth were piled up at each place; a small Christmas tree stood on the table, and everything looked very attractive. All this in a smoky old hole. Thirteen of us gentlemen were there when the general arrived with a gift for everyone: a bottle of alcohol for the senior officers, and something to smoke for the others. Then we had a really good meal, as we'd slaughtered a cow a few days earlier:

soup, tongue with noodles, followed by stewed apple and
cherries which we had found in the quartermaster's stores.
As for alcohol, we had some rum that we drank with tea.
We sat together until eleven in the evening.

The Kessel was still a large geographical area, and there were regional
as well as hierarchical variations in supply. Wilhelm Raimund Beyer,
the soldier who a month before had marched into the cauldron just as
it was closing, was already facing the early stages of starvation.

By Christmas Day there was almost no food left. What was
being distributed can hardly be described as rations: tiny
amounts of tinned bread, tinned sausage, occasionally meat
from a horse that had met its end somehow or other, and
had been crawled over by countless flies. Once we even
caught a donkey – but those times were exceptions – and
eating that meat was forbidden. It was more than unhealthy.
But what starving person is going to bother about that?
Everyone had long since furtively eaten up his 'iron ration'.
When just before Christmas the order reached us that iron
rations could now be broken into, everyone laughed.

Some men in Beyer's unit were even thinking about the ghastly pros
and cons of cannibalizing their own bodies.

Even those accustomed to hunger, who knew how much
pain the disappearance of the last small cushions of fat on
the toes or elsewhere caused, seriously considered taking
this action in defiance of orders.

Werner Lange, an NCO, was richly sardonic about the Christmas fare
in his letters home. This is what he wrote home on 29 December 1942:
'On the first day of the holiday we had goose with rice, and on the
second day we had goose with peas. Only our geese have four legs and
iron shoes on each hoof.' Karl P——, the infantryman who had fondly

hoped to be out of encirclement by Christmas, was one of the few who, despite the hunger, had not yet given up hope.

> Day after day, we're longing for the Kessel to be opened from outside, he wrote on the 27th. Our rations are very poor at the moment. In the morning we get 200 grams of bread, five grams of butter, twenty grams of sausage and a bowl of soup, that's all. But don't imagine it's a lunch like at home, just a load of water. Half of us are even too weak to get up in the morning, let alone do any work. Last week our doctor said if the rations don't improve, he'll be putting all the men into the hospital. Each man looks worse than the last.
>   I haven't had a single little parcel from you. One letter and that's all. The Russians have so far left us in peace over Christmas.

Despite the semblance of a ceasefire, the mundane business of killing and being killed carried on. As soon as the holiday was over, Lieutenant Gross of the 60th Motorized Infantry sat down to write this letter – one of many such notes, no doubt – to a dead man's next of kin.

> It is my sad duty to inform you that on December 26th 1942 your dear husband, Wilhelm Siems fell in battle – approximately 25 kilometres north-west of Stalingrad.
>   On Christmas morning the Russians briefly succeeded in penetrating our line of defence. Your husband was part of a reserve which had the task of forcing the Russians back. As your husband raised his head a little, probably in order to get a better view, he must have been spotted by a Russian sharpshooter. He received a bullet in the head and died instantly. His brother was next to him and will give you an exact account.
>   I know how hard this news must be for you and I send you my sincerest sympathy for this terrible misfortune. It is also an immeasurable loss for the unit. Wilhelm will not be

forgotten by any of us. We have laid him to rest in a military cemetery of the 60th Motorized Infantry Division near the Konnaya Tractor Factory. His effects will be dispatched as soon as possible.

THE MADONNA OF STALINGRAD

The Christmas celebrations were followed with intense interest by Kurt Reuber, both a priest and an army doctor. During the hungry days of Advent he had noted unselfconsciously in a letter to his wife that 'a piece of bread or wood is worth its weight in gold. My patients get such pleasure from half a piece of bread that I put some by for them if I've had enough myself.' After doing his rounds and giving away his food on a Christian whim, he went back to his bunker to have his own Christmas. It began in song, and ended in blood and pain.

At 14.00 hours in one of the balkas, some of the men started singing. The way these men's stumbling voices rang out over the steppe – something you cannot talk about. And as to what was going on inside us: quite a few eyes welled up.

A short, serious address from our commander, not without warmth, and not religious. Then celebration in the bunkers. The adjutant and I prepare our room and set out the table of gifts, just like back home. Calling out greetings, distributing presents. Then, in the end, I am surrounded by a circle of patients and medical orderlies to celebrate. The commander presents the sick with the last bottle of sparkling wine. We raise our field cups and drink a toast to whatever we hold dear.

We are standing with our cups full when we have to hurl ourselves to the ground, as four bombs land outside. I grab my medical bag and run to where the bombs hit. One dead and three wounded. My beautifully decorated bunker turns into a dressing station. One of the wounded men has been hit in the head, and there is nothing I can do for him. But I can help the other two.

The dying man had just that minute left the celebration to go on duty. He had said: 'I just want to sing that carol with you before I go: "*O du fröhliche*".' A minute later, dead. Sad, dreadful work in the Christmas bunker. Our celebration was over.

Reuber's work in the Kessel earned him many admirers. But it was a work of a different kind that made him famous throughout the Sixth Army, and that later made the name of this profoundly decent man a legend in the annals of Stalingrad. Reuber the priest and doctor was also a gifted artist. As he observed the war around him he felt compelled to make a drawing, one that would address the horror of the war, but that would also imbue it with some meaning, with the Christian virtue of hope.

I thought a long time about what I should draw. My mud cave was transformed into a studio. This one room, with not enough space to stand back from the picture! I had to climb up on my plank bed or onto the stool to look at the picture. Constantly bumping, falling, with the charcoals disappearing in cracks in the mud. Nothing to prop the big drawing up against. Only a slanting table which I cobbled together myself. I used the back of a Russian map for paper. The result is a Madonna, or mother and child. Oh, if only I could draw what is in my imagination! This is the picture: the head of the mother and of the child nestling against each other, with a large cloth wrapped around them. The one protecting and embracing the other.

Reuber was a gifted artist – a fine portraitist, in particular – but he would have been the first to admit that the Madonna is not his best work. Given the conditions he had to work in, it could not be. And yet there is something in it that transcends the sketchy draughtsmanship. The cradling gesture of the mother's arm, the almost embryonic form of the helpless baby, the cloak that swaddles them both like the all-encompassing love of God – all this shines through the obviously poor quality of the paper, in which the folds of the Russian map are clearly to be seen. Around the edge of the image Reuber wrote the words of St John: *Licht, Leben, Liebe* – Light, Life, Love. Then he hung the image in his bunker, never suspecting the powerful effect it was about to have on his comrades.

> **There's something I want to say about the reaction to the Madonna**, wrote Reuber. **I followed the old tradition of opening the Christmas door (consisting of rough planks in the case of our bunker) and the comrades trooped in. They stood spellbound, reverent, silent before the picture on the mud wall. A candle on a board was stuck into the clay below it. Everyone stood captivated by the effect of the picture, thoughtfully reading the words. This morning the regimental doctor came and thanked me for this Christmas joy. Late into the night, as the others slept, he and a few comrades lying on their bunks, had felt compelled to keep looking pensively at the picture in the candlelight.**

Reuber's dugout became, in other words, a kind of shrine, and the picture itself was transformed into something more than a mere drawing. It became a sacred object, a focus for the hopes and prayers of the many unhappy men who came in from the cold to gaze at it. It became, in fact, an icon, in the ancient Russian tradition – and it was as if these German invaders had, by some spiritual osmosis, absorbed the deep and simple religion of an older Russia, of Holy Mother Russia.

But the sacramental warmth of the Stalingrad Madonna did not reach everyone in the Kessel. It certainly did not extend to the loneliest man in Stalingrad, General Paulus, who was using the quiet hours of Christmas Eve to grapple with the insoluble logistical problem of distributing supplies to his men. 'On Holy Eve, the commanding general sent for me with an order to bring him the supply tables,' said Gunter Toepke, quartermaster for the Sixth Army.

I was in the middle of working out a new distribution plan, as we had food for three weeks at most at the present rate of consumption. When I climbed out of my bunker I could barely see a thing because of the driving snow. I felt my way over to the commander's bunker, which was a few metres away. He was standing in the open at the door, staring up unblinkingly into the snowstorm.

We stood next to each other in silence for quite a while. Then he spoke, without turning to me, as if he was saying it to himself. He said: 'If God in heaven should forsake us too ...' I thought I should make some reply, but no word came to my lips. I was too much in thrall to his mood at that moment. He didn't say it directly, but with that word 'too' I understood that he felt we had now been abandoned by the people on the outside.

GIVE US THIS DAY OUR DAILY BREAD

The people on the outside meant first and foremost Hitler himself. In the Führer's mind, the plight of the Sixth Army was assuming a kind of Wagnerian grandeur. And though he was not yet admitting the possibility of defeat, Hitler was beginning to see that there might be something rather splendid about an army of noble warriors holding out to the last man against the brutish Slav. He sensed the beginnings of a new national myth, a story that would have the power to inspire the German people for generations to come. He was certainly not about to let any sordid details – such as the filth, the hunger and the stench of Stalingrad – get in the way of that shining Nazi tableau.

One man who tried to puncture Hitler's daydream was General Zeitzler, the Army Chief of Staff. Having lost the tussle with Göring over the airlift, he now made a symbolic decision. In a courageous act of solidarity he put himself on a Stalingrad diet, refusing to eat any more than the ration received by the men of the Sixth Army.

Albert Speer, Hitler's architect and munitions minister, sneered at Zeitzler's attempt to make himself the conscience of the Wehrmacht. His brother was at Stalingrad, and his parents had begged him in vain

Plate 16. 'We covered our boat with green leaves, so that from the air it might look like an island. The Germans didn't see us, but one of the guncrews on the cutter lost its nerve and fired off a salvo. The planes turned full circle and started to drop their bombs randomly in the water.'

Plate 17. A formation of Yak-7 fighters goes into battle. The Yak-7 first saw action in the skies above Stalingrad during the summer of 1942. It was a more powerful version of the nimble Yak-1 – an aircraft which, in the hands of a good pilot, was a match for the feared German Me-109.

Plate 18. *At the start of Operation Uranus one German officer saw 'masses of Soviet tanks and waves of infantry in quantities never before seen'. Vasily Grossman described the onslaught as 'two hammers, one to the north and one to the south, each composed of millions of tons of metal and flesh.'*

Plate 19. *Uranus was a triumph for Andrei Yeremenko (right), commander of the Stalingrad Front. Here he is pictured with Nikita Khrushchev (left), the future Soviet leader who was at that time Stalin's 'Stavka representative'. Jointly they had appointed Chuikov to his command.*

Plate 20. *Some of the Russians' warlike rituals were suspended in the special conditions of Stalingrad: 'We never shouted "For Stalin and the Motherland" when we went in. It would only alert the enemy and put him on his guard. Much better to creep up close and attack out of the blue.'*

Plate 21. *Soviet propagandists made the most of the predicament of the Sixth Army. This cartoon was intended for the Russian public. Against the background of a map of the encirclement, Hitler is portrayed as a babushka who wails: 'I lost my ring – and there are twenty divisions in it!'*

Plate 22. *General Hoth led the tank force that was sent to break through to Paulus. In one of the final engagements of Operation Winter Storm, he hurled 60 tanks against Russian naval infantry – who fought in their striped vests to show their contempt for the cold and for the enemy.*

Plate 23. *Kurt Reuber sent this painting home with a wounded comrade. He included with it a last letter to his children. 'The Fortress Madonna is for you all,' he wrote. 'Mother can tell you how good it is if a person has a fortress inside him to keep him going when times are bad.'*

Plate 24. *'We're coming to the end and every one of us knows it,' wrote one desperate German soldier from the frozen Kessel. 'We're not allowed to surrender, so everything is falling apart. Even now it would be possible to save 200,000 of our comrades, but they're going to be sacrificed.'*

Plate 25. *The Russians were very adept at camouflage. In the Russian winter they used the white of the snow, the dark of the night, and the noise of the battle to hide their movements. Men such as Vasily Zaitsev (on the left), the star sniper of the 62nd Army, became true masters of the art.*

Plate 26. *German troops watch expectantly as a transport comes in to land. The supply chain was chaotic. On one occasion, two Junkers arrived with four tons of marjoram and pepper. 'Maybe we can use the pepper in hand-to-hand fighting,' said the rueful quartermaster.*

Plate 27. *Inside the Kessel, the unburied dead lay everywhere. A corpse was just a bump in the road. As the Russians closed in, loudspeakers blared the same looped message: 'Every seven seconds a German soldier dies at Stalingrad ... Stalingrad is a mass grave ... Every seven seconds ...'*

Plate 28. *The devastation of Stalingrad was so extensive that there were suggestions that the ruins be abandoned, or preserved as a monument, and a new city built elsewhere. German prisoners were put to work removing dead bodies and clearing mines as soon as the fighting stopped.*

Plate 29. *Paulus (left) on the day he became the first German field marshal ever to surrender to an enemy. In all, 22 generals were captured at Stalingrad. Right behind Paulus is his chief of staff, Arthur Schmidt, who remained an implacable Nazi throughout his years of captivity.*

Plate 30. *Barely a single building was left intact in Stalingrad, but almost 8,000 civilians were found still to be living in the ruins of the city at the end of the battle. Many of these survivors were traumatized, severely malnourished, or else sick as a result of eating dead cats and dogs.*

Plate 31. *German soldiers taken prisoner at Stalingrad became part of the vast gulag nation. They were all treated as criminals. Very few survived the long years in prison camps and the forced labour: only 5,000 or so of the 91,000 who surrendered ever made it back home.*

to use his influence with the Führer and get their younger son out, so there was a gnawing sense of guilt behind his scorn. 'The daily rations in Stalingrad have been cut back again,' wrote Speer. It was 5 January, and Zeitzler had been fasting for nearly two weeks.

> In the mess hall of the general staff Zeitzler – rather ostentatiously – would only be served those same rations. He visibly lost weight. Hitler informed him that he considers it unbecoming for the Chief of Staff to use up his strength on such gestures, and told Zeitzler to start eating properly again forthwith. At the same time Hitler decreed that for a few weeks no champagne or cognac were to be consumed.

The men at Stalingrad might have had their own ideas about which of these two gestures was unbecoming: Zeitzler's hunger strike, or Hitler's ban on bubbly. In the trenches and foxholes of the Kessel, hunger was now a more present and deadly enemy than Russian guns. The reduction in rations mentioned by Speer meant that each man was entitled to two slices of bread, a little horsemeat, half a beaker of coffee and one cigarette each day. Joseph Goebbels, the propaganda minister, remarked cynically in his diary that this was 'too little to live on, and too much to die from'. Some soldiers got a little more than the norm; others, isolated in forward positions or just lost amid the chaos of supply inside the Kessel, received rather less. But nobody got enough, and ordinary soldiers were now being completely frank in their letters home about the misery of it all.

> My dear parents, wrote corporal Bruno Kaligo. It's New Year's Eve. I am thinking of home and my heart is breaking. Here everything is terrible and hopeless. Hunger, hunger, hunger, lice and dirt. Soviet planes are bombing us day and night, and the artillery fire hardly ever ceases. If there is not a miracle very soon I shall die here. Sometimes I pray; sometimes I curse my fate. Everything just seems so

pointless and absurd. When and how could we be saved from this? How can a man bear this? Is this suffering a punishment from God?

My dear parents, I should not be writing you this, but I have long since lost all my courage. I have forgotten how to laugh. I am just a shivering bundle of nerves. Everybody lives here as if they are in a trance. If I get put up before a military tribunal and shot for writing this letter, then that will be a release from suffering. I have no hope left. I ask you not to cry if you get a letter saying that I have died. Be kind to each other and thank God for every day he gives you.

Mercifully perhaps, Kaligo's parents never received that letter. It was captured by the Russians and included in an intelligence report on German morale. This anonymous letter also fell into their hands:

Here we have learned the full meaning of God's word: give us this day our daily bread. I am getting 100 grams of bread a day – almost one slice. You cannot possibly imagine how that feels here, when the temperature is minus thirty-five.
Bread, bread, bread!

Horsemeat was the only source of protein. Quartermasters had husbanded the horses used by cavalry and horse-drawn artillery units, and slaughtered them according to a strict plan intended to make them last as long as possible. But they were half-starved already, and there was precious little meat on them. And once the 'official' horses had been consumed, soldiers took their meat where they could find it.

This evening we cooked up some horse again, wrote one soldier on New Year's Eve. You will have to imagine how it tastes, without salt or any other seasoning, and when the animal gave up the ghost a month ago and has been lying under the snow ever since. There are no other dainty little morsels to be had around here.

Some of these 'dainty morsels' had partly decomposed before the frosts came and preserved them. Nevertheless they were exhumed and eaten, and sometimes eaten raw. In these desperate circumstances, a recently killed horse was a valuable find.

> **Meat was being cut from horses lying in the street,** said
> sergeant Helmut Werner of the 16th Panzer Division.
> The daily ration for twelve men was one loaf of bread and a
> little watery soup. If you were really lucky you might find a
> single pea or a bit of noodle floating in it. To begin with no
> one wanted to eat horsemeat, but hunger is really painful,
> and so everyone devoured it. We looked like skeletons or
> walking corpses, some of us on a ration of just a handful
> of oats and a little water.

In January, six weeks after the encirclement, there was a spate of incidents in which German soldiers died for no apparent reason. Often they would go out on guard duty, and be found dead at their posts. The Army High Command decided to send a medical specialist from Berlin to look into this strange phenomenon.

> **So the pathologist arrived,** said Hans Dibold, an army
> doctor. The corpses were thawed out in an operation
> bunker: an earth hole lined and faced with boards.
> The autopsies were made. The findings were these: hardly
> a scrap of fatty tissue under the skin and around the
> internal organs, a water-jellyish content in the intestines,
> all the organs very pale, the bone marrow not red and
> yellow but a glassy, quivering jelly, the liver blocked, the
> heart small and brown, the right ventricle and auricle
> greatly enlarged. The distension of the right ventricle was
> deemed to be the immediate cause of death.
>   Immediately after the pathologist's visit the doctors of the
> division were called together to discuss the result of the
> autopsies. I made a report to this conference. In peacetime

we had found that weakness of the right ventricle was a common cause of sudden death in old people. Here, in Stalingrad, it caused death in the worn-out, prematurely senile bodies of German soldiers.

The doctor from Berlin was not the last visitor to the Kessel. In the middle of January a Luftwaffe officer was sent in to discuss the pathetically inadequate airlift with General Paulus. If he was expecting a businesslike talk about logistics, he was mistaken. What he got was an angry tirade about the realities of Kessel living. Here is a frank excerpt from the Luftwaffe's report.

A reliable officer and group commander of the Luftwaffe flies into the Kessel to make contact with the Commander-in-Chief of the Sixth Army, in order to discuss the critical supply situation. General Paulus and his Chief of Staff, Major-General Schmidt, are bluntly outspoken in describing the hopelessness of the situation. The commander-in-chief's words were to the effect that: If there are to be no more landings this spells the death of the army. And it's too late now anyway. Dropping supplies doesn't help at all. Many of the canisters aren't recovered, we don't have the fuel to collect them. The men are too weak to go searching. It's now four days since they've had anything to eat. The last of the horses have been eaten.

Can you imagine people flinging themselves at an old horse corpse, tearing open the head and swallowing its brain raw? What am I supposed to say when a man comes up to me and begs: 'Commander-in-chief, sir, a scrap of bread?'

THE LAST OF 1942

Christmas was an ordinary fighting day for the 62nd Army, but the Russian soldiers did have cause for celebration on the 25th. On that day, the six-week-long siege of Lyudnikov's Island in the Barricades Factory came to an end. Around this time Vladimir Sokolov, who had been on the Island throughout, came across a ragged little girl, about three years old, who was snuggled up to the dead body of her mother. One of Sokolov's colleagues, an older man, brought the girl to the command post of the 138th Division. None of the soldiers there had seen a child for months, and when the girl spoke, many of the Red Army men began to weep sympathetic tears. 'So far as I know,' said Sokolov, 'the girl was adopted by one of our officers.'

In the meantime, communications were re-established with the depleted, exhausted men of the 138th Rifle Division, and supplies began to move across the river. But as regimental quartermaster Vladimir Borisov found, the process was still fraught with danger.

In the winter it was still extremely difficult to guarantee supplies. The Germans remained in a position to fire on all approaches to the Volga, and to smash the ice on the river. From sundown and all through the night they would hang out 'lanterns' – parachute flares – and shoot at anything that was exposed by the light.

So supply was carried out by small groups of people using little sledges – that way there was very little noise. Everybody wore white overalls when they crossed the river. The best time to walk across was just before morning. True, you were dying to go to sleep, but the Germans were pretty dozy at that time of day too and so did not keep such careful watch. I remember one crossing when I was ordered to accompany a high-ranking officer across to our command post.

Since I knew the way, I went in front. I was keeping an eye out for the enemy. We were getting close to the right bank, and I was paying so much attention to the enemy's positions that I did not notice a hole in the ice made by a German mortar shell, and I fell straight in.

Some sort of preservation instinct made me stick my arms out to stop myself from going under. My comrades quickly pulled me out. Dripping wet and covered in icicles, I had to wait while my comrades ran on to the dead zone. If I had gone with them, the squelching and rustling might have alerted the Germans and got us all killed. As soon as they were under cover I ran to catch them up. I reached them safely: the Germans must have been sleeping soundly that night. As soon as we reached the command post I quickly got out of the wet clothes, someone gave me some vodka, and the regimental commander, Konovalenko, told me to get into his cot in the dugout to warm myself up.

Borisov was lucky to escape with his life. He would certainly have frozen to death within a few minutes had he been delayed or diverted on his way to the command post. As it was he survived to grapple with the budgetary problems faced by any bureaucratically minded front-line quartermaster: how do you keep tabs on death?

In spite of the dangers and difficulties, it was important at that time to maintain systematic links with the regiment and to keep strict accounts, otherwise it was easy to lose track and as a result find yourself short of supplies that the men needed to take into battle. All the more so as reinforcements usually went straight in: they would arrive in the evening, and by morning many of them were dead. So it was hard to keep any sort of inventory when you did not always see what kit they went in with, and when the official record books always said they were issued with a complete uniform.

Borisov was doubtless poring over his books at New Year, when another short and peaceful hiatus – like the accidental Christmas lull – descended on Stalingrad. For the Russians this was a special day, not just because New Year was the only non-political public holiday in the Soviet calendar (no martial music and Kremlin speeches, just family and feasting) but also because it was now clear that the battle for Stalingrad was nearing its conclusion. They already knew they were going to win.

So New Year 1943 was a memorable night in Stalingrad. Valentin Orlyankin, the newspaper photographer whose black camera had made him a target on the ice, was invited to a party by one of the young officers in the 13th Guards Division. Since the officer was in command of a forward machinegun unit, just to respond to the invitation was a life-threatening undertaking.

My friend, press photographer Grisha Zelma, went with me to mark the holiday with the soldiers under Lieutenant Linnik. It was evening. We made our way stealthily to the lieutenant's dugout. There was half-hearted shooting from both sides: it was New Year for them as well as us, after all, and no one really wanted to fight.

We tumbled into a cosy, homely dugout, where a samovar with an amusing little teapot on top was already boiling away. It was warm. There were rugs on the walls, and on a table there shone a 'front-line lamp' made of a shell case. Everyone had contributed some titbits, put by from their rations. We had brought some mutton soup. Linnik and his soldiers, freed from having to keep watch, were in a festive mood.

Now and then we could hear the muffled sounds of salvoes from one of our machineguns, which was set up behind the dugout, in a gap in the ruined wall of a house. Amid all the chatter, midnight crept up on us unawares. We poured some more mugs of wine.

The host was just about to propose a toast when suddenly, from both sides, there burst out a blaze of machinegun fire. We leapt out of the dugout, leaving the wine on the table. It was dark here, there was nothing for my camera to do, so I set about loading the cartridge belts with ammo. In the embrasure made in the wall of the house, a stream of gunfire poured from our Maxim gun, banging away at the German dugouts and trenches that were situated around seventy metres away from us. The shooting stopped as suddenly as it had started. There were no losses on our side, nor, probably, on the Germans'. It had been nothing more than a New Year salute among enemies, random fire, a mutual greeting.

Similar congratulations were exchanged in many parts of the front. In some places the Germans were observed to shoot tracer bullets vertically into the air along the line of the forward trenches. The effect was a kind of cascade of light the length of the line, an improvised firework display for men who had long since become inured to the sound of war. Once the trivial nature of the gunfire in his sector became clear, Orlyankin and his hosts returned to the party.

We went back to our mugs of wine. We didn't celebrate for long – there was still a war on, after all. We talked of our families far away, wished each other health and happiness, and then Zelma and I got up to return to our trench quarters closer to the bank of the Volga.

'Stop, cameraman!' Linnik suddenly said to me, 'You've earned a trophy. Here, take it!' and he held out a violin-case. 'You're an artist, you can put it to good use. It's in danger here, so let it sing and tell tales of us, the men of Stalingrad!' I was grateful to the lieutenant and moved by the gift. I didn't stop to ask how such a noble thing had ended up in such an unsuitable place. I took the gift back to my dugout.

I didn't even know how to play the violin, but I kept it with me as a keepsake of New Year 1943 in Stalingrad. And this mute instrument travelled with me for a long time on the roads of the front, perhaps waiting for its time to come, for someone's skilled hands to tease from it sounds that would be worthy of what this violin had heard and seen in Stalingrad.

On the German side, inside Fortress Stalingrad, the young corporal Werner R—— had survived another week. As the new year rolled in he was in less optimistic mood than at Christmas, when he had been so soothed by the sight of the peaceable moon. 'The last hours of this year are slowly ticking away into eternity,' he wrote to a distant friend:

> As the year comes to an end it's customary to look back, and the more difficult the situation in which one finds oneself, the more urgent is the review. The typical Landser reaction is just to say 'to hell with it all'. There's absolutely nothing I can do to influence the situation I'm in. But I hope that one day I'll have a life of my own again. Meanwhile, I'm playing hide-and-seek with destiny. Yes, I have the feeling that life is just a gamble, no matter how worthwhile it is to live it.
>
> I probably shouldn't be writing to you now, for we're really not in a good way. I'm referring to danger from the enemy. Yet I don't have to tell you, do I, that in these last hours of the bygone year in my heart I'm with you? Totally!
>
> I'll be on guard duty from 12 till 1 in the first hour of this New Year. I'll keep my thoughts about this hour for a fresh sheet of paper.

Werner continued his letter the next day, but in the cold light of morning he was more preoccupied with the workaday business of the fight than with the meaning of his own existence.

> Yesterday the Reds launched an assault which was meant to get them back into Stalingrad before the old year was out. By way of reply, our old hymn 'Now thank we all our God' rang out at midnight to greet the Russians across the Volga, where the Bolshevik loudspeaker was tastelessly blaring out 'Dawn, dawn, and still no bread ...' This is no way to trap any of the Landsers whose haggard faces now resemble the faces of those soldiers from the last war, the faces that stare out from many photos. The German soldiers' response to the pathetic leaflets inviting them to give up their pointless resistance is a midnight fire display, sending the Reds the message that their propaganda will make no impression.

The Russians will be trying to use the winter again to subject us to a 'Napoleonic fate', which they didn't succeed in doing last year. I hope and believe, and I'm making it a New Year wish now, that the battle for our position here may be absolutely crucial in bringing the war to an end. The Russian posters are virtually inviting German officers to surrender, saying there's no more holding out against the 'Red Ring' (Wagner!) of the Red Army. That just makes us wonder: well, why don't you come and burst our balloon?

LAST CHANCE TO SURRENDER

The Russians had every intention of bursting the Germans' balloon, of puncturing the Kessel and reducing it to nothing. Plans were already in train for a new offensive that had as its goal the total annihilation of the Sixth Army. This, the final phase of the battle of Stalingrad, was given the transparent designation Operation Ring.

But first the Russians intended to give the Germans an opportunity to surrender, hence the propaganda leaflets that had looked to Corporal Werner R— like a pathetic bluff. The mass leafleting from the air was now to be followed with a formal approach to the German commanders. Semyon Ozerinsky was a battalion commander involved in the tricky task of organizing the delivery of a letter.

The Chief of Reconnaissance, Ilya Vinogradov, went to see the Chief of Staff of the front, General Malinin, with a proposal that envoys be sent to the encircled group of Germans with an ultimatum to surrender. Malinin listened attentively to Vinogradov, as did General Sergei Galadzhev, the head of the Political Department of the Stalingrad Front, who was there with him at the time. They discussed the matter among themselves, and took the preliminary decision to approve the idea in principle and immediately notify General Voronov, who along with his staff was based in the same village. Galadzhev assumed responsibility for drafting the ultimatum.

The document that Galadzhev prepared was a judicious mix of threats and promises – what the Russians call *knut i pryanik* ('whip and gingerbread'). In this instance the whip was the prospect of a crushing offensive against the starving army; the gingerbread was an assurance that prisoners would be decently treated.

But the document began with a pitiless assessment of the Germans' present situation:

> To the Commander of the Sixth Army encircled at
> Stalingrad, General Paulus, or his deputy.
> The Sixth German Army, the units of the 4th Tank
> Army and their reinforcements have been completely
> surrounded since November 23rd, 1942. The forces of the
> Red Army have drawn a secure ring around this German
> army. All hopes of rescue by means of a German offensive
> from the south and south-west have proved unfounded.
> The forces which were rushed to your aid have been
> destroyed by the Red Army, and the remnants of these
> forces are withdrawing towards Rostov. The German
> transport planes which are supplying you with a bare
> minimum of food, ammunition and fuel are being forced to
> move between airfields, and to fly from great distances to
> reach your positions. Moreover, the Russian air force is
> inflicting great losses on German transport planes and their
> crews. Air transport is unlikely to continue for much longer.
> Your encircled troops are in a grave situation. They are
> suffering from hunger, sickness and cold. The harsh
> Russian winter is only just beginning: hard frosts,
> cold winds and snowstorms are still to come, but your
> soldiers do not have winter uniforms and are living in
> unsanitary conditions.
> You, as commander, and all the officers of the surrounded
> troops know very well that there is no longer any realistic
> possibility of breaking through the encirclement. Your
> position is hopeless and further resistance is pointless.

After this came the Russians' two-point demand, followed by the carefully worded 'gingerbread':

> Given the inescapable position that your forces now
> find themselves in, and in order to avoid unnecessary
> bloodshed, we propose that you accept the following
> terms of surrender:
>   1. All surrounded German troops, with you and your staff,
> are to give up further resistance.
>   2. You are to hand over to us, in an orderly fashion and
> intact, all men, arms, weaponry and army property.
>   We guarantee the lives and the safety of all officers,
> non-commissioned officers and men who cease resistance.
> We also guarantee that at the end of the war they will be
> returned to Germany, or to any other country of their choice.
>   All surrendering forces will be allowed to keep their
> uniform, insignia and decorations, along with their
> personal belongings and valuables. High-ranking officers
> will be allowed to retain their service daggers.
>   All officers, non-commissioned officers and men who
> surrender will immediately be issued with normal rations.
> All those suffering from wounds, illness or frostbite will
> receive medical attention.
>   We expect your written reply on January 9th, 1943, at
> 15.00 hours, Moscow time. It should be brought by a
> representative whom you have personally appointed, and
> who should proceed in a car flying a white flag along the
> road from the Konny railway halt to the Kotluban station.
> Your representative will be met by Russian officers in
> Region B, 0.5 kilometres south-east of railway halt No. 564.

Then, finally and brutally, the threat of the whip:

> If you choose to reject our proposal for your capitulation,
> be warned that the forces of the Red Army and the Red Air

Force will be compelled to take steps to destroy the surrounded German troops, and that you will bear the responsibility for their annihilation.

Signed, Colonel-General of Artillery, Voronov; Supreme Commander of the Don Front, Lieutenant-General Rokossovsky.

The wording of the document met with the approval of the Soviet commanders. It certainly looked like an offer that Paulus could not refuse. But there remained the tricky problem of how to deliver it to him. Any envoy was likely to be shot on sight, long before he had a chance to ask for a parley. And in any case, nobody on the Russian side knew the etiquette of such things: how, in the midst of total war, do you declare a truce?

Colonel Vinogradov declared his willingness to be the postman, but it was thought that, as head of reconnaissance, he knew too much to risk his being killed or (even worse from an operational point of view) captured by the Germans. Instead he was ordered to find some lower-ranking officers to do the job.

Out of the large number of volunteers, Major Alexander Smyslov was chosen to head the group of envoys, said Semyon Ozerinsky. This seasoned soldier combined all the qualities required for such a responsible and dangerous mission. He was well-liked by all the staff at the front. He was a somewhat shy, reserved, laconic and composed man, good-looking, well proportioned and smartly dressed. In his brown eyes there sparkled an exceptional intellect, and his determined Russian face reflected the confidence of a man who knew exactly what he was doing. An indefatigable scout, he knew all about all the commanders of the enemy grouping, right down to the commanders of the smallest sub-units, and had a good command of German.

On the night of January 7th, our wireless stations broadcast an address to the command of the surrounded troops several times, informing them of the time and place of the envoys' crossing and demanding that they do not launch any military operations, that they cease firing, and that they send some of their officers out to meet our envoys.

Smyslov, who belonged to army intelligence, was to be accompanied on the mission by an NKVD man, a young captain named Nikolai Dyatlenko.

At dawn on the 8th our envoys went out past our front line into the 'neutral zone', along a path through a minefield that had been cleared by the sappers, said Ozerinsky. At first everything was quiet, and the envoys continued moving forwards with a white flag without encountering any officers from the German side. But then the enemy's front line gradually started shooting – first single shots, then sub-machinegun salvoes – and our lads had to dodge the bullets and lie down. Two bullets went through Smyslov's hat. True to form, the fascists were behaving like scum.

Despite repeated calls to cease fire from the loudhailers on the propaganda trucks, the enemy carried on firing. As soon as our lads stood up, the Germans would start shooting again. The envoys lay there for several hours, pinned to the ground on top of a sharp frost. Vinogradov, who had observed the whole event through a stereoscopic telescope from a trench at a combat outpost, sent two soldiers out with orders to get the envoys to the safety of a ravine seventy or eighty metres to the left of where they were lying. This they managed to do, but now instead of single shots the enemy started firing shells at our front line.

Colonel Vinogradov decided to get the envoys out of the line of fire and terminate the operation. Exhausted, frozen, dispirited by their brush with death, and frustrated by the failure of their mission, the envoys and the support team returned to the command post of the front headquarters.

We knew about the Germans' habits and were not
surprised by their hospitality, but no one thought that in
their hopeless situation they would reject the favourable
surrender terms and opt instead for suicide. The failure
did not shake our determination to repeat the attempt at
persuading the fascists to give in. The wireless station of the
front headquarters sent another message to von Paulus
calling on him to surrender, and indicating a new route.

In the space of a few hours the front's Political
Department produced ten thousand leaflets, which were
then dropped onto the German positions from aircraft.
The leaflets gave the surrender terms but also highlighted
the treachery of the German command in recklessly
condemning tens of thousands of soldiers to a certain death.
The leaflets called on the German soldiers to cease resistance
and give themselves up. Dozens of propaganda trucks
broadcast the same message across the whole front line.

After this psychological softening up, the Russians tried again to
deliver their letter. Smyslov and Dyatlenko were informed at breakfast
that they had been awarded the Order of the Red Star for their work
the previous day. They were also told that they had now done enough,
that other volunteers could be found for the second attempt. But
Smyslov and Dyatlenko were loath to let anyone else take on the job.

Despite their exhaustion and the nerve-racking experience
of the first attack, they begged to be entrusted once again
with this trip, continued Ozerinsky. This time around, it was
decided to cross the front line at a point near the village of
Marinovka, in the zone of the 21st Army. A bugler was
added to Smyslov and Dyatlenko's group. He was First
Lieutenant Sidorov, a bandmaster from the 96th Rifle
Division, which was defending the sector in which our
representatives were to cross over on that frosty morning
of January 9th.

Smyslov, carrying a letter sealed with many seals, Dyatlenko, bearing an unfurled white flag, and Sidorov, continuously blowing trumpet-calls on his bugle, climbed out of the trench and began their second procession to the fascists' camp. Vinogradov, along with a large retinue of assistants (including myself), nervously tracked the three of them through binoculars from their trenches as they made their way towards the enemy.

So far, everything was going according to plan. This time, not a single shot was fired from the enemy side. More and more enemy soldiers started popping their heads over the tops of their trenches, watching our envoys.

When they reached the open battlefield a ground blizzard was in full swirl. The whole battlefield was strewn with shell cases and spent cartridges – mute witnesses to fierce and bloody battles. Vinogradov picked a smashed tank to be his 'observation post', and climbed inside it to get a better view.

But soon the envoys disappeared out of sight. The three Russians were now on the far side of no-man's-land, in German-held territory. Captain Dyatlenko picks up the story.

Junior German officers approached us and asked in a bitter tone of voice: 'What do you want?' We replied: 'We are envoys, official representatives of the Soviet command, here to hand over a letter to your commander-in-chief, and we therefore request that you take us to him.' They then asked us to hand the letter over to them, which we categorically refused to do, since the letter had to be handed in person to Paulus or to a general of his staff.

They conferred amongst themselves for a while, and then proposed that we hand over our pistols and that they blindfold us. We agreed to the proposal. Luckily we had brought blindfolds with us in our pockets, and so avoided being blindfolded with dirty rags.

We were led by the hand and taken somewhere down in the ravine. We could feel ice beneath our feet, and were obviously walking along the floor of the ravine. Then we started going up a steep bank, falling over several times, and after a tiring journey we finally reached a dugout. They removed our blindfolds.

There were several senior officers there. This was clearly the observation post of the German divisional commander. The officers talked to their superiors over the telephone and scurried back and forth; this went on for several hours. Finally, we were informed that the division commander had spoken with Paulus, and that he knew the content of the letter from Soviet radio messages and refused to surrender. Smyslov then demanded that the division commander officially sign a letter on behalf of Paulus, stating that the ultimatum was rejected, but this demand too was turned down.

We were then blindfolded and led back the same way as we had come to the point on the front line from where, that morning, we had set out in the hope of accomplishing something worthwhile: hastening the end of hostilities in that sector of the front.

When we reached the place where the officers of the two sides had met that morning, the Germans removed our blindfolds, gave us back our pistols, and told us to walk forwards without turning round. That was one agonizing, nerve-racking walk.

No further word was received from Paulus within the deadline. By his silence, the German commander-in-chief condemned his army to another month of agony.

8
OPERATION RING

There was never the slightest chance that Paulus would agree to the Russian surrender terms. He believed in Hitler, and perhaps he still had faith that the Führer might find some way to turn the situation around. From a military point of view, he could tell himself that by tying up Russian forces here on the Volga he was aiding the withdrawal of the rest of the German armies in the south. And in the end, he had an absolute personal commitment to the idea that a soldier should do as he is told. '*Ich stehe hier auf Befehl,*' he wrote laconically to his wife in his last letter from the Kessel: 'I'm here because I'm ordered to be.' Paulus needed no other justification for his actions.

Operation Ring began the day after the second parley attempt. It was a freezing, bitter Sunday. The Germans seemed to be holding their breath, steeling themselves as they waited for the blow to fall.

The morning of the tenth of January was a cold one, wrote one Russian officer. The wind was whipping up into a blizzard. Everything was ready. In the fascists' camp there was a deathly, oppressive silence. No wailing from the German six-barrel mortars, no crackling of machineguns. It was as if the enemy was hiding, waiting for death to come. They knew from our leaflets, and from the warnings that had been blasting out from the propaganda trucks for the past three days, that they were about to be dealt a killer blow.

At 08.00 came the preliminary commands 'In position!' and 'Set watches!', followed after a brief pause by signals over the radio and telephone giving the command 'Ready

fuses!' and, finally, at 08.05, the command 'Fire!'
For 55 minutes, a tornado of fire raged over the German
trenches. The enemy was pounded by seven thousand
guns and mortars.

At 09.00 the infantry went in to the sound of the
'Internationale' with their regimental standards unfurled.

The Kessel was attacked from all directions at once: the 57th and 64th
Russian Armies went to it from the south, the 65th, 24th and 66th
Armies from the north. Chuikov's 62nd Army maintained its terrier-
like grip on the Germans at the eastern side of the Kessel, in the
howling ruins of Stalingrad itself. From the west came the hardest
blow of all, from General Chistyakov's 21st Army out on the open
steppe. This part of the offensive was directed against the protuberance
of the Kessel known as the 'Marinovka Nose'.

The aim was to smash through the defences on the outer rim and
drive towards Pitomnik, the airfield in the dead centre of the Kessel.
To capture Pitomnik would be to stab at the heart of the German
Sixth Army, because it would make it well nigh impossible for the
airlift to continue. Here too was the main hospital, along with the
nerve centre of communication for the Germans and, under tarpaulins
and armed guard, the last supplies of food and ammunition.
If Chistyakov's men could take Pitomnik then push on into the city,
they would cleave the Kessel in two like a clean knife slicing through
a rotting apple.

The German forces were in a catastrophic position, said
Matvei Kidryanov, an intelligence officer with the 21st Army.
Transport planes were dropping provisions, munitions and
fuel. But recently they had been dropping them ever more
frequently right into our laps, as we knew all the ground
signals that told the planes where to drop their cargo, and
we were making good use of this knowledge.

A group of German transport planes appeared above the
observation post, protected by fighter planes. They circled

OPERATION RING

ANNIHILATION OF THE SIXTH ARMY

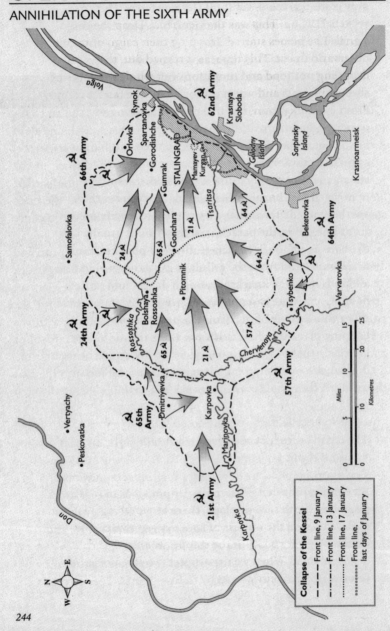

Collapse of the Kessel
- – – – Front line, 9 January
- –·–·– Front line, 13 January
- ·········· Front line, 17 January
- ░░░░░░░░ Front line, last days of January

above the steppe like kites, searching for their troops. True, only yesterday there were still Germans here. Our orange rockets flew up. This was the Germans' 'Drop the cargo!' signal. The planes started dropping their cargo onto our observation post. This time, as it turned out, they were dropping not food and munitions but whole packages of sheepskin coats and warm uniforms for the fascist troops. From every direction, our troops were running out to the packages and dismantling them.

No sooner had the planes dropped their cargo than our anti-aircraft gunners started shooting at them. Several enemy planes were shot down. The soldiers would run up to downed and burning German planes to see if there was anything inside them that they could use for life on the front line. From the parachutes, they would usually sew themselves camouflage jackets, tobacco pouches, even underwear. And from the celluloid glass they would make all kinds of knick-knacks: beautiful dagger and knife handles, cigarette cases, pipes, cigarette-holders, and many other things. One of our scouts, Zhezhera, ran up to a burning plane that had fallen not far from us. A little later he returned with his booty. Bathed in sweat, he was dragging the remains of a burnt parachute, the pistols of the dead crew, and some fragments of plastic.

Three days after the start of Operation Ring, Kidryanov's forward unit was closing in on its first objective – when suddenly it happened upon a mysterious sight.

We were approaching Pitomnik. Up ahead of us, in the middle of the deserted steppe, there appeared against the night darkness the outline of some large town that was not on the map. 'It's a city in the steppe', someone said, 'It's like Serafimovich!' When we drew closer, we saw a mass of vehicles: it was a city of cars.

The Germans had abandoned around 5,000 vehicles here. They were parked in orderly rows according to their make, and from a distance they looked like a town with many streets. There were covered trucks, repair trucks, armoured personnel-carriers, tanks, light vehicles, Opels of every type. The witty lance-corporal Zhezhera said to me: 'Comrade Lieutenant-Colonel! There's every make of car here: Opel 'Captains', Opel 'Admirals'. The only one missing is the Opel 'Corporal', so I guess Corporal Zhezhera will have to fight on foot!'

The following morning there began a kind of pilgrimage to the city of cars. Our men started stripping the cars for spares, or taking the tyres. The drivers went about this task with particular zeal. The city of vehicles gradually started thinning out. A lot of dodgy characters showed up from various different units. They picked vehicles and drove them away. Army booty details turned up to make an inventory of the vehicles, but they arrived too late. All the good vehicles had already been taken by combat units.

Outside Stalingrad nearly all the officers, right down to the platoon commander, and in some cases even sergeants with their scouts and signallers, were driving around in captured vehicles. Only once the fascist forces had been routed were all the non-regulation vehicles handed over to the army booty depots.

There were still plenty of Russian fighters doing their job without the benefit of personal transport. For the mass of infantry, Operation Ring was a seemingly endless succession of route marches punctuated by vicious skirmishes. The walking was almost a greater hardship than the fighting.

Our battalion was ready to advance as soon as we received the order to break through, said a sergeant Kudryavtsev. There was no transport of any kind, the conditions were difficult, we made only short halts, and our provisions had run out. Night came, it was snowing and raining, and everyone, officers and soldiers alike, was encrusted in a freezing rind of ice. The command to halt was given, but no one could get to sleep beneath the rain and sleet. The night passed in the gloomy wood. Early in the morning the battalion moved out. Day was already breaking, and we wanted to eat, but there was no food, nor any command to halt. We were exhausted, and those who were starting to slow down held on to the carts so as not to be left behind.

Every weary soldier was feeling the sting of the frost. Nothing could be discerned of the Stalingrad steppe – just snow and more snow, blending into one with the horizon. However tired we were on the march, we had to keep going and hold out against the frost and the fierce winter. After a long march, we slept a deep sleep on the steppe of Stalingrad, in the open air, on snow and frost, and the next morning we got up, and there was ice underneath every one of us. But no one so much as coughed, no one had frozen to death or even got frostbitten. What willpower the Russian soldier has, what endurance and steadfastness! This is the secret of his victories.

The secret was not so much steadfastness as good supply and iron discipline. The Russian forces were all dressed in warm winter uniform consisting of quilted jacket and trousers, fur hat and felt boots. They all knew how to wind footcloths so as to protect the toes from cold (woollen socks were seen as an oddity by the Russians). Consequently, frostbite was practically unknown among Russian soldiers, and when it did occur it was treated as a punishable offence because it was so obviously preventable. In the German ranks, by contrast, frostbite was almost universal.

By 14 January Russian tanks and mobile artillery were within striking distance of Pitomnik, which was already under almost constant bombardment from the air. The Germans were reeling back towards the city in utter disarray, just as the Russians had done the previous August. Sergeant-Major Wallrawe was in one of the infantry units that felt the Russian fist to the Marinovka Nose. He was a tankman with the 16th Panzer Division, but had been transferred to infantry duties. For three days he had been pulling back, trying to do his part to keep the retreat orderly. His unit had withdrawn to the village of Karpovka. Wallrawe was defending the railway station when a Russian rifleman gifted him a ticket home.

> I was wounded with a Russian bullet right through the stomach. With utter disregard for their own safety, Corporals Klaus and Ranz dragged me two kilometres on a strip of canvas. I was loaded on to a lorry along with several other wounded and taken towards the airfield. When we were still three kilometres away from our destination we ran out of petrol. Orders were given for the vehicle to be blown up. The wounded were left to their fate.
>
> I crawled the rest of the way. Meanwhile night had fallen. I received first-aid inside a large tent. Several tents for wounded were hit or swept away in a hail of bombs from Russian aircraft. At 03.00 in the morning I was flown out of the Kessel in a Junkers. On that day the enemy was only 12 kilometres away.

Wallrawe was told that he survived the perforation of his stomach only because he had eaten nothing for the past six days. His life was saved by hunger. That is something he must have thought of often as he recuperated in a safe hospital bed.

Hordes of other Germans, wounded or merely crippled with famine, were meanwhile gathering at the airfield, desperate to win the right to be evacuated before the Russians arrived. Many thousands more were on the open road, where the temperature was around 35 degrees below zero.

Alexander Dohna-Schlobbiten, an East Prussian officer of impeccably aristocratic descent, was ordered to accompany General

Hube on a visit to the front line. Though Dohna was old enough to have fought in World War I, he had never seen anything to compare with the horror now unfolding before his eyes.

> It was the most profoundly shocking thing I have seen in
> my life. On the short drive to the front line there was an
> endless train of retreating soldiers, all of them streaming
> towards us. They had no weapons, often no shoes. Their feet
> wrapped in rags, their emaciated faces encrusted with ice,
> suffering from their wounds, they dragged themselves
> deeper into the Kessel. At the edge of the road lay the dead
> and dying. I saw people crawling on their knees because
> their feet were entirely consumed by frostbite.

Among this crowd was Raimund Beyer, who in November had been one of the last to enter the Kessel, and was now about to become one of the few to get out. He had been shot in both legs, but made it to the airfield. Yet before he could receive an official pass to be flown out he had first to be examined by a doctor, to check his injuries were genuine and that they conclusively put him out of the fray. 'In my case the examination was over very quickly,' he said. 'Age, high blood pressure and two heavily bleeding leg wounds seemed to have tipped the balance. I still remember his exact words as the doctor said to me softly, perhaps enviously: "Send my greetings to the homeland."'

Now Beyer and the hundreds of other stretcher cases waited for a plane to emerge like an angel of salvation from the freezing fog.

> I was driven to the airfield, that is, to one of the miserable
> barracks that were dotted about. There were military police
> all around, but not at all unpleasant, actually giving us a
> feeling of security, mingled with the feeling that this might
> be the first step towards being flown out. They followed
> every movement of those lying stretched out. But not for
> medical reasons, but to make sure that no unauthorized
> soldiers smuggled themselves in.

We lay in the barracks and waited. Night fell. We were arranged in rows in three groups, but in such a way that you could talk to those in the group lying directly behind you. All sorts of rumours were flying. At first I just listened, but then I stopped even doing that. All that concerned me was that I was lying in the first row, so that I could count on being on the first flight out. Then I dozed off again. Soon people stopped talking to each other.

Some were crouching, if they only had wounds in their arms or the like. The night dragged to an end. No plane arrived, three were scheduled. It got steadily colder. Weak tea and a crumb of bread did nothing to warm us up. At last the first plane arrived, landed, was unloaded and medical orderlies with three or four stretchers began loading the first row of those waiting as well as the few able to walk. Then suddenly out of the line waiting for the third plane, my old mate Leo Goschka, a real rough and ready Berliner, came hobbling over to me and called out: 'Raimund, Raimund, stay where you are, we've always been together,' and turning to the military police who'd rushed forward: 'Let me come along, I want to go with this lot.' But they instantly began to fend him off with the butts of their guns, thinking this was someone who was trying to fiddle his way in or jump the queue.

I called out to one of the military policeman. 'Look, I'll stay, and let someone else waiting for the third plane go. I'll change places with him and stay with my pal.' The man nodded and waved to two bearers who immediately carried me back. To avoid trouble, and so as not hold things up, he simply allowed the man lying next to Goschka to be brought forward. It was all done at top speed and the good old Ju took off with about 15 men.

It leaves a bitter taste to see others being flown out of the Kessel while you're left to wait, unsure whether another plane will arrive. All eyes were fixed on the flight approach, that is in the direction from which the first rescuing 'King's horseman' had come. Then – it was already getting light – two came almost at the same time. Some of the men quietly called out 'There they are'. Others deliberately kept quiet, shivering with anxiety as to whether it would be their turn now. Things went even faster this time, and soon I was lying in the third plane, beside Leo Goschka. He lay down next to me.

I said something to Leo. Then the pilot half-turned his head and called out 'That's someone from Nuremberg, I can tell by your accent.' I told him I was born right on the market square, opposite the Schöner Brunnen. He answered: 'And I was born on the Förther.' And immediately after that he said: 'Here, this is for you.'

It was a loaf of bread, like the ones we were given by the slice in the Kessel. A corporal cowering in the corner now barged over to me, snatched the loaf of bread from me, hugged it to his chest, and forced his way back to his corner. He began to tear the bread apart like a madman, ripping hunks off and chewing. At the same time he was warding off several other hands that stretched out towards the loaf, long thin arms leaning over begging for some. He gobbled and gobbled. I was so taken by surprise that I couldn't say a word and just indicated my displeasure with several dismissive waves of the hand. But nobody noticed. Everyone was so shocked that silence fell. After a short while the fury of those who'd lost out blew over, as the glutton who had wolfed down the bread now started getting stomach cramps and was rolling about and screaming and writhing. He was carried out dead from the plane when it landed.

Russian tanks overran Pitomnik airfield on 15 January, just as the selfish corporal was eating the last meal of his life. Many hundreds of Germans, including the helpless wounded, were killed in the attack on the airfield. Anybody who could walk or crawl now tried to escape to the east, towards the smaller airfield at Gumrak, which was just outside the city.

One soldier highlighted the surreal absurdity of this new retreat, which took him and his comrades deeper into the enemy's country: He said : 'This flight wasn't towards the homeland – by which we meant the old homeland – but further away in the opposite direction. The line from the song 'Long is the road back to the native land ...' just didn't apply. Backwards and forwards formed a dialectical unity – backwards meant eastwards, in other words forwards.'

A crazy, ragged caravan of German soldiery shuffled towards Stalin's city. The doctor Hans Dibold joined the traffic when his field hospital came under attack from the west. It was a nightmare journey that ended for him with a kind of glimpse of the apocalypse.

We had put on a few dressings when Grosch and Bellowitsch came up with their ambulances; the bodies were shot away, but the engines and chassis were still whole. Bellowitsch, always serious, calmly asked: 'Where to?'

'To Gumrak.'

Bellowitsch was a Viennese workman. He had saved many hundreds of soldiers, had driven them through fire and enemy troops to the dressing station, and had had no qualms about pointing his gun at a German officer who tried to stop him. Nor was he at a loss for an answer when a hospital doctor snarled at him one night: 'Why didn't you bring in the wounded earlier?' 'Beg to report, sir, that they were not wounded any earlier.'

Under Russian rifle-fire from thirty paces and despite two shot-up tyres, Bellowitsch turned his ambulance round in the bog and brought the wounded – head and abdominal cases – safely back. And so he drove this time too.

He, Grosch, and Strohbach came once more into Stalingrad to get their last orders. I never saw them again, never shall see them, and shall never forget them.

When the ambulances had driven off I stood freezing in front of the bunker. An orderly hastened up: 'Come quickly to Major X.' He resided some hundred yards or so away, but I had never been to him, he had always come to us. I went in. A shell splinter had shattered the window and split open the knee of a fair-haired Russian girl who was sitting on a bunk. Her trouser leg was in shreds, the knee-cap gleamed like ivory, fluid was dripping from the wound, and the thighbone gaped through. The woman whimpered as she nursed her white thigh. I put it in splints and bandaged it as best I could, and had no time to wonder where this woman had come from.

After a night spent between Pitomnik and Bolshaya Rossoshka we occupied quarters in one of the many so-called 'death ravines'. Russian infantry advanced towards us slowly over the undulating ground to the west and north-west. Late in the afternoon things grew quieter. During the night I was to get the last wounded out of Bolshaya Rossoshka. From an enormous derelict barn we picked up all who were left, while the divisional doctor Andreesen nervously paced to and fro, and the usual Russian plane dropped its flares and small bombs. On the way back I was asked to take an anti-tank gun in tow. I refused, saying: 'I've got wounded on board.' Then the diesel truck got stuck in the snow. Tanks and assault guns passed us, going eastward. 'We've got wounded inside.' No one would take us along.

Our driver went off to get a tractor from a nearby unit. Meanwhile I remained in his cab and wrestled with sleep, for the night was very cold, the temperature being down to around minus twenty-five degrees. The wounded lay together under the awning and were in tolerable shape, but I had to climb out to avoid falling asleep. Then my feet began to burn like fire, for my boot soles were full of ice. So I climbed in again and wrestled with sleep, climbed out, could stand it no longer, climbed in and so on until our driver came with a small tractor, which hauled the truck free, and we went on to Gumrak.

At Gumrak station, outside Stalingrad, a great assembly point for the wounded had been set up. The streets were overcrowded, anyone who could move at all was making his way to the assembly point. Others were lying along the edges of the road and against rubbish heaps. As soon as they got up, the whistle of bombs and the rattle of stones sent them crouching down again.

I forced my way through to the assembly point. Our wounded men asked to be allowed to stay. We unloaded them, and they joined the hundreds of their fellow sufferers along the edges of the road. A few more were flown out from Gumrak after that.

Dibold now drove on towards Stalingrad. He knew there was a medical team, the First Company of the Medical Corps, established in a balka close to the city.

We arrived, frozen to the bone and feeling rather sorry for ourselves at the First Company ravine, entered a light and warm bunker, and were delighted to learn that there was to be horseflesh for lunch, for the First Company had been 'mounted'.

Clean plates, knives and forks added to the amenities. Here there was an air almost of formality. The active service men sat bolt upright and ate with decorum, but I leaned rather wearily against the earthen bank under the bunker window. The last to arrive was the senior surgeon, an elderly Berlin ear specialist. I have forgotten his name, but I still remember the photographs of his children. We enjoyed the warmth, and the hot food, which we hadn't had for a long time, and felt secure among our comrades.

There was a sudden whine of steel. The Berlin specialist sank back into his neighbour's arms. It was the senior physician, Zwack, who now held him as a mother holds her child. A bomb fragment had trepanned him cleanly right across the top of his cranium above the eyebrow. The upper part of his skull hung down behind, over the limp neck, and a thick stream of bluish-red blood slowly oozed out of the large blood vessels. The brain had spattered our clothes with fine grey sprinkles. 'Poor fellow!' Zwack said softly.

My chief's face took on a greenish pallor, he gasped for air and cried: 'I'm choking!' A transverse blow had knocked in several of his ribs. Oxygen and caffeine eased his breathing. That was his fourth wound, and the third since the encirclement. We managed to fly him out, together with another man who had already lost one eye and now was wounded in the other. Of the eight people in that bunker, only Zwack and I escaped uninjured.

I had to go back to the 'death ravine', and I looked around for my Volkswagen. Great caverns had been dug into the left-hand slope of the ravine. They had been stables for horses, but the animals had all been killed and eaten. These bunkers were now being used to accommodate seriously wounded cases. There was no hope for them.

I stepped out of the twilight of the bunker and walked towards the mouth of the ravine. The ground was littered with wreckage. I attempted to raise my eyes. Before me rose the dome of a white hillock. On that hillock stood three large slender crosses, marking the military cemetery. As I looked they seemed to tower endlessly into the clear grey sky; they were gently quivering as though alive.

That place was no longer Gonchara. The place where crosses are alive is Golgotha: the end.

By 19 January the Kessel had been reduced to half its original size. The dead of the Sixth Army were uncountable, and the living were being compressed into an ever-smaller space. And with every short advance, the Russians were overrunning abandoned German positions.

I could not find a piece of earth for my motor company just to shoot, so many of the German weapons lay on the ground, said Mikhail Alexeyev, who was an infantryman with the Russian 64th Army. As the circle was becoming smaller and smaller, the mounds of German guns grew higher and higher. So many, and so close to one another.

I was looking for a place to hide until morning, to get some sleep. There were many German positions safe, but nothing was available. I couldn't use them, because the bodies of the German soldiers took up all the ground. They were everywhere, piled high on the fields and in the dugouts. I could find not one piece of open field nor any unoccupied dugout. There were also so many maggots because of the dead bodies. And oh, the lice, the lice.

I saw a dugout in the snow. I had warm clothing so I went in there and bumped against something very stiff. It was dark, so I couldn't see what it was. I thought they were sacks of something. So I made myself comfortable lying on these sacks. In the light of the morning, I saw that I was sleeping on the bodies of killed German soldiers.

Now the Russians were approaching Gumrak. Some planes were still managing to take off from here, so this airfield was the last chance any soldier had to be whisked out of the cauldron. The awful scenes that had been played out at Pitomnik were repeated – only this time, it was worse. In his post-war novel, *The Forsaken Army*, Heinrich Gerlach described the horror of Gumrak, where dying men crammed into train wagons to keep out of the cold.

Gumrak was nothing but a transit camp for the immense burial ground that stretched farther and farther into the steppe. There they lay, badly wounded cases or men who could not walk any further – 30 or 40 in a single wagon, wrapped in rags and bedded down on dirty straw or simply on the floorboards, keeping themselves warm by huddling together or by means of bonfires which they lit between the lines. There was no one there to attend to them, and if there had been it would not have helped them much, for the Army Staff had cancelled the 60-gram bread ration for the wounded on the grounds that those who cannot fight, shall not eat. The walking cases dragged themselves to a nearby pump to wait for the horse-drawn carts. Before the unsuspecting driver understood what was happening they would throw themselves with pocket-knives, pieces of metal, or just their bare hands onto the trembling horse and cut it to pieces, carrying away with them shreds of steaming flesh.

Before the door of one of the high goods-wagons they had made a stairway of hard frozen corpses. Then there was the soldier in front of the railway building. He lay there, weeping and begging to be taken in, clasping the sentry's knee. The sentry shook him off, saying good-humouredly 'No, it can't be done – don't make trouble.' The next day the man was there again, lying on his side with his arms outstretched. His mop of ash-blond hair had been trodden into the snow. And frozen tears, like pearls of ice, glittered on his face.

The imminent fall of the airfield drove one German officer to take a desperate risk. This incident quickly made the rounds of the Sixth Army. Joachim Wieder, who knew the soldier, tells the story.

Our quartermaster, a young general staff officer, had suddenly disappeared. His driver, who had taken him to Gumrak airbase in his *Kübelwagen*, had waited in vain for his return. The lieutenant-colonel was missing. He had silently left the Stalingrad pocket, the zone of death and destruction, on his own initiative. Probably it was a mixture of nerves, fear, cowardice and the vain hope that in the general confusion he might be able to fly out and save his life, that had tempted him to desert. The commanding general had made inquiries by radio. The deserting staff officer had shown up at Army Group, claiming to have flown out on an official assignment from corps on matters of supply. Our general was wild with indignation and rage. He declared that he would have the criminal flown back into the pocket and shot before our eyes. We were all deeply depressed and anticipated with horror the terrible scene that had been announced, and that we were spared to our relief. Our quartermaster was shot outside the pocket on the spot where, in his fatal weakness, he had hoped to find the door to freedom and life.

Russian tanks rumbled onto the cratered, wreck-strewn runway of Gumrak on the morning of 22 January. Hundreds of German wounded, those who could not move, had been left behind. Many were crushed under the tracks of T-34s, or else were finished by a Russian infantryman's bullet. There was a highway, about 8 miles (13km) long, that led from the airfield to the city. That snowy road was filled with suffering Germans. Joachim Wieder joined the tortured procession.

The dispersed, the starving, the freezing, the sick, but also those still fit for fighting, had only one objective to which they were attaching the last glimmerings of hope, and this objective was Stalingrad. In the protective walls and cellars of the ruins they might be able to find some warmth, food, rest, sleep and salvation.

And so they streamed by, the remains of the shattered and decimated formations, trains and rear echelon services, with vehicles that were being slowly dragged and pushed by wounded, sick and frostbitten men. There were emaciated figures among them, muffled in coats, rags; pitiful wrecks, painfully dragging themselves forwards, leaning on sticks and hobbling on frozen feet, wrapped in wisps of straw and strips of blankets.

Drifting along through the snowstorm, this was the wreck of the Sixth Army that had advanced to the Volga during

the summer, so confident of victory. Men from all over
Germany, doomed to destruction in a far-off land, mutely
enduring their suffering, tottered in pitiful droves through
the murderous eastern winter.

   These were the same soldiers who had formerly marched
through large parts of Europe as proud conquerors. Now
the enemy was at their backs and death lurked everywhere.

Any one of the Russians on Wieder's heels might have pointed out to
him that nobody had invited these proud conquerors to come to their
part of Europe, and that the Germans had inflicted plenty of suffering
on many thousands of entirely innocent people along the way. The
men of the Sixth Army had sown death across Russia, and now they
were reaping it. A hundred thousand of them had already died in the
two weeks since the launch of Operation Ring. And there was a special
kind of poetic justice in the fact that the final reckoning would take
place inside the city that they had fought so hard to subdue, within
sight of the wide river that they had travelled 1,250 miles (2,000km)
to possess.

THE SQUARE OF THE FALLEN

The main square of Stalingrad was a just a short walk from the banks
of the Volga. Before the Revolution, this broad open space was called
Alexandrovskaya Square, after the beautiful Byzantine cathedral of
St Alexander, which stood at its eastern end.

   The cathedral had been demolished in the 1930s as part of Stalin's
nationwide drive to eradicate religion, and a modern plaza had been
constructed in its place. On the northern edge was a brand-new
department store, the Univermag. On the opposite side was a plush
19th-century hotel, which had been a headquarters for the Red forces
during the Russian Civil War. Between these two ensembles the
planners of Stalingrad had created a little park with a monument to
the Bolshevik dead of the Civil War. The square had been renamed in
their honour: it was the Square of the Fallen Fighters. The Germans,
for their part, never used the Soviet name. 'Square of the Fallen

Fighters' was too much of a mouthful in German, and the reference to Communist heroes was in any case rather unpalatable for Nazi ideologues. So the Germans always referred to this point on their maps as Red Square, by analogy with Moscow.

Now, in the last week of January 1943, the Soviet name was gruesomely apt, for the square was strewn with dead Germans, or with Germans who would be dead very soon. Waves of soldiers flowed like grey floodwater into the fetid cellars of the buildings around the square: the Sixth Army was retreating underground. Both able-bodied and wounded men crammed into the bowels of the city theatre, just opposite the hotel, and set up firing points in windows and doorways. Many thousands more occupied basements throughout the diminishing patch of ruins that remained in German hands. They continued to resist the Russian advance from the west, and ferocious battles were still being fought in the outhouses and machine rooms of the factory district.

But on 26 January, the Russians broke through to the Volga in the region of Mamayev Kurgan, splitting the German resistance in twain as they had planned to do from the start of Operation Ring. There were now two small Kessels, one in the north and one in the south of the city.

General Friedrich Paulus, along with his staff, was lodged in the crowded maze of rooms beneath the Univermag, in the southern Kessel. He had set up his command post in a dark, narrow little room deep inside the subterranean labyrinth. Here he had a respectable but battered desk and, behind a curtain, his camp bed.

The bed was where Paulus spent most of his time. He lay there in a mood of fatalistic apathy, expressionless apart from the nervous tic that twisted his face violently and spasmodically every few seconds. Command of the army had in effect devolved on General Arthur Schmidt, who occupied a little room across the corridor from the commander-in-chief. In this dark and monkish cell, the devoutly Nazi Schmidt perused his operational maps, issued orders, and kept a large commercial safe full of documents: the red tape of total war.

Here are some extracts from those papers. They are transcripts of radio messages which, when taken together, form a kind of collage of confusion and defeat: defensive positions are given up one by one; generals commit a soldierly kind of suicide by charging at the Russians, guns blazing; officers receive promotions – mostly posthumously – or simply vanish without trace into the maelstrom of destruction.

> Daily Bulletin from Don Headquarters, Jan 24th.
> Romanian 1st Division and Romanian 20th Division fought to the last with distinction, shoulder to shoulder with their German comrades. Their deeds deserve to be singled out in the history of this unique battle ...
> Morning bulletin from Don Headquarters, Jan 25th.
> Swastika flag hoisted on tallest building in the town centre, last battle to be fought under this symbol ...
> Intelligence report, January 26th.
> 4th Corps south of Tsaritsa collapsing in face of enemy army's superior numbers. Last report from there received 07.00 hours, that Generals Pfeffer, von Hartmann, Stempel and Colonel Crome with few men are making a stand on the right-hand side of the railway embankment, firing into the Russians who are advancing in large numbers ...
> General von Hartmann, Commander 71st Infantry Division killed at 08.00 hours by a bullet through the head during close combat. General von Dresser, Commander 297th Division, overrun by Russians in his command post at noon on January 25th, presumably taken prisoner ...
> Daily bulletin, January 26th.
> Croatian 369th Infantry Regiment participated in the fighting around Stalingrad with 1st Croatian Artillery Division, and distinguished itself outstandingly. Heavy enemy artillery fire over the entire town area. Defence of same massively hampered because of 30,000–40,000 unattended wounded and scattered personnel.

Energetic leaders making every effort to form units out of scattered personnel, and are fighting alongside them offering front-line resistance. Apart from a few scraps, all rations have been used up ...

German Gold Cross awarded to Major-General Wulz ...

January 26th.

Don Headquarters. Request posthumous promotion for Lieutenant-General Hauptmann, Commander of the 71st Infantry Division, whose outstanding conduct was a shining example, and who fell today in close combat. Signed, Paulus ...

January 27th.

We are keeping the flag flying to the last. Greetings to Nienhagen and Leipzig. Signed, Lieutenant General Schmidt ...

January 29th.

Don Headquarters. Lieutenant Antlebert Zuhlenkamphs, nephew of General von Seydlitz-Kurzbach, killed in action. Please notify next of kin.

Also in Schmidt's safe was a message from Paulus to Hitler in which, at long last, he pleads for the right to give up the struggle.

Troops are without ammunition and food, wrote Paulus. We have contact with some elements of six divisions only. There are signs of disintegration on the southern, western and northern fronts. Unified command is no longer possible. Little change on the eastern side. We have 18,000 wounded who are without any kind of bandages or medicines at all. The 44th, 76th, 100th, 305th and 384th divisions have been annihilated. As a result of strong incursions the front has been torn open. Firing points and shelter are available only inside the city. Collapse is inevitable. The army requests permission to surrender so as to save the lives of those that remain.

Hitler categorically refused once more. He had one last dramatic set piece in mind. The tenth anniversary of the establishment of the Nazi regime was coming up, four days hence. This was an important occasion for Hitler personally, and it was a fine opportunity to make some propaganda capital out of the situation at Stalingrad. But for this piece of theatre to work, Hitler needed the army to continue the struggle until then – to remain on stage, as it were, until Hitler himself decided it was time to bring down the curtain. The centrepiece of the anniversary celebration was a speech, which Hitler delegated to his corpulent sidekick Hermann Göring. The Reichsmarschall knew his master's mind, and made an address that was intended to lay the foundations of a National-Socialist legend. It was broadcast to the nation on the evening of 30 January.

The speech was a dreadful piece of faux-knightly bombast, a classic piece of Nazi rhetoric, in fact. 'There will come a day when future generations will speak with pride of the struggle of the Sixth Army,' intoned Göring. Then, placing Stalingrad alongside other great battles in the annals of German feats of arms, he said:

> Every German will one day speak in solemn awe of this
> battle, and will recall that in spite of everything the
> foundation of Germany's victory was laid here. They will
> speak of a Langemarck of daring, an Alcazar of tenacity, a
> Narvik of courage, and a Stalingrad of sacrifice. In days to
> come it will be said thus: when you come home to Germany,
> tell them that you have seen us lying at Stalingrad, as the
> rule of honour and the conduct of war have ordained that
> we must do, for Germany's sake. It may sound harsh to say
> that a soldier has to lay down his life at Stalingrad, in the
> deserts of Africa or in the icy wastelands of the North, but if
> we soldiers are not prepared to risk our lives, then we would
> do better to get ourselves to a monastery.

The speech was listened to with sullen humour or impotent rage in the cellars of Stalingrad. Many remarked ruefully on the irony that the fattest man in the entire Reich had the gall to place himself alongside the starving wretches of the Sixth Army. Others screamed at the radio where they lay wounded, or shouted for it to be turned off. One unit stranded in the northern pocket sent a curt radio message to Berlin. 'We can do without premature funeral orations,' it said.

THE BROKEN-HEARTED FIELD MARSHAL

But the oration was not all that premature, as the death of the Sixth Army was imminent. Russian troops appeared on the fringes of the Square of the Fallen Fighters on Hitler's big anniversary. Crossfire sputtered and cracked around the Univermag and the theatre. But the gun battles that day were almost desultory. The Germans knew it was all over, and individual units were unilaterally laying down their arms and surrendering.

That same day, having sent his anniversary congratulations to Hitler ('the swastika still flies over Stalingrad' said the message) Paulus gave his permission for talks to be held with representatives of the Red Army, whose soldiers were now gathering on the other side of the square. While the formalities of capitulation were being set in train, a message came in from Führer headquarters. It was a promotion for Paulus: he had been raised to the rank of field marshal. Paulus knew what this parting message from Hitler meant: in all German history, no field marshal had ever been taken prisoner. The award of the baton invited Paulus to carry out a death sentence on himself, and so add a pleasingly tragic grace-note to the future legend of Stalingrad.

Paulus was possibly mulling this over on the morning of 31 January, when the Russian envoys arrived to discuss surrender terms. These first emissaries were fairly low-ranking: Lieutenant Colonel Vinokur, who was a commissar with General Shumilov's 64th Army, and First Lieutenant Fyodor Ilchenko. A more senior delegation led by Generals Laskin and Mutin soon followed. It arrived on the square while Vinokur and Ilchenko were still inside the Univermag. Leaving General Laskin behind for now, Mutin took some men and headed boldly across the square.

We walked over to the department-store building where the headquarters of the German Sixth Army was located. As we approached it, we saw that the muzzles of artillery pieces and rifles were poking out of all the windows and doors on every floor, including the basements, pointing at the opposite side of the street that ran past the department store, where soldiers of our 38th Brigade were lying on the ground with their weapons aimed at the enemy.

All this enemy weaponry had been blazing away only fifteen minutes before our arrival, and was now bristling, ready to start firing again at any moment. In the rest of the city, only five or six hundred metres from the department store, the Germans were continuing to fire from all types of weapon. There was a ceaseless rumble of cannon.

Pavel Lyamov, an intelligence officer with the 64th Army, was with General Mutin. He vividly recalled their descent into the eerie underworld of the Univermag.

Nobody was shooting at us, said Lyamov. At the entrance to the basement stood five tall SS officers with swastikas on their sleeves, sub-machineguns around their necks and pistols on their belts. It was sleeting. Individual groups of our scouts had taken up positions on top of smashed German tanks and cars, and on the walls of ruined buildings. All was quiet, except for the sound of gunfire coming from the north.

It felt as if they were expecting us. The guard checked our credentials, and on his signal a young SS colonel came out, introducing himself as Colonel Adam, an aide of Field Marshal von Paulus. He asked all four of us to follow him into the basement. It was dark. We entered the basement via a ramp. Our general was walking behind Colonel Adam, followed by the Army's head of reconnaissance, the interpreter and myself. At the bottom of the ramp we

turned right and went down a narrow corridor, our way
lit by Colonel Adam. We hadn't thought to bring along
any torches.

In the basement there was a deathly quiet. After about
80 metres, we all turned to the right again and entered an
intercommunicating room lit by lamps. What was the first
thing we saw? Straight in front of us there hung a dark-
pink velvet banner with fascist swastikas on the bottom,
to the left stood a round table, the top of which was
entirely covered by a Nazi swastika. Behind the table
stood a tall general with an iron cross. The generals
swapped credentials.

The German general, Rosske, announced that the Führer
had conferred on Colonel-General von Paulus the highest
German military rank of field marshal, evidently hoping
that our delegation would be deeply impressed by this and
express hearty congratulations. But no one spoke.

Mutin, unlike Lyamov, was not unnerved by the devilry of the Nazi
décor, nor was he amused by the smug smalltalk of the German
officers. It was the gaunt spectres milling around in the shadows that
troubled him.

The Germans started shouting and kicking up a racket.
They shoved each other aside to make way for us.
Colonel Adam had to go to the front and lead us.
We walked along a narrow, dirty corridor, poorly lit
with lamps made out of artillery-shell cases, past rows of
Germans standing to either side.

The room that Colonel Adam led us to was poorly lit
by a dying candle and a dim lamp. The room was a mess:
suitcases, clothes and furniture were strewn about all over
the place. All the officers under Lieutenant-General
Schmidt and Major-General Rosske, somewhat nonplussed
by the appearance of our delegation, stood up and then

introduced themselves. We, in turn, then introduced
ourselves as representatives of the front commander
General Rokossovsky, and said that we were authorized
to negotiate the capitulation.

Our names were known to them through their
intelligence, and a kind of hiss ran round when they heard
my name. 'Commissar, commissar, commissar,' and they
started staring at me as if looking for my devil's horns
and tail.

When we entered the headquarters room, there were
Lieutenant-Colonel Vinokur and First Lieutenant Ilchenko.
I straight away instructed Ilchenko to expedite the
installation of a telephone so that we could communicate
with our army's headquarters, and then to take advantage
of the bewilderment and confusion in the enemy's camp to
disarm the German headquarters guards and replace them
with our own guards. Comrade Ilchenko left the room
immediately to carry out the order, while Vinokur stayed
behind with us.

From the outset, General Schmidt came across as an
inveterate fascist. All his clothes were ironed and polished
to a sparkle, he was clean-shaven, his hair was combed and
greased, he had a little black Hitler moustache, thin lips and
small, black, round eyes that kept darting about, and his
pronunciation was clipped like a dog's bark. Outwardly, he
was all pomposity, but on the inside he was trembling in
some kind of agony, as if in his death throes, waiting for
something terrible to happen. Colonel Adam was very quiet,
and did not join in the conversation. He was taciturn and
worried-looking, and as soon as the introductions were out
of the way he went off to his room on the pretext of
gathering some things that he needed.

Colonel Adam was in fact darting backwards and forwards to the dark
corner where Paulus lay waiting. His job was to keep the field marshal

informed of developments in the other room. Paulus had made plans for his own personal surrender, which were about to be put before the Russians.

> We presented the printed ultimatum signed by Generals Voronov and Rokossovsky, and asked that all personal weapons be handed over, continued Mutin. Our demand was carried out immediately, with no resistance. Everyone in the room handed over their firearms and removed their daggers from their belts. Thus began the disarming of German forces of the entire southern group in Stalingrad.
>
> In response to our delegation's demand to be taken at once to Field Marshal von Paulus, Lieutenant-General Schmidt said that von Paulus was in a separate room, that he was unwell, and that he was no longer in command of the army, as it had been broken up into independent combat groups. Von Paulus himself was now a 'private citizen', and he, Chief of Staff Lieutenant-General Schmidt, would be conducting the negotiations.
>
> We insisted that Lieutenant-General Schmidt notify Field Marshal von Paulus of the arrival of our delegation for negotiations, and that von Paulus himself receive us and sign the order for the capitulation of the German forces. Lieutenant-General Schmidt immediately carried out our demand, and reported everything to von Paulus.
>
> Von Paulus confirmed, through General Schmidt, that he was no longer in command of the army, that he was a private citizen and would therefore not sign the capitulation order. He refused to receive our delegation, but asked that, as a field marshal, he be personally taken prisoner and escorted by one of our generals.
>
> To keep the negotiations going, our delegation then told General Schmidt to issue an order for the immediate cessation of resistance and the complete capitulation of the

German grouping. Fallen Warriors' Square was designated the place where weapons and equipment were to be surrendered and prisoners received.

All these preliminary capitulation terms were accepted by the German command, but with the following conditions. Firstly, the delegation was not to interrogate Field Marshal von Paulus in any way, since he would supply information on military arrangements only to Colonel-General Rokossovsky; secondly, von Paulus's safety had to be guaranteed, to ensure that he would not be attacked and killed en route or when leaving the building; thirdly, even though von Paulus was a 'private citizen', his soldiers were not to be disarmed until he had left the building, and once he had left he was not to be held responsible for the actions of his subordinates. General Schmidt reported this last request in an emotional tone, and then added that 'it would break the Field Marshal's heart to see his soldiers disarmed.'

The Russians chose not to be moved by the delicacy of the German commander's feelings. They waited for General Laskin to come over before proceeding to the next stage of this strange rite, which was the formal arrest of Paulus.

General Laskin arrived at around 08.40, and took command of our delegation. We then went to Field Marshal von Paulus's room, where we found him dressed in an unbuttoned greatcoat and pacing up and down the room. It was partitioned off by a chest of drawers. A desk stood by a basement window looking onto the department store's yard, and behind the chest of drawers, in the dark part of the room, there was a bed.

When he saw us, Field Marshal von Paulus stopped in his tracks but did not say anything. General Laskin gave his name and rank, declared von Paulus a prisoner, and told him to surrender his personal weapons. Field Marshal von

Paulus then gave his own name and rank, and stated that he was surrendering to Soviet forces, that he did not have any personal weapons on him and his aide-de-camp had his pistol, and that he had only been made a field marshal on January 30th, and had not yet received his new uniform – which was why he was dressed in the uniform of a colonel-general. He went on to say that he would not now have much use for the new uniform.

General Laskin then told the field marshal to present his army-commander identification card. In response, von Paulus pulled a soldier's card from his tunic pocket and handed it to General Laskin, stating that all he had was his soldier's card, and that he didn't have any other documents attesting to his identity as army commander. General Laskin, having checked the soldier's card through the interpreter Stepanov, returned it to von Paulus.

General Laskin and I then briefly discussed the situation and decided to search Field Marshal von Paulus. The search was carried out by myself. I carefully checked all his clothes and pockets. The reason this had to be done was that some German generals had committed suicide rather than be taken prisoner. So we had to take all precautions to stop von Paulus doing the same thing. Although he seemed a little put out by the search, he did not offer any resistance or objection. And then, when General Laskin asked von Paulus whether he was ill, he replied that he was well but had been affected by the poor diet and the long-drawn-out, agonizing experience of the ignominious capitulation of his army.

And then he took out of his trouser pocket some small cubes of baked bread, like we used to make with oil. He showed them to us and said: 'A hundred and fifty grams a day – that's all I've had to eat for many days now. I've been sharing my starvation rations with my soldiers, who only get fifty grams a day.'

With that contradictory and self-serving admission – that he got three times the rations of his ravenous men – Field Marshal Friedrich Paulus, commander-in-chief of the Sixth Army, became a Russian prisoner of war.

TRIUMPH AND DISASTER

Afzal Khairutdinov was an 18-year-old infantryman from Kazakhstan. Like all the Red Army men in Stalingrad, he was aware that the day of victory had arrived. 'On January 31st the character of the fighting changed completely, as the Germans were completely demoralized.' It was only a matter of a few weeks since he and his classmates had been plucked from their military academy and sent to fight in the city. Khairutdinov had been attached to the 173rd Rifle Division. In less a month he had gained more knowledge of practical soldiering than he could have hoped to acquire in a decade of attendance at the training school. Now he was daring to wish that his luck would hold, and that he would live to see the end of the battle – and after that, the end of the war.

But today there was still work to be done.

On that morning the frosts were strong – it was 35 or 40 degrees below zero. The remains of our battalion were gathered together and formed into two units, one of which was put under my command. There were very few officers left. The commander of our platoon had already been wounded.

The lieutenant in charge of our company ordered us to blockade a building about 150 metres away from our position and to clear it of Germans. The building was in ruins, and the windows were empty, like eye sockets. We advanced. We went in single file, one behind the other. We began to notice packages on the snow, supplies that had been dropped on German positions during the night. We picked one up: it was frozen loaves of bread. We gathered together a few of these packets.

We could see the heads of some Germans bobbing in and out of view at the dead windows. They did not shoot. We were walking upright in broad daylight, so I suppose we were not expecting them to shoot. Their situation was hopeless, after all. We approached a little niche on the front of the building, where once there must have been a front door. The shadow of a soldier passed across it. I shouted: 'Kamerad, komm!' After a few shouts there appeared the dirty, stubbly face of a crawling soldier. We again called to him to come out to us. After a little hesitation he stood up. I told the lads not to point their guns at him. I held out the brick of bread that we had picked up. He grew bolder and came nearer, grabbed the bread and straight away began to gnaw at it. Then a second soldier came. We asked them: are there many of you down there? 'Oh, lots and lots,' came the answer. This surprised us. We gave them all the bread that we had picked up and told them to go back down into the basement and come out with all the others. Then we waited.

After about five minutes the same two came back with three or four others. We said: is this all of you? They replied that there were others, but they were afraid to come out – especially the officers. So we sent this party back too and said that everybody had to come out. A long time passed. We prepared for the worst. We could hear dull shots coming from the basement. Something was going on down there. Then we heard noises getting nearer, talking. First out were our new acquaintances, and many more came behind them. We saw that they were carrying a wounded officer – he was tied up and lying on a stretcher. We asked: why has he been tied up? It turned out that he had woken up to see the soldiers preparing to give themselves up, and had drawn his pistol to threaten them. Someone had shot him in the leg. Then they all tied him up.

They all had their hands up and were unarmed. We asked: where are your guns. 'Down there,' they said. We told them all to go back (apart from the officers – there were some of them too) and to come back with their weapons. They very quickly did as we asked and piled up their guns in the place we told them to. We were astonished by how many people came out of that basement. A whole battalion at least! Around that time our own officers turned up and began to organize the process of taking them prisoner.

Our commander came over to us and said: 'Well done, you good lads. I have just one more job for you today. Go and clean out that building across the square, and then you can relax.'

It was about two in the afternoon by now. It was extremely cold – so much so that my tommy-gun would barely fire because the grease had frozen. I had to swap it for a different one; the lieutenant gave me his. We went forward to carry out the order. We went about it the same way as before: single file, one behind the other, me in front.

Suddenly we realized that we were in a minefield. Here and there we could see the tiny wooden crosses poking above the ground. This meant there were anti-infantry mines, the kind we called 'frogs'. If you touched the wire and set one off it jumped up in the air and exploded. They could take out everything in a four- or five-metre radius. We stopped in our tracks, and discussed what would be for the best: to go on or to turn back. The lads all said: 'We've seen this before, let's go on. Going back is just as dangerous.'

No Germans were shooting at us, and there were none to be seen. I began to take forward steps, slowly and carefully. The lads (there were six or seven of them) followed in my steps. I should say that the square was full of ruts and holes. There were abandoned rifles lying around on the ground, helmets, all kinds of kit, bits of bricks, pieces of broken equipment. It was very hard to make progress. I had not gone ten steps when I stumbled and fell forwards. Before I could straighten up I heard the deafening sound of a mine exploding three or four metres behind me. In that instant I felt a hard blow in my right shoulder, and something wet on my back. I knew it was blood, but strangely, I felt no pain. I glanced behind me in time to see my lads falling down – some of them frontways, others onto their backs. It was sickening. A mine must have gone off at their feet. I managed to see not only my lads as they went down, but also all the sharp and jagged objects on the ground around me. I managed not so much to fall as slowly lower myself onto the snow. I remember nothing more. I lost consciousness.

Khairutdinov lay unconscious for some hours. It was pitch black by the time he came round, and even colder.

I woke up with the sensation that someone was pulling me about, rifling through my pockets and taking away my documents. Then I heard a voice: 'Hey, this one's alive, he's moving.' A second person came close. I was slowly coming round, and with great difficulty I opened my eyes. I could see the clear night sky and the twinkling stars. I felt a dreadful pain in my neck and my right shoulder; I felt weak. The medic, leaning over me in the darkness, was trying to find out whereabouts I was wounded. He was saying: 'Where is he hurt? His arms and legs are in one piece, his head too. I see no blood.' Seeing that I had opened my eyes he asked me: 'Where were you hit?' I tried to answer but I could not open my mouth or make a sound. I was completely numb. He could see me trying, and waited. 'Where then, where, where?' At long last I forced out some kind of sound. The medics were prodding me all over: my face, my nose, the top of my head. I managed to pronounce the word 'neck'. One of them shoved his hand down my collar and brought it back out covered in blood. 'There it is!'

The medic got a pair of scissors and cut all the way up the sleeve of my quilted jacket (I wasn't wearing an overcoat). He cut as far as the place where I was wounded. Then he put a field dressing on the wound and bandaged it. After that he bound up the sleeve of my jacket with some wire and put me on a sled.

I asked them to help my lads. 'They are just here,' I say. One of the medics showed me a wedge of Red Army pay books and said: 'There is no one here who needs our help. They are all goners. You are the only one we found alive.' I was horrified. All my boys were dead.

As for me, I was dragged across the bumpy, shell-pocked square. It was pure torture. Though the field hospital where they were taking me was not far away, they had to take me over all kinds of obstacles and rough ground to get there. At one point they tugged at the rope as we went over a shell hole and the sled shot out from underneath me. I ended up in a hole full of snow. They swore out loud, hauled me out and told me to hold on tight to the edge of the sled, then ... the same thing happened again. My hands were freezing: I couldn't hold onto anything. Finally they dragged me to a large canvas tent and put me down on straw near the entrance to the operating room.

Inside the tent there was a surgeon and his team of helpers. I waited there till deep into the night, and all the time there were operations going on. A helper would come out from time to time and pick out the most badly wounded person, who would then become the next to go in. As the rest of us waited for our turn, we could hear the screams and groans of the wounded being operated on without any anaesthetic. It made you shudder.

I was one of the last. They led me in and sat me down on a chair. One of the helpers held me very tightly. The doctor opened up the entry wound with a kind of pair of scissors, rooted around in there and found a piece of shrapnel –

which he pulled out and showed to me. 'That's what got you,' he said, and tossed it into a big bowl.

Afzal Khairutdinov was lucky. He had got the perfect wound, the one that less enthusiastic soldiers than Afzal dream of: something bad enough to put you out of action, but not disfiguring and not permanently crippling. Thousands of Germans had been praying for such an injury for months – they called it the *Heimschuss*, the 'home shot' – but now it was too late. Captivity was the best remaining option for them.

Captivity, or a soldier's death. In the centre of Stalingrad, not all the Germans had heard of the general surrender, as the Russians were discovering. Ivan Vakurov was with the 173rd Rifles, like Khairutdinov. On 31 January he too was detailed to round up prisoners, but he had an additional task: to raise the red flag on a tall building known as the 'Black House' near the so-called Nyeftesindikat factory on the banks of the river. Inconveniently, there were still Germans inside it. Right at the last, Vakurov's weary riflemen were going to have to employ the tried and tested street-fighting tactic.

The storming of the house began in the morning, after an artillery bombardment. The Germans, hiding behind the thick stone walls, were firing from all the windows and out of the basement. The storm groups moved forwards in short hops, covering each other's approach with gunfire. Lieutenant Rostovtsev was first to get to the doorway of the Black House.

Using grenades and machineguns we carved out a path up the stairs. Right behind Rostovtsev were Lieutenant Titov, Sergeant Kozachuk, and infantrymen Khoroshev, Zapolyansky and Matveyev. There was a struggle on the staircase landing at the second floor, and an enemy bullet felled Lieutenant Rostovtsev. Sergeant Zhernov took his place. While the battle continued on the second floor, more storm groups burst into the building. There were battles in every corner of the house.

Khoroshev covered Matveyev as he climbed up into the attic, found a way out onto the roof, and attached the flag to the chimneystack. All the fighters attacking the Nyeftesindikat saw it, and we heard their loud 'hurrah'. They pushed forwards more strongly after that. The enemy's resistance weakened and soon ceased altogether. More than 700 prisoners were taken.

Elements of the 173rd Rifles reached the river. Some of them were sure the battle for the city was now over, and were shooting their guns into the air in celebration. Then they turned to their right and headed south, towards the town centre. Everywhere Germans were giving up and emerging from cellars with their hands up. Vakurov and his men were expecting at any moment to happen on the men of the 65th Army as they pushed north. But there remained one last hurdle for them along the way.

The regiments of our division cleaned out Kirov Street, Sovetskaya Street, Parkhomenko Street and Pushkin Street. It was not until we reached Ninth of January Street that we encountered strong resistance. The enemy had dug himself in inside the building of the State Bank, and was directing machinegun fire at us.

A company under the command of Sergeant Sklyerov found a way into the Bank via holes in the walls, and forced their way to the stairwell. There was a short skirmish, which resulted in our taking 70 Germans prisoner. Private Gorbatko raised the red flag above the State Bank building.

We had not yet cooled down after the tension of that heated battle when we heard more shots coming from the street below. Gorbatko stuck his head out of the window, and shouting above the gunfire he called out: 'It's our lot! We've joined up!'

That is how the 173rd Division connected with the forward units coming from the south. It was decided to commemorate the moment in an official document.

This is what the document said: 'We, the undersigned, Major Vasily Ivanovich Telegin and Captain Nikolai Nikitovich Remizov on the one hand, and Major Ivan Pavlovich Akhmatov and Senior Lieutenant Ivan Yefimovich Titov on the other, have drawn up this deed in testimony of the fact that our respective units, acting in Stalingrad from two directions, defeated the enemy in battle and joined forces on Ninth of January Street, where we exchanged greetings.'

With that little piece of pomp the fighting in the city centre came to a stop. However, there was still a war going on in the factories. One of the last outposts of the Kessel was centred on the large brick building of Workshop No. 32 of the Barricades Factory. Here a handful of Germans had been fighting a desperate battle all through the last week of January. They were not in contact with Paulus, and had not heard the news when he gave himself up. Probably they would have fought on anyway: Workshop No. 32 was the alamo of the eastern front.

The Russians, for their part, could not flush these Germans out or make them surrender. A kind of unstoppable momentum was leading Russian commanders to throw more and more men at the workshop. A group of Russian infantrymen was holed up somewhere inside the building, and had been there for some days, but many of their comrades had been killed to gain that foothold. Now they were cut off from HQ, and the telephone line was broken.

Some junior officers at HQ were incensed that their officers were employing the wasteful tactic of full-frontal assault at a time when the battle for the city was clearly drawing to a close. One of the angry young men was Alexander Lukash. He was with the naval infantry of the 92nd Independent Rifle Brigade, the tough band of naval infantrymen who had fought in the grain elevator during the autumn. He was convinced that the time for suicidal bravery was past. Lukash was not inclined to sacrifice himself or his men for the sake of some colonel's arbitrary schedule. Yet orders were orders in the Red Army, just as surely as they were in the Wehrmacht. Lukash's orders were to get inside the workshop and make contact with the stranded group, to end the German resistance, and to do it right away.

I began to object that it was impossible to do that in broad daylight, but the brigade commander Yelin coarsely interrupted me and demanded that I carry out my orders immediately. I put together a team of 15 men – all volunteers, of course. Among them were platoon commander Semyonov and company commander Lieutenant Ageyev. Rukavtsov was already in a forward position with a group of scouts.

Naturally, we did not begin the attack in daylight, but lay in the neutral zone under enemy fire until darkness fell. It was night when we made our way into the workshop building. The scene inside was indescribable. Bodies, nothing but dead bodies, everywhere you looked. There were wounded who lay there bleeding. No one was going to their aid. There was no ammunition and nothing to eat or drink. The only place there was anyone alive was the washroom: tired, hungry men. On the command of one of the junior commissars, they were occasionally shouting 'Hurrah' – and that alone was giving the Germans a fright.

The commissar gave me a quick report on the situation, but I could see for myself what was happening. That night, under cover of darkness, we attacked the other end of the workshop and made some progress, but in the morning the Germans forced us back to the washroom area. Medical instructor Kolomitsev took some of the scouts and they gave what first aid they could to the wounded. All the food we had was shared out.

That morning the scouts found the break in the cable that was preventing us making contact with HQ. It was right by the telephone itself. The line was re-connected, and I personally reported to Yelin all I had seen, and proposed to bring the men out right away as only 20 or so were still alive. Yelin did not believe me, and told me once more to carry out my orders. A few minutes later contact was lost again.

We remained in the workshop for several days. We fought till we were ready to drop. At one point we were grabbing some sleep in a toilet cubicle when we were woken by a powerful explosion. There was dust everywhere, and bits of grit and brick flying through the air. The Germans had blown up the roof of the workshop, and what was left of our brigade was now buried under concrete.

This crudely effective blow put paid to Lukash's attack. He was not badly hurt himself, but many of his men were killed. There were not enough men left alive in the washroom to carry on the fight. Lukash did not know it, but by now Paulus and the southern pocket had capitulated. His men and his enemy were among the very few soldiers in Stalingrad who were fighting. Still seething with anger at his own leaders, Lukash decided to call off the offensive and return to base.

That same night three of us – me and two scouts – made our way back to brigade HQ. We were hungry and worn out. We were not the only survivors, but it nevertheless felt like a miracle that we were still alive. About 15 men made it back from the workshop over a period of time.

Brigade commander Yelin gave us a cold reception. He said he was sure we were all dead. This was an affront not just to me, but to all those fine sailors who had pointlessly laid down their lives. That their brigade commander should so glibly write them off, the living as well as the dead! That was the tragic conclusion of the battle for Workshop No. 32.

And that, more or less, was also the conclusion of the Battle of Stalingrad. The last few pockets of German resistance, including the men in Workshop No. 32, laid down their arms a few hours later, on 2 February.

By the Russian way of reckoning, the Battle of Stalingrad had begun on 17 July, when the as yet unblooded 62nd Army first exchanged fire with the Sixth Army. That initial encounter had been a running battle on the open, sun-drenched steppe, where the Germans were bowling towards the city like an unstoppable train. Precisely 200 days had passed since then, and the final shots were exchanged between men of the same two armies. Only now they fought in the cold, static ruins of the Barricades Factory – a few hundred yards from the indifferent river.

Alexander Lukash, recovering at his command post, must have been close enough to hear the crack of the last bullet fired in the battle of Stalingrad. He was waiting for it. He had a personal errand to run once the guns fell silent; then he could put aside his rage.

We went back into Workshop No. 32, hoping to find someone alive. But we found nothing but corpses. On that raw, snowy ground lay the bravest of the brave, the very best sailors and officers we had. Senior Lieutenant Semyonov died there, and so did Lieutenant Ageyev.

Yet that day, February 2nd 1943, was the most joyful and happy day of my life. It was joyful first and foremost because we had won, we had defended the city of Stalingrad and held on to it. But I was happy too because I had come out of that inferno alive, and I was not the only one who was celebrating. I saw men weep, young ones and grey-haired elderly ones. Everywhere people were embracing and kissing each other. How sad that so many did not live to see that day.

That is why I bow my head before those who fought on the banks of the Volga and sacrificed the most precious thing they had – their life.

9
AFTER THE BATTLE

Someone came and woke me up at two o'clock in the morning, and took me to the military council.

It was the night of 31 January. Nikolai Dyatlenko, the NKVD officer who had delivered the ultimatum to the Germans on the eve of Operation Ring, was about to receive a new and interesting mission.

The car carried me swiftly to the far end of a long village, to the little house which was occupied by the representative of the Stavka, marshal of artillery Nikolai Voronov. Still half-asleep, I was thinking to myself: what do they want me for? I had heard that the General Staff had been wondering whether to send another delegation to the Germans. Probably it was something to do with that.

Voronov was in his office, along with Rokossovsky (the commander of the Don Front) and Telegin (a member of the military council). Voronov spoke first. 'Right then, Captain,' he said, once I had announced myself. 'It seems Paulus is regretting not talking to you before, and now he has requested an audience. You will speak with him.' So I was to be Paulus's interpreter.

Dyatlenko was nervous – but so, apparently, was everybody else. As with the ultimatum, the etiquette of the occasion was obscure. These leaders of the Workers' and Peasants' Red Army were suddenly worried about looking oafish in front of a German they assumed –

quite wrongly – to be a Prussian toff, and to whose name they often added (erroneously) the aristocratic preposition 'von'. This crisis of gentility suddenly generated a great deal of nervous discussion.

It was getting crowded in Voronov's cottage. Apart from his adjutants, there now appeared members of the staff of the military council. Everyone who had permission wanted to be around for such an unusual event.

Out of Voronov's dark bedroom came a photographer. Without paying any attention to the high-ranking personnel he began changing the lamps, checking camera angles, working out how to photograph Paulus once he was sitting down. Something was bothering him. He moved the empty chair which was opposite Voronov then he said: 'General Voronov, if he realizes that you are the highest-ranking commander present and decides to sit next to you, then when he turns his chair towards you all I will get is a picture of the back of his head and his left ear.' I wanted to make myself useful in this unusual company, so I jumped in with a suggestion: 'I'll hold the chair: if he is a well brought up person he won't try to turn it.' We grew tense as we waited. The generals whispered to each other. I was concerning myself with the question of how we should go about meeting Paulus. So I asked Voronov: 'Should we stand up when he comes in or not?'

'Well, you stand up if you want to,' came the answer.

'Should I introduce you to him?'

'Tell him my name and General Rokossovsky's.'

At last a car drew up outside the cottage. Everything went quiet in the front room and the adjutants' room. We could hear that several people had entered the house, and were wordlessly taking off their overcoats. It seemed that the whole process was taking much too long.

Then a man appeared in the doorway – tall, lean, slightly hunched, greying, unshaven, wearing the crumpled uniform

of a colonel-general of the Nazi army. Having bowed
his head to cross the threshold, he silently and rather
indecisively raised his arm forwards and upwards, and held
that pose for a moment.

The Soviet officers were rather taken aback by Paulus's Hitler salute. For all their worrying beforehand, it was the German who had made the first faux pas of the evening. Paulus was invited to sit down at the chair that Dyatlenko had prepared for him. The Russian captain then introduced the two generals, as he had been told to do. Paulus lifted himself from the chair and bowed to his adversaries. Then General Voronov opened the discussion with a suave little speech.

'It's really rather late,' began Voronov. 'And you, colonel-
general sir, are clearly tired. We have been working hard the
past few days too, so today we will limit ourselves to one
extremely urgent matter ...'
'Pardon me,' Paulus interrupted the first phrase of my
translation. 'I am a field marshal. Two days ago I received
a message in my headquarters informing me of my
promotion. But I am afraid I've not had an opportunity to
change my uniform.'
Our generals, smiling ironically, exchanged meaningful
glances. 'Yes, well then,' continued Voronov. 'We are asking
you to sign an order for the capitulation of the part of your
army which is still resisting, and so prevent the needless
death of many officers and men.'
'That would be unworthy of me as a soldier!' objected
Paulus, but Voronov parried easily.
'How can it be unworthy of a soldier to save his men,
when the commander himself has already given himself up?'
'I did not give myself up. I was captured by surprise.'

The Russians knew full well that this was a lie. And Paulus knew that they knew it. But both the Communists and the Fascist understood that a lie spoken with utter conviction is almost as good as the truth. Voronov was too clever to get involved in an argument about the exact circumstances of Paulus's surrender. Instead, the Russian general began to pile on the pressure. Dyatlenko continues his account of the discussion.

'I am proposing a humane act here,' said Voronov. 'We have the force and means at our disposal. In a couple of days, or even in the course of a few hours, we could annihilate the group of your soldiers who are still fighting. Their resistance is pointless. All it can bring is the senseless death of tens of thousands of your officers and men. It is your duty as commander-in-chief to save their lives, which is all the more logical since you have saved your own life by surrendering.'

Paulus tried to wriggle out once again. 'Even if I were to sign such an order, they would not obey it. The very fact that I have become your prisoner means that I have ceased to be commander of the army.'

'But you fulfilled that role until just a few hours ago,' countered Voronov.

'From the moment that my forces were split into separate groups, I have only nominally been their commander,' said Paulus, pushing the same line. 'General orders came directly from Führer headquarters, and each group was under the command of one of the generals.'

'Nevertheless,' insisted Voronov. 'Your personal authority is not to be discounted when it is a question of saving many thousands of men.'

'They would not submit to my authority. A warrior's duty ...'

'Duty is duty, but these are unusual circumstances,' interrupted Voronov. 'You now find yourself in complete safety. Surely in this situation, as a matter of conscience, your duty before the men who are still under siege, before their relatives and loved ones, is to prevent the senseless destruction of those who for many years have been under your command.'

It was getting harder for Paulus to refuse to sign the order, and his arguments grew more and more nit-picking. He started saying that he was sure that a new commander had been appointed by now, or that his signature on the document would be taken for a forgery. Paulus was assured that one of the officers already captured could go with our emissaries and vouch for his signature. If necessary, a meeting could be arranged between Paulus and a delegation from his forces. At times it seemed to me that the old man was about to break. But the field marshal continued to refuse though he had been backed into a corner and all his arguments were spent. Voronov, convinced that there was no sense in continuing the discussion, brought it to a close in this way:

'In that case you must know that by refusing to sign the order you bear a weighty responsibility before the German people and Germany's future for the lives of many of your subordinates and comrades.'

Paulus listened to the translation of Voronov's last word, then looked through him towards the wall. He sat there, crushed and silent. His cheek and his nose twitched. After a short but painful pause, Voronov asked the field marshal if there was anything he needed – special food, say, given the state of his health. Paulus said that he was quite content with the conditions, and so had no requests. 'I would just like to ask,' he said in conclusion, 'that the many prisoners-of-war be given food, and that the wounded receive medical attention.'

'Very well,' said Voronov. Paulus thanked him, stood up, made a small bow and went to put his coat on. I had met many captured fascist officers before then, and it now occurred to me that they always remembered international

law when it is in their interest to do so. 'They are all the
same,' I thought to myself.

The northern pocket surrendered a day later without the additional
validation of Paulus's signature. As for the stubborn field marshal, he
remained in captivity in the USSR where, after months of reflection,
he renounced his faith in Hitler. He joined the Union of German
Officers, an ineffectual anti-Nazi organization sponsored by the
Soviets and fronted by high-ranking German POWs. After the war
Paulus was brought from Moscow to be a witness for the prosecution
at the Nuremberg Tribunals. The newspapers called this broken
shadow of a man 'the ghost of Stalingrad'. He was released in 1953
and allowed to return to Germany – Communist East Germany. He
chose to live out his days in Dresden, the city that was razed by aerial
bombardment in one night in February 1945 – just as, on his orders,
Stalingrad was obliterated in one afternoon in August 1942. He died
in 1957.

STALINGRAD HAS FALLEN

The capture of Paulus was announced in a brief Soviet communiqué.
The news was picked up and flashed around the world. For the Allies
it was a day of rejoicing: the Battle of Stalingrad was over at last.

In Germany, where Dr Goebbels had been carefully preparing
the nation for the worst, three days of mourning were declared.
But Germany's soldiers, especially those on the eastern front, did not
need to be told to grieve. They knew instinctively that this was a blow
from which the Wehrmacht would never recover. Guy Sajer's unit was
on the move in Russia when the news came through.

A sergeant ran down the length of the convoy, blowing the
whistle for assembly. The captain came over to us, followed
by his two lieutenants and three feldwebels. He didn't lift
his eyes from the ground, and his expression was one of
despair. A shiver of anxiety ran across our shaggy and
exhausted faces.

'*Achtung*! *Stillgestanden*!' shouted a feldwebel. We stood at attention. The captain gave us a long look. Then slowly, in his gloved hand, he lifted a paper to the level of his eyes.

'Soldiers,' he said. 'I have some very serious news for you; serious for you, for all the fighting men of the Axis, for our people, and for everything our faith and sacrifice represents. Wherever this news will be heard this evening, it will be received with emotion and profound grief. Everywhere along our vast front, and in the heart of our fatherland, we will find it difficult to contain our emotion.'

'*Stillgestanden*!' insisted the feldwebel.

'Stalingrad has fallen!' the captain continued. 'Marshal Paulus and his Sixth Army, driven to the ultimate sacrifice, have been obliged to lay down their arms unconditionally.'

We felt stunned and profoundly anxious. The captain continued after a moment's silence. 'Marshal Paulus, in the next to last message he sent, informed the Führer that he was awarding the cross for bravery with exceptional merit to every one of his soldiers. The Marshal added that the calvary of these unfortunate combatants had reached a peak, and that after the hell of this battle, which lasted for months, the halo of glory has never been more truly deserved. I have here the last message picked up by short wave from the ruins of the tractor factory. The High Command requests that I read it to you.

'It was sent by one of the last fighting soldiers of the Sixth Army, Heinrich Stoda. Heinrich states in this message that in the southwest district of Stalingrad he could still hear the sound of fighting. Here is the message: "We are the last seven survivors in this place. Four of us are wounded. We have been entrenched in the wreckage of the tractor factory for four days. We have not had any food for four days. I have just opened the last magazine for my automatic. In ten minutes the Bolsheviks will overrun us. Tell my father that I have done my duty, and that I shall know how to die. Long live Germany! Heil Hitler!'"

A man in the ranks began to whimper. His white temples made him look like an old man. Then he quit his rigid posture and began to walk toward the officers, crying and shouting at the same time. 'My two sons are dead. It was bound to happen. It's all your fault – you officers. It's fatal. We'll never be able to stand up to the Russian winter!' He bowed almost double, and burst into tears. 'My two children have died there ... my poor children ... '

'At ease,' ordered the feldwebel.

'No. Kill me if you like. It doesn't matter. Nothing matters ... '

Two soldiers stepped forward and took the poor man by the arms, trying to lead him back to his place before anything worse happened. Hadn't he just insulted the officers? Unfortunately he struggled, like someone possessed by demons.

'Take him to the infirmary,' the captain said. 'Give him a sedative.' I thought he was going to add something else, but his expression remained fixed. Perhaps he too had lost a relative.

We returned to our trucks in small, silent groups. By now it was full night. The rolling white horizon was tinged with a cold bluish grey. I shivered. 'It's getting colder and colder,' I said to the fellow walking beside me.

'Yes. Colder and colder,' he answered, staring into the distance.

Adolf Hitler received the news of the Sixth Army's subjugation at the Wolf's Lair. Before lunch on 1 February, when the northern pocket was still holding out in the factories, Hitler held a meeting with his senior staff. He was livid with Paulus for failing to do as he was told and blow his own brains out: the sheer disobedience of it seems to have troubled him more than the loss of a quarter of a million soldiers. He expressed his disappointment in the form of an odd little story about the suicide of an affronted woman. He told this tale to General Zeitzler (who had resumed eating proper meals, and was therefore back in the Führer's good books).

> They have given themselves up formally and completely, complained Hitler. In such situations it is usual to form a hedgehog defence and then to use one's last bullet to shoot oneself dead. Given that a woman who hears just a few insulting words is proud enough to go and lock herself away and shoot herself dead immediately, then I have no respect for a soldier who is afraid to do the same and prefers to go into captivity.

'I can't believe it either,' replied General Zeitzler. 'I'm still of the opinion that it may not be true, that he may be lying there, badly wounded.

> No, it's true, said Hitler. Now the Russians will immediately take them to Moscow, to the GPU, and they'll blurt out orders for the northern Kessel to give up too. That Schmidt will sign anything. If a man doesn't have the courage at this hour to take the path that everyone will have to take one day, then he will not possess the strength to resist either. We have insisted too much on training the intellect and too little on building strength of character.

'It's quite impossible to explain how this happened,' wheedled Zeitzler, comfortably back in the role of chief courtier. But Hitler had an explanation to hand. He recalled the flurry of radio messages generated by the Russian ultimatum three weeks before, on the eve of Operation Ring:

> I had my doubts before, when I received the report that he was asking what he should do. How can he even ask about such a thing? When the nerves break down, there is nothing left but to admit that one can't cope and to shoot oneself.

The man should have shot himself just like the Roman commanders who threw themselves on their swords when they saw that the cause was lost. In this war, no more field marshals will be made. But we had to make the assumption that it would end heroically.

General Zeitzler tut-tutted and shook his head. 'How could one imagine anything else?' he said.

This hurts me so much, continued Hitler, because the heroism of so many soldiers is nullified by one characterless weakling. What is life? Life is the nation. The individual must die anyway. I don't understand it at all. He could have freed himself from all care and ascended into national immortality. It just doesn't make sense. It is tragic that such heroism is spoiled at the last.

At this point a group of officers arrived to discuss the situation in North Africa, where the British Eighth Army had taken Tripoli and were chasing Axis forces into Tunisia. Zeitzler took the opportunity to leave the meeting. But even after Zeitzler had gone, Hitler could not forget his analogy with the lady suicide. He rambled vaguely on, and as he spoke she seemed to take a more concrete form in his imagination: 'Such a beautiful woman, she was ... first class. It was just a small matter, insulted by a few words. So the woman went away ... wrote farewell letters ... shot herself ... '

THE QUICK AND THE DEAD

No Western reporters were allowed inside Stalingrad during the battle. British and American correspondents in Moscow had to content themselves with reading the reports in the Soviet press and trying to pick up on arcane hints and clues. 'Fighting south-west of the city ...' Did that imply a counter-attack? 'Such and such a village has been recaptured ...' But when did the Germans take it in the first place? It was an immensely frustrating way to gather news. So when, as soon as the fighting stopped, the Soviets offered to take a group of journalists on a tour of the now-quiet city, Alexander Werth of *The Sunday Times* leaped at the chance.

> Stalingrad left one with an unforgettable impression, wrote
> Werth. Until then I had seen Coventry and Portsmouth
> and the East End of London. But that was bombing and it
> was somehow impersonal, as the results of a hurricane
> would have been. Moreover it was patchy destruction.
> But Stalingrad, every inch of Stalingrad, was a battlefield.
> For five months it had been, to use the gruesome but
> picturesque Russian phrase, a mincing-machine, a meat-
> chopper. Walking over the frozen, tortured earth of
> Stalingrad you felt that you were treading on human
> flesh and bones. And sometimes it was literally true.

Werth was surprised to hear explosions as he was shown round the ruins. Perhaps the front was closer than he had been led to believe by the Russian propaganda chiefs. But he was reassured to be told that the bangs were not falling shells; sappers were blasting the ice-hard ground to make mass graves. These were for the German bodies that littered the ruins like so many dead leaves.

The grisly tour led north to the Red October Factory.

> We walked up the ravine which had come to be known as
> the Gully of Death. There had been houses on the sides of
> the ravine; now there was hardly anything left. But as we
> passed a woman with three children came out of a dugout
> and told some disjointed story of how she had lived
> through it all, how she had washed clothes for the soldiers.
> She became slightly hysterical and one of the children
> began to cry.
>   In the main building of the October Plant, trenches ran
> through the factory yards, through the workshops
> themselves. At the bottom of the trenches there still lay

frozen green Germans and frozen grey Russians and frozen
fragments of human shapes, and there were tin helmets,
German and Russian, lying among the brick debris, and the
helmets were half filled with snow. There was barbed wire
here, and half-uncovered mines, and shell cases, and more
rubble and fragments of walls, and tortuous tangles of rusty
steel girders. But, strange to say, though riddled with holes,
a large red-brick factory chimney was still standing, rising
from all this.

How anyone could have survived here is hard to imagine.
And someone pointed to a wall with something written on
it, where one of the units had died to the last man.
Everything was silent and dead in this cold fossilized hell, as
though a raving lunatic had suddenly died of heart failure.

Werth and the other Westerners trooped back to the centre of the city,
where the Germans in the southern Kessel had made their last stand.

In the middle of the pavement lay a dead German. He must
have been running when a shell hit him. His legs still
seemed to be running, though one was now cut off above
the ankle by a shell splinter, and with the splintered white
bone sticking out of the frozen red flesh it looked like
something harmlessly familiar from a butcher's window.
His face was a bloody frozen mess, and beside it was a
frozen pool of blood.

We crossed the square, and went into the yard of the Red
Army House. Here one realized more clearly what the last
days of Stalingrad had been to so many of the Germans.
In the porch lay the skeleton of a horse, with its skin ripped
off and only a few scraps of meat still clinging to its ribs. In
the yard there was an enormous, horrible cesspool –
fortunately frozen solid.

And then suddenly, at the far end of the yard, I caught
sight of a human figure. He had been crouching over

another cesspool, and now, noticing us, he was hastily
pulling up his pants. And then he slunk away into the door
of a basement. But as he passed I caught a glimpse of the
wretch's face, with its mixture of suffering and idiot-like
incomprehension. For a moment I wished the whole of
Germany were there to see it. The man was perhaps already
dying. In that basement into which he slunk there were still
two hundred Germans – dying of hunger and frostbite.
'We haven't had time to deal with them yet,' one of the
Russians said. 'They'll be taken away tomorrow, I suppose.'

An anonymous British Communist visited the city a month later,
when most of the Germans were gone. He was in any case more
interested in providing a sympathetic description of the great loss to
the Bolshevik cause that the ruin of the city represented.

Hardly a house stands in all the six miles between the
Square of the Heroes of the Revolution in the city's centre
and the famous Red October Works in the north. Around
the central square, tall buildings show their bones to the air,
the skeletons of buildings that house the skeletons of men.
The trees, the lovely squares, the roofs which the birds
quitted last August, are no longer there. Millions of
shellpocked bricks and mountains of twisted metal are
all that remain of the famous Dzerzhinsky Tractor Works,
the factories of Red October and the Red Barricade.
  Deep thousand-pound bomb craters, filled with ice, pit
the almost trackless streets. And here and there a frozen
corpse stares up pale through the ice. All over the city hangs
the sick smell of rubble and death.

Ilya Ehrenburg, the polemicist who had declared that there was
nothing jollier than a dead German, was now in his writerly element.
As the battle drew to its close, he dashed off a series of newspaper
articles, all of them full of righteous *schadenfreude*. One of Ehrenburg's

favourite devices was to comment ironically on something that the enemy had said. Sometimes he would use the sharply gleaming scalpel of his sarcasm to dissect a speech by Joseph Goebbels or Benito Mussolini. On this occasion he penned a piece based on the captured postbags of the Sixth Army. 'A German lady named Erna Kraus has sent a letter to her husband,' he wrote, then quoted the letter.

'The children would like you to send us the gift of victory. I'll be modest and ask only that you send some soap, and if it is not too difficult some fur, so I can have a jacket like Betty's.' But in the steppe by the Don, amid thousands and thousands of German corpses, lies the body of Major Kraus. Beside him is a trampled German banner.

Erna will not be getting her little fur jacket; and Germany will not have her victory.

The image of masses of slaughtered Germans was no mere literary device. For anybody living or working between the Don and the Volga they were an inescapable and entirely unremarkable feature of the landscape. Corpses were as common as grass.

There were so many dead bodies around Stalingrad that the horses had ceased to be afraid of them, said one Russian woman. Usually they are scared. A horse will never step on a dead man. We gathered our own dead, but the Germans were left frozen on the ground. They were everywhere. I was a driver and carried boxes of artillery shells in my lorry. I could hear their skulls crack beneath my wheel. Bones too. And I was glad.

Burying the German dead was not a practical proposition until springtime: the ground was too hard frozen to dig. But at the beginning of March the journalist-poet Konstantin Simonov happened upon evidence that this Herculean task was under way. It was a sight so macabre that at first he could not make sense of it.

We were driving through wasteland and ruin towards Beketovka. Suddenly, at a bend in the road, the lead car came to a stop. Our car stopped too. I climbed out of the car and saw a sight the meaning of which I could not understand. It was something like a foundation pit, or a big snowy ravine with a very level base. And on this flat white surface were piled huge stacks of planks. My first impression was that this was a gigantic woodyard.

And then it hit me. Here, at the bottom of the pit, were stacked several thousand corpses. They were neatly piled like the logs in a well-organized sawmill, with little paths and alleyways between the tall stacks. Each tidy pile consisted of several hundred dead Germans.

I don't know, but it seems to me that this strangely precise way it had been done was not the result of anyone on our side having given an order, but was done purely on the initiative of the people who brought the corpses here. It turned out that this was the place for German bodies that had been pulled out of the cellars of Stalingrad. It had been done so that, come the spring, there would not be an epidemic when they thawed out and began to rot and disintegrate.

The intention, it seemed, was to blow up the side of the pit and so create a mass grave. But somehow, in spite of the fact that it was a sensible measure, and even though it all became a woodyard once more when we got back in the cars and drove on a distance, I could not help but shudder when I turned and looked at it, there behind me.

The living as well as the dead were removed from the city in the course of February 1943. Of the quarter of a million Germans who were locked in the Kessel, around 90,000 were still alive at the end of the battle. These survivors were formed up into columns and marched across the frozen Volga and into long years of forced labour. Viktor Kondratenko, who was a correspondent with one of the Red Army newspapers, watched the defeated Germans go.

It was snowing a little and the day was bleak. Suddenly, after 200 days of constant cannonade and shooting, there was silence. Everyone was asking each other: what's happening? It is so quiet in the streets. Someone says: the Germans are surrendering. They are putting their weapons on the ground. Just hills of weapons.

Then I see this snake, this giant snake of the wounded and the captured. This long, twisting line. The snake was green and dirty. It looked like many frogs. Their ragged suits were camouflage, green, white and black. The line is moving towards the horizon. You don't see the end and the beginning of it. It is growing darker and darker. Dirty snow is everywhere. Our lorries are moving along with this column and picking up the wounded and the fatigued German prisoners.

Toward the end of the column, I saw a German field lieutenant who was so fatigued he collapsed on the ground. As his friends shuffled ahead, his cry was like a wolf. A howl: 'Paul! Paul! Peter! Peter!' His friends just put their ragged collars up, hunched their shoulders and moved on. They never turned their heads.

As the Germans left the city, Russian civilians made their way back to their smashed homes. For Nikolai Razuvayev, the signaller who had witnessed the initial bombing of his hometown in August, the end of the battle was a day of unfathomable sorrow.

The annihilation of the Germans at Stalingrad was in its final stage. The southern group had already been taken prisoner, though the northern group, at the Tractor Plant, was still holding out. It was already safe to walk through the district where I lived. I was only 400 metres away from my house, and with my commander's permission I went there to find out the fate of my family. When I got to the place where my house had stood, I saw only ruins. I found some

neighbours living in a dugout, and was told by them that
my whole family – my wife and two daughters – were dead.
My younger daughter Galya had been killed along with her
mother by an exploding shell, which had injured my elder
daughter, Lyuba, who was eight years old. She had passed
away only ten days before my arrival. A neighbour told me
that my daughter kept saying that she was sure her dad
would be coming to get her. She had waited and waited,
but never lived to see that day.

Similarly dreadful discoveries were being made as people trickled back
to their homes, dragging their belongings on sleds across the static
river. Vasily Grossman described this reverse exodus in his post-war
epic novel *Life and Fate*:

People had immediately begun crossing the Volga into the
city itself. They had heard that the remaining inhabitants of
Stalingrad endured terrible hunger during these last weeks;
the officers, soldiers and sailors from the Volga fleet all
carried little bundles of tinned food and loaves of bread.
A few of them also brought some vodka or an accordion.
   These unarmed soldiers who entered Stalingrad during
the night, who handed out bread and kissed and embraced
the inhabitants, seemed almost sad; there was little singing
or rejoicing.
   The morning of 2 February, 1943, was very misty.
The mist rose up from the holes pierced in the ice and from
the few patches of unfrozen water. The sun rose, as harsh
now in the winter winds as during the blazing heat of
August. The dry snow drifted about over the level ground,
forming milky spirals and columns, then suddenly lost its
will and settled again. Everywhere you could see traces of
the east wind: collars of snow round the stems of thorn-
bushes, congealed ripples on the slopes of the gullies, small
mounds and patches of bare clay.

From the Stalingrad bank it looked as though the people crossing the Volga were being formed out of the mist itself, as though they had been sculpted by the wind and frost. They had no mission to accomplish in Stalingrad; the war here was over and no one had sent them. They came spontaneously, of their own accord – soldiers and road-layers, drivers and gunners, army tailors, mechanics and electricians. Together with old men wrapped in shawls, old women wearing soldiers' trousers and little boys and girls dragging sledges laden with bundles and blankets, they crossed the Volga and scrambled up the slopes of the right bank.

Something very strange had happened to the city. You could hear the sound of car-horns and tractor engines; people were playing harmonicas, soldiers were shouting and laughing, dancers were stamping down the snow with their felt boots. But, for all this, the city felt dead.

The normal life of Stalingrad had come to an end several months before: schools, factories, women's dressmakers, amateur choirs and theatre groups, crèches, cinemas, the city police had all ceased to function. A new city – wartime Stalingrad – had been born out of the flames. This city had its own layout of streets and squares, its own underground buildings, its own traffic laws, its own commerce, factories and artisans, its own cemeteries, concerts and drinking parties.

Every epoch has its own capital city, a city that embodies its will and soul. For several months of the Second World War this city was Stalingrad. The thoughts and passions of humanity were centred on Stalingrad. Factories and printing presses functioned for the sake of Stalingrad. Parliamentary leaders rose to their feet to speak of Stalingrad.

But when thousands of people poured in from the steppes to fill the empty streets, when the first car engines started up, this world capital ceased to exist. At the same time, an

everyday, working city was coming into being – with
schools, factories, maternity homes, police, an opera
and a prison.

A world capital is unique not only because it is linked
with the fields and factories of the whole world. A world
capital is unique because it has a soul. The soul of wartime
Stalingrad was freedom.

Freedom was not a word that the 90,000 captured Germans would
have associated with the name of Stalingrad. For many of them, the
close of battle was only the beginning of their ordeal. Hans Dibold,
the doctor who had seen a vision of the Crucifixion in the pitiless
steppe, was now in a new and different hell: a holding camp that the
Germans christened the Timoshenko Bunker.

The men lay on the cold earth, clothed in filthy, dank rags,
shirts black with dirt, ragged socks, worn-out footwear.
They were tortured by sores on the shoulder-blades and
loins, the thighs and elbows; their bluish-black, mortified
toes, one mass of pus, slowly dropped away from the deep
red swollen feet, or had to be removed with the knife
because of the intolerable pain. The sick could not wash,
for there was barely sufficient water to ease their thirst.
They relieved themselves into tin cans standing on the
floor beside them, and frequently knocked them over.
Anyone who could drag himself along hobbled, groaning,
to the bucket. Cries of pain and angry shouts marked their
progress there and back as they pushed against another
patient's foot.

Hunger ate its way into their innermost being and
deprived many of them of the power to reason clearly.
They snapped at the bread, their eyes had an insane gleam.
Fever had not yet started to rage among them; but the
smoke burned their throats and grated in their windpipes,
their thirst grew more and more intense.

The lice were the worst of all, the sick men said.
All organized delousing had ceased even during the
investment of Stalingrad. The worse the living
accommodation, the more troublesome was the plague
of lice. Whosoever was fit spent every free minute searching
for them. At any given moment twenty or thirty insects
could be cracked in a collar-band alone. Every inch of the
body was red with bites, and the furious itching took away
the one remaining blessing, sleep.

Only when fever set in did the lice wander off to the
next man, and infect him. The sick, less agile than the
fit, tried to delouse themselves, but without success.
Their pullovers were grey with lice and seemed to be alive.
Wherever the wool of socks or vest sleeves protruded they
swarmed. When a man was near to death the ground
around him was grey with lice abandoning him. Lice could
be scooped out from the men's sunken abdomens like
flour from a bin.

Yet the deepest misery was caused by man himself: by the
thieves who stripped the corpses. Even while the dying still
lay in their last agony they lost their footwear, their coats
and their rings. One man sold sips of water for money.
When he himself died, he had eight thousand marks
in his pocket.

The interpreter Schlösser, formerly a waiter in Romania,
robbed, stole and traded incessantly. During his rounds
devoted to prying and plundering he infected himself with
an unbelievable quantity of typhus germs. When he expired
like a beast, a sack full of gold rings was found at his side.
More and more frequently we found that the sick and dying
had been robbed of their wedding rings. I still possessed
mine. It was made of gold from my dead father's ring, like
the one which my wife at home wore. No stranger should
ever touch that gold. I crushed my ring into a ball in the fire
and concealed it.

Dibold kept his ring, but lost a treasured pocket edition of Goethe's *Faust*. It was snatched away from him by a Russian guard, who tore out its pages and rolled fat cigarettes in its Bible-thin paper. Meanwhile the incipient typhus, noted by the careful doctor, swept through the mass of sick men like an invading horde. The lice carried it, and soon an epidemic was raging in the overcrowded camps. It wiped out half of the remnant of the Sixth Army before the summer came.

The rest of the prisoners were put to work clearing rubble, and then reconstructing the places that they had destroyed. This punishment was enough to kill most of them over the course of the next decade, but as Vyacheslav Molotov, the Soviet foreign minister, had said: 'They will not go home before Stalingrad is rebuilt.'

Kurt Reuber, the Christian doctor who drew the Madonna of Stalingrad, continued to do good work in the POW camps, but never did go home. He died in a Russian camp in 1944 at the age of 38. His charcoal Madonna survived. It was brought out of the Kessel on one of the last transports to leave, and passed to his wife. She bequeathed it to the Kaiser Wilhelm Memorial Church in Berlin, the ruined spire of which is itself a symbol of peace and hope. It hangs there still.

Reuber's fellow physician, Hans Dibold, survived captivity and came back to Germany in the 1950s. He was one of only 5,000 members of the Sixth Army to make it home from Stalingrad. For him, to have lived through it was a kind of miracle. After his return he wrote an impassioned book on his experiences, which ends with this little parable from the first days of his captivity:

This was in Stalingrad, 23 September, 1943.

We were being transferred to the heart of the Soviet Union, that was all we knew. We stood and waited. Once more an uncertain fate lay before us. We stood erect and supported our sick.

At the roadside, under the small fruit trees, a Soviet woman was waiting with her daughter. The little girl was wearing a small red cap on her black curls. She ran up to us and gave us an old newspaper as cigarette paper for the smokers. Great tears of compassion glittered in the eyes of the Soviet woman. That picture long followed us; it seemed to us as though the glitter of those tears would not fade even if the whole world were to descend once more into the underworld night of a new war.

THE SWORD OF STALINGRAD

For the victors, of course, the immediate meaning of Stalingrad lay not in its spiritual lessons, but in the brutal military facts of the matter: Germany had suffered a mortal blow, and everybody apart from Hitler knew it. The front line in Stalingrad, two minutes' walk from the Volga, represented the absolute high tide of Nazism. From this point on, the geographical extent of the Reich would always be decreasing as the strength of the Wehrmacht ebbed away.

Ilya Ehrenburg, in typically catty fashion, remarked that Stalingrad was surely the 'beginning of the end' that Churchill had not wanted to name when he called El Alamein 'the end of the beginning'. But the implied accusation of churlishness was unfair. Churchill was well aware that a corner had been turned, that events had swung decisively in the Allies' favour, and he was planning to commemorate Stalingrad's achievement in a special way: he wanted to give the city a gift.

So Churchill commissioned a sword, to be designed and forged by British artists and craftsmen. The finished Sword of Stalingrad was 4ft (1.2m) long. The points of the crossguard were decorated with leopards' heads wrought in silver. A large crystal was mounted on the pommel, and the scabbard was covered in crimson Persian lambskin. The blade was made of Sheffield steel and inscribed in English on one side with the words, 'To the steelhearted citizens of Stalingrad, the gift of King George VI, in token of the homage of the British people.' The text on the other side was in Russian and read slightly differently: 'To the citizens of Stalingrad, strong as steel ...' The Russian wording made the most of a pun on the Russian word *stal* – 'steel' – which was the root of Stalin's revolutionary *nom de guerre* ('man of steel'), and which was given apt and concrete form in the shining blade.

Churchill presented the sword to Stalin in person at the opening of the Teheran conference in November 1943. Roosevelt was there, at the Soviet Embassy, when the ceremony took place. So was Valentin Berezhkov, a Russian diplomat and interpreter. His underlying dislike of Churchill exactly reflects Soviet foreign policy at that moment, and is palpable in his account of the presentation of the sword.

The hall began to fill up long before the ceremony started. All the delegates and the leaders of the armies, fleets and air forces of the countries making up the anti-Hitler coalition were present when 'The Big Three' arrived.

Stalin was wearing a light grey tunic with his marshal's shoulder-boards. This time, Churchill also appeared in military uniform. From that day onwards, the British Prime Minister wore his uniform constantly in Teheran, and everyone regarded it as his peculiar reaction to Stalin's marshal's dress. At first Churchill had worn a dark blue pin-striped suit, but on seeing Stalin in uniform, he had immediately ordered himself a blue-grey full-dress coat of a senior officer of the Royal Air Force. This uniform arrived just in time for the ceremony of the presentation of the sword. Roosevelt, as usual, was in civilian clothes.

The guard of honour consisted of Red Army and British officers. An orchestra played the Soviet and British national anthems and everyone stood at attention. Then the music stopped and a solemn moment of silence ensued. Churchill slowly went up to the large black box lying on the table and opened it.

The sword, inside its sheath, rested on a claret-coloured velvet pillow. Churchill took the sword in both hands and, holding it suspended, he turned to Stalin and said: 'I have been commanded by His Majesty King George VI to present to you for transmission to the City of Stalingrad this sword of honour, the design of which His Majesty has chosen and approved. The sword of honour was made by English craftsmen whose ancestors have been employed in sword-making for generations.'

Taking a few steps forwards, Churchill presented the sword to Stalin, behind whom was standing the Soviet guard of honour, with sub-machineguns atilt. Stalin took the sword and pulled it out of its sheath. The blade glinted coldly. Stalin raised it to his lips and kissed it. Then, holding the sword in his hands, he said in a low voice:

'On behalf of the citizens of Stalingrad, I wish to express my deep appreciation for the gift of King George VI. The citizens of Stalingrad will value this gift most highly, and I ask you, Mr Prime Minister, to convey their thanks to His Majesty the King.'

There was a pause. Stalin slowly walked round the table and went over to Roosevelt to show him the sword. Churchill held the sheath while Roosevelt looked carefully at the huge blade. Then he gave it back to Stalin who went over to the table and put the sword in its sheath. Then he gave it to Voroshilov who carried the sword into the next room, accompanied by the guard of honour.

Berezhkov fails to mention that the ceremony almost ended in low farce. As Stalin passed the king's gift to Klimenty Voroshilov, his long-time crony, somehow the hilt tilted downwards and the sword started sliding slowly out of its scabbard. Voroshilov, who according to some witnesses had been drinking, lurched sideways and caught the sword just before it clattered to the floor. Everybody pretended that nothing had happened and quickly moved outside, where the three leaders sat side by side and had their photograph taken for posterity.

THE RED ARMY TRIUMPHANT

As the Battle of Stalingrad came to an end, a number of symbolic reforms were instituted in the Red Army. Most visibly, the inelegant uniforms that had been in use since the civil war were abolished, and smart new forms of dress were introduced. Officers now had well-cut tunics with high collars; dashing peaked caps replaced the forage caps that were also worn by lower ranks; shoulderboards – the hated symbol of the Tsarist army – were reintroduced. Henceforth, rank was signified on the shoulderboards by a system of stars and other symbols analogous to the pips and crowns of the British Army. (British officials were astonished when, at the height of the struggle in the east, they received an urgent request from the Soviet Union for a large quantity of gold braid.)

The word 'officer' (*ofitser*), which like the shoulderboards had distinctly pre-Revolutionary associations, was officially rehabilitated as a synonym for the more egalitarian 'commander' (*komandir*). Moreover, new medals were instituted that underlined the Red Army's reconnection with an older military tradition. The Order of Suvorov and the Order of Kutuzov celebrated the spiritual link with martial heroes of previous centuries: Mikhail Kutuzov was the general who had defeated Napoleon's invasion force in the 'patriotic war' of 130 years before; Alexander Suvorov had fought and defeated the Poles – another old enemy in the west – at the end of the 18th century.

But there was a separate reform, enacted at the height of the battle for Stalingrad, that ran much deeper than the cosmetic changes to the Red Army. In October 1942 the system of 'dual command' – military and political – was abolished. Commissars were made subordinate to their corresponding field commanders, and their role became advisory rather than supervisory.

It was as if, collectively, the Red Army had earned its spurs at Stalingrad. The officer corps, freed of the nannyish ideological interference of the commissars, now saw itself as a professional institution that commanded the respect of the ranks, and of Soviet society at large. The new attacking Red Army was to be a different fighting machine from the defensive Red Army, the one that had been crippled by purges, made fearful by defeat and retreat, bled almost to death by casualties beyond number.

And yet, at the time of the Teheran conference – ten months after the fighting stopped in Stalingrad – there were still German soldiers fighting well inside Soviet borders. Kiev, which had been captured by the Germans in the course of Operation Blau in the summer of 1942, was liberated only in November 1943. During the fighting this beautiful city, with its wealth of golden-headed monasteries and its ten centuries of architectural tradition, was almost as thoroughly destroyed as Stalingrad.

Chuikov's 62nd Army, renamed the 8th Guards Army as a mark of its achievement at Stalingrad, was in the vanguard of the Soviet advance across Russia and the Ukraine. The same men and women who fought with their backs to the Volga now moved beyond the Dnieper, rolling back the German front line as the enemy withdrew to the west. The fighting was no less ferocious than it had ever been. Here is a German account of a small incident that occurred near the River Donets in 1943.

A Russian tank was apparently rendered immobile by a direct hit. When German tanks approached, it suddenly reopened fire and attempted to break out. A second direct hit again brought it to a standstill, but in spite of its hopeless position it defended itself while a tank-killer team advanced on it. Finally it burst into flame from a demolition charge and only then did the turret hatch open. A woman in tanker uniform climbed out. She was the wife and co-fighter of a tank company commander who, killed by the first hit, lay beside her in the turret.

This story also casts a light on the profoundly personal commitment that many Russians had to the war. The deep-rooted devotion that many Russians felt towards their native soil meant that abstractions such as 'motherland' and 'patriotism' became almost indistinguishable from the reality of 'family' and 'love'. Russian soldiers and civilians alike were outraged by the damage that Germany did to the land, both as they advanced and as they retreated.

That harm was long lasting, and took unexpected and sometimes chilling form. 'It was 1944, and we had been liberated,' said Nadya Savitskaya, who was 12 years old at the time and living in Belorussia.

We received a letter saying that my brother had been killed. My mum cried and cried and went blind. We lived in the countryside then, in German dugouts, because the village had all been burned. Our old cottage was burned and so was the wood we had put by to build a new one. We had nothing left at all. We would find soldiers' helmets in the woods and use them to cook in. German helmets were like big iron pots.

We fed ourselves from the forest. But it was scary to go looking for berries and mushrooms. Lots of German dogs had been left behind. They attacked people and sank their teeth into the children. They had been given a taste for human flesh, for human blood. If we went into the forest we did so only in big groups. Our mothers taught us that you have to keep shouting all the time you are in the forest, to scare the dogs off. While you picked berries you would be shouting so much that you would lose your voice, go hoarse. But the dogs were as big as wolves. And they were drawn by the human smell.

The German dogs remained long after the German soldiers had all been driven from Russian soil. The last of the human invaders fell back across the border in February 1945. Vasily Chuikov's Eighth Guards were among the forces that pushed the Wehrmacht across the Vistula and into Poland. They stayed in action right to the end of the war. Many of the men who fought in the streets of Stalingrad did the same again more than two years later in the streets of Berlin. In the last days of April 1945, Chuikov himself conducted surrender negotiations with German officers in a command post on the edge of the Tiergarten, less than a mile from the bunker where Hitler lay dead. The Germans who negotiated their surrender with Chuikov were astounded and awed to learn that this was the same man who had grappled with the Sixth Army and won.

It was a special badge of honour within the Red Army to have fought every step of the way from Stalingrad to the German capital. One who did so was Yakov Pavlov, the eponymous hero of Pavlov's

House. After the war he made a kind of career speaking to school-children about his experiences. But eventually he tired of telling the tale – or perhaps he was troubled by the fanfare and jingoism that became a feature of Soviet pronouncements on the war years. At any rate, Pavlov changed. Late in life, he became a Russian Orthodox monk. He took the name Kirill, went to live in the hallowed monastery city of Sergiyev Posad, and spoke no more of the many men that he had killed.

GLOSSARY

Army Group A German military formation consisting of two or more armies.

Balka Russian dialect term for a ravine or gully in the flatlands of the southern steppe. Some are big enough to accommodate or conceal large numbers of troops and tanks.

Coffee grinder See U-2.

Commander Usual term for an officer in the Red Army until the reforms of 1943.

Commissar A 'political officer' in the Red Army. Commissars were responsible for conducting propaganda among the troops, and for taking an ideological view of the work of military commanders.

Communist In Soviet parlance, a full-fledged member of the Communist party. As with the Nazi party in Germany, only a small percentage of the population belonged to this political élite.

Corps A military formation consisting of two or more divisions. Soviet tank and cavalry divisions were sometimes termed 'corps'.

Division A military formation consisting of a number of battalions, regiments and support units, and comprising 10,000 to 15,000 men. A full-strength Panzer division would have about 100 tanks.

Feldwebel A German NCO rank, roughly equivalent to a corporal.

Front The Soviet term for an Army Group. A front consisted of several armies and comprised between one and two million men. Fronts were given geographical names ('Stalingrad Front', 'Don Front'), but the term denotes the forces at the front commander's disposal rather than the physical location of the front line.

Frontovik Informal Russian term for a front-line soldier.

Frontschwein Literally 'front pig'. Wehrmacht slang for a front-line soldier.

Führer German 'leader', Hitler's honorific title within the Nazi party.

GPU Russian acronym for 'Gosudarstvennoye Politicheskoye Upravleniye' – State Political Administration. The name of the Soviet secret police in the early 1920s. Hitler's use of the term in the 1940s is redundant.

Guards Honorific title given to Soviet units, usually divisions, that had distinguished themselves in battle.

Heinkel 111 A German long-range bomber, which was used as a transport plane during the Stalingrad airlift.

Il-2 Short form of Ilyushin-2, the main ground-attack aircraft of the Soviet air force at Stalingrad.

Junkers 52 German transport plane, known as 'Tante Ju' – Auntie Junkers.

Junkers 87 German dive-bomber.

Katyusha Russian term for a mobile multiple rocket launcher, usually mounted on a truck. The Germans called them 'Stalin organs'.

Kommandantur German military HQ in occupied territories.

Komsomol Russian acronym for the Communist Youth League, a kind of junior version of the Communist party for teenagers and young adults. Membership was more or less compulsory.

Kübelwagen Literally 'bucket car' – the German military jeep.

Landser German military slang for an ordinary soldier, equivalent to the British term 'tommy' or the American 'GI'.

Leninist In Soviet parlance, a high-flown term for a card-carrying member of the Communist party.

Luftwaffe The German air force.

Machinegun Usual rendering of Russian *pulemyot*, which denotes a heavy weapon supported on a mount or a tripod and fed by a cartridge belt. Compare Sub-machinegun.

Maxim gun A heavy machinegun, mounted on wheels. The wartime Maxim was an updated version of the pre-revolutionary design.

National-Socialist Short form of National Socialist German Workers' Party (NSDAP), Hitler's political movement. The word 'Nazi' is an abbreviation of National-Socialist.

NKVD Russian acronym for 'Narodny Kommissariat Vnutrennykh Del' – People's Commissariat of Internal Affairs. The official name of the Soviet secret police from 1934 to 1943.

Oberfeldwebel German NCO rank, roughly equivalent to a sergeant major.

Pravda Soviet newspaper, the official organ of the Communist party.

Red Army Name of the Soviet armed forces from 1917. After the Second World War the name was officially changed to 'Soviet Army'.

Red Star The newspaper of the Soviet armed forces.

Reich German word for 'Empire', and the Nazi term for Germany together with all its conquered territories.

Reichsmarschall German, 'marshal of the Reich'. Honorific title of Herman Göring, commander of the Luftwaffe.

Shtrafbat Russian acronym for *shtrafnoi batalyon* – punishment battalion.

Shturmovik General Russian term for low-flying attack aircraft.

SS German acronym for *Schutzstaffel* – protection squad. The SS was a paramilitary organization within the Nazi party that provided Hitler's bodyguard and constituted the German security forces.

Stalin organ See Katyusha.

Stavka Russian word for 'headquarters'. The term was usually reserved for Stalin's supreme HQ in Moscow.

STZ Acronym of the tractor plant, the full name of which was the 'Stalingrad Tractor Factory named after Dzerzhinsky'.

Sub-machinegun Usual rendering of the Russian *avtomat*, which denotes a light, portable machinegun such as the Russian PPSh-41 or the German MP-38.

Tommygun Usual English term for the Russian PPSh-41 which, with its drum-shaped magazine, closely resembled the Thompson sub-machinegun.

Tsaritsyn The original pre-revolutionary name of Stalingrad. The city was rechristened 'Stalin's city' in 1925. Then in 1961, during the process of 'destalinization', its name was changed again – this time to Volgograd.

U-2 A small Russian reconnaissance plane. Known as the 'maize cutter' by the Russians, and as the 'sewing machine' or the 'coffee grinder' by the Germans.

Univermag Russian acronym of *universalny magazin* – department store.

Untermensch Nazi pseudo-scientific term meaning 'sub-human'. Usually applied to the Jewish race, but sometimes extended to include the Slav peoples.

Wehrmacht The German armed forces as a whole.

Zagradbat Russian acronym for *zagraditelny batalyon* – blocking battalion.

CHRONOLOGY

1941

22 June Three German army groups invade Soviet territory. No declaration of war is made beforehand.

3 July Stalin speaks on the radio to the Soviet people and declares that this is a 'great patriotic war'.

2 October Operation Typhoon, the German offensive against Moscow, begins.

6 December The Soviet counter-offensive outside Moscow is orchestrated by General Georgy Zhukov.

1942

28 June Operation Blue begins – this is the start of the German summer offensive on the Eastern front.

14 July Martial law is declared in Stalingrad.

17 July Elements of the Soviet 62nd Army encounter forward units of the Sixth Army for the first time near the River Chir. The battle for Stalingrad is under way.

28 July Stalin's 'Not One Step Back' order is issued to the Red Army.

15 August General Paulus's Sixth Army reaches the west bank of the Don.

23 August General von Richthofen's Fourth Air Fleet bombs Stalingrad; Panzer troops reach the Volga north of the city.

14 September The first German ground assault on Stalingrad is launched. Battles rage at the railway station and on Mamayev Kurgan. Rodimtsev's 13th Guards Division crosses the Volga from the east bank with orders to hold off the Germans inside the city.

26 September The second German assault begins. It is directed against the factory district north of the city centre.

30 September The Germans are in possession of most of the city centre.

14 October A third German offensive drives the Russian defenders out of the Tractor Factory and the Barricades Factory.

22 October The German Sixth Army and the Russian 62nd Army fight for possession of the Red October Factory.

30 October The German assault on the factories grinds to a halt.

19 November Operation Uranus, the great Soviet counter-offensive at Stalingrad, is set in motion.

22 November Paulus's army, a quarter of a million men, is surrounded between the Volga and the Don.

25 November Start of the German airlift to supply the Sixth Army.

12 December Operation Winter Storm: a German relief column strikes north from Kotelnikovo towards the encircled Sixth Army.

23 December The relief column stalls on the River Myshkova, short of the surrounded group.

1943

8 January The Soviet High Command issues an ultimatum to the Sixth Army: surrender or be destroyed.

10 January Operation Ring: the annihilation of the surrounded German forces at Stalingrad begins.

25 January The German forces are split into two pockets inside the city.

31 January Paulus surrenders inside the southern pocket.

2 February The northern pocket surrenders, and the battle for Stalingrad comes to an end.

CONTRIBUTORS INDEX

Publications

[Quoted in] *19 Noyabrya 1942*, Nikolai Yakovlev, Molodaya Gvardiya 1979 136, 161–2, 162

[Quoted in] *Bitva za Stalingrad*, A.M. Borodin (ed.), Nizhne-Volzhskoye knizhnoye izdatelstvo 1969 240–1, 282, 283–4, 284, 285–7

Days and Nights, Konstantin Simonov, tr. Joseph Barnes, Simon and Schuster Adult Publishing Group 1945 48

Doctor at Stalingrad: the Passion of a Captivity, Hans Dibold, Hutchinson 1958 227–8, 252–4, 254–5, 300–1, 302–3

[Quoted in] *Dvesti ognennykh dnei*, B.V. Druzhinin, Voennoye Izdatelstvo MO SSSR 1967 108–9, 109

[Quoted in] *Eastern Front 1941–1945: German Troops and the Barbarisation of Warfare*, The, Omer Bartov, Macmillan 1985 (tr. Omer Bartov from *Die Wehrmacht im NS-Staat*, M. Messerschmidt, Hamburg 1969) 64

Echolot, Das, Walter Kempowski (Ed.), Albrecht Knaus Verlag 1997 212, 225–6, 249

Feldzug nach Stalingrad, Der, Hans Doerr, Darmstadt 1955 103–4

[Quoted in] *Fighting in Hell: the German Ordeal on the Eastern Front*, Peter Tsouras (ed.), Ivy Books 1995 307

Forgotten Soldier, The, Guy Sajer, Weidenfeld & Nicolson 1976 287–9

Forsaken Army, The, Heinrich Gerlach, Weidenfeld & Nicolson 1958 256–7

Good War: an oral history of World War Two, The, Studs Terkel, Hamish Hamilton (UK) Donadio & Olson Inc. (USA) 1985 256, 297

History in the Making, Valentin Berezhkov, Progress 1982 304–5

[Quoted in] *Hitler: Reden und Proklamationen 1932–1945*, M. Domarus, Neustadt: Schmidt 1962 9, 63–4

Krasnaya Zvezda, 16 November 1942 111

[Quoted in] *Kriegsbriefe gefallener Studenten 1939–1945*, W. & H.W. Bähr, R. Wunderlich 1952 18, 18–19, 19–20, 20–1, 21–2, 22–3, 23–4, 221–2, 222, 223

Life and Fate, Vasily Grossman, (tr. Robert Chandler) The Harvill Press, Random House Group Ltd 1995 298–300

[Quoted in] *Marshall Zhukov's Greatest Battles*, Georgi Zhukov, Macdonald 1969 61, 71, 73–4, 74–6

[Quoted in] *Moryaki v bitve za Stalingrad*, Mikhail Gryaznov, Nizhne-Volzhskoye knizhnoye izdatelstvo 1982 47–8, 57–8

Moscow Under Fire: A Wartime Diary 1941, Erskine Caldwell, Hutchinson 1942 15, 16–17

Nachalo puti, Vasily Chuikov, Voennoye izdatelstvo MO SSSR 1959 81, 82, 82–3, 84–5, 85–6, 95–6, 97, 97–8, 99, 100, 123–4

[Quoted in] *Other Side of the Hill, The*, Basil Liddell Hart, Cassell 1951 27

[Quoted in] *Paulus and Stalingrad*, Walter Goerlitz, Methuen 1963 (tr. R.H. Stevens from *Ich stehe hier auf Befehl*, Citadel Press 1963) 51

[Quoted in] *Peredovaya nachinalas' v tsekhe*, L.P. Ovchinnikova, Nizhne-Volzhskoye knizhnoye izdatelstvo 1983 46, 46–7

[Quoted in] *Perelom*, Petr Popov (ed.), Izdatel 2000 37–8, 44–5, 101–2, 107, 108

[Quoted in] *Pisma iz Kotla*, L.F. Petrova, in *Stalingradskaya bitva: materialy nauchnykh konferentsii*, Institut Voennoi Istorii MO RF 1994 225

Poslednie Svideteli, Svetlana Aleksievich, Palmira 2004 308

Raznye dni voiny: dnevnik pisatelya, Konstantin Simonov, Molodaya Gvardiya 1977 296

[Quoted in] *Russia at War*, Alexander Werth, Barrie 1964 92–3, 182–3

Russian Newsreel, Charlotte Haldane, Secker and Warburg 1942 65–6

Shadow of Stalingrad, The, Heinrich von Einsiedel, Allan Wingate 1953 51–2, 53

Siege of Stalingrad, The, Communist Party of Great Britain 1943 294

[Quoted in] *Soldaty*, A.P. Dudkin (ed.), Nizhne-Volzhskoye knizhnoye izdatelstvo 1979 162–3

[Quoted in] *Stalin*, Isaac Deutscher, OUP 1949 10, 15, 16–17

Stalingrad, Vasily Grossman, Sovetsky Pisatel 1943 93–4, 198

Stalingrad, Theodor Plievier, Time Life 1966 154–5, 158

Stalingrad, Andrei Yeremenko, Voennoye Izdatelstvo MO SSSR 1961 165–7

[Quoted in] *Stalingrad: ein Armee wird geopfert*, Joseph Vilsmaier, München 1992 172, 213, 214

Stalingrad: memories and reassessments, Joachim Wieder/Heinrich Einsiedel, Cassell 1995 257–8, 258–9

Stalingrad: unten wo das Leben konkret war, Wilhelm Beyer, Athenäum 1987 169–70, 219, 249–51

Stalingrad: wie es wirklich war, Gunter Toepke, Stade 1949 170–1, 224

[Quoted in] *Stalingradskaya Epopeya*, I.I. Basik (ed.), Zvonnitsa-MG 2000 29–30, 88–9, 89–90, 219

[Quoted in] *Stalin's War Through The Eyes of His Commanders*, Albert Axell, Arms and Armour 1997 12, 175

[Quoted in] *Stopped at Stalingrad: the Luftwaffe and Hitler's Defeat in the East, 1942–43*, Joel Hayward, University Press of Kansas 1998 205

[Quoted in] *U voiny ne zhenskoye litso*, Svetlana Aleksievich, Palmira 2004 295

[Quoted in] *Und die Wolga brannte: Überlebende*

aus Stalingrad erinnern sich, Frauke
Eickhoff (ed.), Verein zur Förderung der
Städtepartnerschaft 2003 62, 62–3
[Quoted in] *V nebe Stalingrada*, V.S. Melnikov,
Nizhne-Volzhskoye knizhnoye izdatelstvo
1983 54–5, 177, 177-8
Voina, Ilya Ehrenburg, OGIZ 1943 66–7, 295
Völkischer Beobachter, 10 November 1942 152–3
Völkischer Beobachter, 31 January 1943 263

Year of Stalingrad, The, Alexander Werth, London
1946 292, 292–3, 293–4
'Yesli dorog tebe tvoi dom...', Konstantin
Simonov, in *Sobranie sochinenii* v 6–i tomakh,
Khudozhestvennaya literatura 1966 67–9
[Quoted in], *Yesterday's Britain*, Jonathan
Bastable (ed.), Reader's Digest 1998 12

GENERAL INDEX